Covenant and Kingdom

The DNA of the Bible

MIKE BREEN

Dedicated to the members of the Order of Mission—my wider family,

may this help you grow in community and mission

as we follow Jesus together

Acknowledgements

This book began when Mrs. Demarest took a Bible from the shelf in her high school classroom and gave it to me. I was immediately captivated by its contents. She stood in a long and illustrious line of godly people down the years who have given the Bible to others. But she was the one who actually placed the Book in my hands.

Since then, it has been one of the great passions of my life to study this Book, but it is only in recent years that I have come to record my reflections. In doing this, many have helped along the way. Some, like the congregations I have served over the years, have helped by patiently listening to my discoveries. Others have recorded and transcribed my spoken words. Still others, such as the members of the various teams that I have led, have reflected and discussed the subject matter with great enthusiasm. To all of these dear people, I owe a great debt of gratitude.

In the last few years, this project has been served by the diligence of Helen Cockram, who has edited and prepared the manuscript with great care and attention to detail.

Thanks to Gavin and Libby who were so careful to help with all the layout and notes.

My wife and ministry partner for thirty years, Sally, and my three children, Beccy, Libby and Sam, have readily encouraged me when my zeal has flagged.

I am grateful to all these people and know that this book would probably never have been attempted without them.

Contents

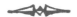

Contents Continued

INTRODUCTION

$\mathcal{T}$he Bible is translated into virtually every known language and is presented to every possible niche market. The Bible is essentially a simple book. So why do we find it so complicated?

For the average person, Scripture appears to be in the same category as modern sculpture or Shakespeare: enjoyed by most, valued by many but understood by very few. There seems to be an alienation, a distance between the ordinary person and the text of Scripture. And yet the Bible has a preeminent place of influence within our world and particularly within Western culture. Surely, when literacy is so commonplace and education so available, we must seek to better understand this greatest of all books.

To understand where this sense of alienation came from, we need to take a brief historical journey.

PUTTING THE BIBLE INTO THE HANDS OF THE PEOPLE

Toward the end of the medieval period, there was an upsurge of scholarly interest in the Bible, and some began to demand that it be made available to everyone. For hundreds of years, the Bible had been the exclusive property of popes and priests. Since the Bible was written in a language accessible to only a few (Latin) and reproduced by hand in incredibly small quantities, the "common people" were told that they needed professional clergymen to be their interpreters and guides. An individual relationship with God and access to Scripture were mediated through someone in the ecclesiastical hierarchy.

A few brave souls decided that the Bible should be translated into the languages of the common people. It was arguably John Wycliffe, the fourteenth-century scholar, studying first in Oxford and then alone for long hours in his Lutterworth vicarage, who first began this revolution. His life's passion was to translate the Bible into English. His work was continued and finally completed by William Tyndale, who was exiled from his native England for his efforts. Others on the European continent translated the Bible into Flemish, and of course, there was the giant of the Protestant Reformation, Martin Luther, who struggled against constant threat to reform the Church. He fueled the movement by his teaching and by translating the Bible into German. These remarkable men strived to put the Bible back into the hands of people.

With the invention of the Gutenberg printing press, the cost of producing the Bible in the common languages of Europe greatly decreased, and over time, the Bible became available to everyone.

The intellectual liberation that came through the Renaissance led to the Reformation. In time, the freedom that came after the Reformation led to the Enlightenment.

With the Enlightenment and its new era of intellectual freedom came all kinds of philosophical, social and scientific breakthroughs, but the "light" of the movement's name did not shine equally in all areas. The place of the individual within the universe was explored, social democracy was born and "the scientific method" was perfected. This method proved so powerful that in the coming centuries it began to be applied to the study of literature and in particular the Bible. Perhaps inevitably, this led to an evermore detailed analysis of the literary styles found within Scripture. Layers of complexity were added to the disciplines of biblical research, and in time, only experts schooled in "higher criticism" were able to understand the simplest of narratives.

The Bible, once wrested from the grip of spiritual potentates, for a short time widely available to read and wrestle with, was by the nineteenth century placed in the hands of professors working in the great universities of Europe. These professors trained the pastors, and together, as they taught the people, replaced the popes and the priests. And again ordinary people needed "mediators" to understand the text of Scripture!

As in medieval times, the spiritual lives of many were colored and defined by the teaching of a few. Confidence in God was thinly founded on the faith of these teachers who themselves were often uncertain of the truth they were teaching. In time, this led to serious decline in many denominations of the Western Church.

Of course, many church leaders and theologians have tried hard to rectify this malady, especially in the middle part of the twentieth century. But though the battle for the Bible was bravely fought and won by those who trusted its truth, the dependence upon the "experts" has continued, albeit in a different form.

CONSUMER CHRISTIANS

Too often in Christian circles, we hear the comment that people go to church to "get fed." To me, this suggests that people have become spiritually dependent upon their pastors and teachers. Somehow the rank-and-file members of congregations have become "spiritual consumers" rather than "producers." The Bible is no longer in the hands of the people but in the hands of an elite. I'm certain that this dependency relationship is not intentionally cultivated by pastors, but it continues nevertheless.

Perhaps we church leaders need to set aside our emphasis on glittering exegesis and swashbuckling exposition—all our clever tools for impressing people with our biblical erudition—and teach people instead how to read the Bible for themselves. This passion lies at the heart of this book.

You may be wondering what my qualifications are for such a task.

I am not a professional theologian, but I am a thinker, and over many years, I have reflected deeply on the themes of Scripture. I have discerned a pattern, a simple code. Not the esoteric codes of the occultist or Gnostic, but rather something more like a genetic code—the "double helix" of spiritual DNA running through the Bible. The two themes of this "double helix" are relationship and responsibility, and their theological names are Covenant and Kingdom.

I am not a biblical archaeologist or an anthropologist, but I am an enthusiast, and I have held the artifact of Scripture in my hands for long enough to feel its texture. I have seen the warp and the weft of the richly woven fabric. I have traced the threads of Covenant and Kingdom in their respective directions. The warp—Covenant or relationship—reveals how to be one with God, and the weft—Kingdom or responsibility—tells us how to do something for him.

My call has not been that of the academic but that of the church leader and spiritual guide. In my heart and mind, I have traversed the landscape of Scripture many times, and I have found its mountains and valleys to be places of challenge and refreshment. I have discovered the guiding coordinates—the latitude and longitude—that orient the journey.

My prayer is that, as you read this book, your passion to study the Bible will be rekindled and that as you hold that greatest of all books in your hands you will discover at a deeper level that you are held in the hands of another.

AN INTRODUCTION TO COVENANT AND KINGDOM

The Bible was the first book I ever read.

When I was 16, a missionary—Mrs. Demarest—returned from work in Africa and spent a few months at my high school teaching religious education. She was a great character who often incited debate on important religious questions. After one such classroom discussion, I told her that I felt incapable of arguing with her because I did not know the Bible well enough. Promptly, she handed me a Bible from the classroom shelf. It was the newly published Living Bible, written in contemporary English for people just like me.

I had struggled with dyslexia throughout my childhood years, which caused me to fail academically and feel isolated in the classroom. Books were enemies to me, not friends. By the age of 16, I had never read a book from cover to cover, but as I looked at the Bible, something seemed to happen in my brain that enabled me for the first time to read properly. The Bible became my friend, and learning to study it has never been a chore for me.

Since then, I have read thousands of books, many of them relating to the Bible. I have carried it throughout my life, and the Bible is the one piece of literature that I consistently refer to for help, hope and guidance.

This book offers the simplest framework of interpretation that we can use as we read the Bible for ourselves. I am not suggesting that in-depth Bible study is not important. On the contrary, I believe it should be part of every Christian's experience. This book is simply offered from a different perspective.

You can study the Scripture by starting with its details, or with its largest themes. This is true of every kind of study. If we study the Earth from its surface, we are conscious of many different elements that make up the atmosphere, biosphere and lithosphere—a grain of sand, a blade of grass, insects foraging for food.

Viewed from space, however, the Earth is blue.

Both perspectives are correct, but reality for the majority of us is lived out somewhere between the two. Human beings live at neither a microscopic nor a macroscopic level. We may be conscious of the details that lie beneath our perceptions of the world; we could be mindful of the smallest life forms, microbes, bacteria and atoms, but frankly few of us ever think of these things. It is enough for our senses to be bombarded by the colors, smells and touch of our surroundings. Similarly, we may be aware that our planet is little more than a speck of dust in our galaxy (the Milky Way), but again, few of us approach life from this perspective. It is enough for us simply to interact with the other people who daily fill our lives.

The same is true as we approach the Bible. We may be aware of the details—often microscopic—that lie beneath a simple reading of the text. We may be conscious that viewed from afar the Bible is simply a book about God and us. However, for most of us, life is lived out in the "in-between"—between the largest and smallest realities. Our lives are about friendship and hope, fear and aspiration. As we read the Bible, we discover that the characters we meet have similar stories, needs and challenges. The Bible's worth is found in its application to our ordinary experience—how we make relationships and how we take responsibility for our lives and the lives of others.

This book offers a perspective, not from space or under a microscope, but from an everyday vantage point. Here, we will study the Bible in terms of the two fundamental themes of Covenant and Kingdom—relationship and responsibility—worked out in the lives of some key characters who stirred nations and changed history. We will need to cover the whole Bible, from Genesis to Revelation, but we will not cover every kind of literature found in the Bible. There is little space to include a study of the poetry, wisdom and various kinds of prophetic writings. We will have to restrict our perspective to that which can be drawn from the narrative portions of the Bible. To do this, we will need to take in the stories of many of the characters of Scripture, major and minor. However, our journey will principally follow the lives of Abraham, Joseph, Moses, David and Jesus.

From the first page to the last, we will discover that the Bible is riven through with the "double helix" of Covenant and Kingdom. Perhaps a brief explanation of how I understand each would be helpful.

COVENANT

Covenant is the way in which the Bible describes and defines relationship: first our relationship with God and then our relationship with everyone else.

In the next chapter, we will see how, in the beginning, when we lived in perfect union with God, the only thing necessary was to maintain the "oneness" that God had already created. Sadly, we will also discover that, as simple as this responsibility appeared, the first people found it impossible to keep. The story tells us that human beings became alienated from God. However, as it unfolds, the story also tells us that time and again God took a gracious initiative toward them. As we read on, it becomes clear that although we could never make our own way back to God, he built a bridge to us. Beginning with Abraham and Sarah, God reconnects with humankind.

This reconnected relationship is ratified and reconfirmed in the lives of Moses and David.

By the time we reach the New Testament, we see a deepening in our understanding as Jesus reveals his relationship with his Father. As we follow his story, we see him invite his followers into a depth of Covenant relationship not seen before. He invited them to experience the same depth of relationship that he enjoyed with his Father.

Throughout this book, I hope to explain the three essential elements of Covenant. First, the Fatherhood of God. He is our Creator, and we live our lives under his loving and generous gaze. Second, identity. This flows from our relationship with God. Our identity and therefore our sense of security and confidence come from outside ourselves as God tells us that we are his children.

Third, obedience. Although this sounds rather heavy, we will discover that obedience is simply acting in a way that is consistent with our identity.

KINGDOM

Kingdom is the way in which the Bible describes and defines responsibility: first, our responsibility to represent God to the people we know and then to everyone else.

As we will see in the next chapter, human beings, as well as losing their relationship with God, also lost their ability to represent him as King. When the relationship through Abraham and Sarah was restored, the process of rebuilding our capacity to represent him also began.

First, with Joseph and later in numerous other women and men, God's Kingship was expressed in his Covenant partners. In time, the Kingship of God would be seen most perfectly in the life of Jesus.

Joseph was the first example of someone being called to carry the responsibility of Kingdom representation. In his life, we see God's Kingship expressed, revealed in the context of submission and human frailty.

In the New Testament, Jesus deepens our understanding of the Kingdom (or Kingship) of God. He came as the King incognito, revealing to his disciples that they should represent him by living as he lived, doing as he did and loving as he loved.

As with Covenant, I believe there are three essential elements to a complete understanding of Kingdom. First, there is the King himself. God is the majestic ruler of heaven and earth, and he seeks to extend his loving rule through the lives of all people. Second, authority. As King, God clearly has the authority to act, but remarkably, he expresses his authority through people who choose to carry the responsibility of representing him. Third, power. As the Creator and sustainer of the universe, God holds incredible power. He chooses to use this to express his love to people and, more surprisingly, through people who carry his authority as King.

Now that I have given a brief overview of the journey we are about to make, our preparations are complete, and we can now begin. We will see both themes of Covenant and Kingdom writ large in the lives of the great characters of the Bible. We begin with the Creation and the place of bliss called the Garden of Eden.

Notes

You will notice that in the main sections of this book there are margins like this one. These are for your own notes and will include extra thoughts that will further our understanding of the Bible story we are studying.

Chapter 1

Creation

To understand the Bible, we need to start where it begins, with the book of Genesis.

Let's try to read it from the perspective of those who first heard these words. In their world of wonder, day and night, the skies spoke of the Creator. The people knew that somehow, beyond the spiraling expanse of the heavens (the skies), the Lord was seated above the highest vault. The angelic beings were thought by some to be lesser gods, and they were represented in the heavens by stars of greater or lesser brightness. Surrounded by this royal court, God the Creator was enthroned. As Genesis opens, these first readers and listeners would have imagined God speaking from this throne using the first person plural ("we") of royalty:

"Then God said, 'Let us make man in our image, in our likeness, and let them rule over the fish of the sea and the birds of the air, over the livestock, over all the earth, and over all the creatures that move along the ground.' So God created man in his own image, in the image of God he created him; male and female he created them." (Genesis 1:26-27)[1]

With these words, God revealed the wondrous scope of his creative activity. Incredible though it may have appeared to those first readers, God intended that people would bear his imprint, and even rule the world. They would reflect his identity and represent him to all of creation. Even the angelic court of heaven was to be secondary to God's purposes in this. Humankind would be his sole representatives on the earth. They and they alone would be the means by which God would govern the earth.

1: The image of God is borne by both man and woman. We are equal in our connection to God.

Human beings were intended to rule the world on God's behalf.

FORMED FROM DUST

The poetic language of Genesis renders a vision of creative beauty:

"the Lord God formed man from the dust of the ground and breathed into his nostrils the breath of life and the man became a living being." (Genesis 2:7)

With the words of creation still hanging in the air and with all of heaven looking on in breathless wonder, God reached down from his throne and scooped up the clay of the earth, shaping it with his fingers into a new being designed for his purpose. And then he gave it life! The clay turned to flesh, the eyes opened and Adam began his existence looking into the face of his Creator:

"Then the Lord God made a woman from the rib he had taken out of the man, and he brought her to the man. The man said, 'This is now bone of my bones and flesh of my flesh; she shall be called "woman," for she was taken out of man.'" (Genesis 2:22-23)[2]

Adam's human partner Eve began as flesh of his flesh. They were always intended to function together as one—as partners together with their Creator.

With this epic story, the first book of the Bible begins, and its two main themes are introduced.

COVENANT

From the beginning, God created us in his likeness. He wanted to tie our identity to his. When creation was pristine and unsullied by the stain of sin, God placed us in prime position, the crown of his creation. We were the pinnacle, the high point of all that he had made. And unlike all of his other creatures, God made us in his image.

The word translated as "image" also means "imprint." When God created us, he pressed the imprint of his presence upon us. Building on the figurative language of this ancient account, it is as though God had left his handprint in the clay from which we were made. The imprint was always intended to be filled by the hand that made it. His presence was always meant to fill human existence and experience. When Adam and Eve asserted their independence and pulled away from the hand of God, his Spirit no longer filled that imprint. They began to feel empty, uncovered and vulnerable.

"Covenant" is the fundamental concept that lies at the heart of this truth. Covenant is all about relationship: the word means "to become one." God's desire was that we should live in unfettered union with him. God's desire was that, when anyone looked at us, they would see him!

Covenant means becoming or being one. We were made to be one with God.

Kingdom is the expression of God's Kingship on the earth, which he chooses to express through us.

KINGDOM

Alongside the theme of relationship expressed in the language of Covenant, there is also responsibility, expressed in the language of Kingship or Kingdom. Kingdom follows Covenant because responsibility always follows relationship. Our fundamental responsibility was to represent God. Adam and Eve and all successive generations of human beings were designed and destined to be God's representatives:

"The Lord God took the man and put him in the Garden of Eden to work it and to take care of it." (Genesis 2:15)

Their task, still ours today, was quite simple: to steward, oversee and care for all creation. They would begin this task in a place specially prepared for them—the "Garden of Eden." Here Adam and Eve's work would directly express God's kingly rule.

When we read the early chapters of the Bible from this perspective, there is no doubt that human beings were intended to be God's co-regents on the earth. Standing in God's place, Adam names all the animals, giving them their identity, and thereby asserting his authority over them. "So the man gave names to all the livestock, the birds of the air and all the beasts of the field." (Genesis 2:20a). So if this was our Creator's initial intention, what went wrong?

THE FALL

In the beginning, the Covenant partnership between God and us was defined by our dependency on him. Together, Adam and Eve would be "one" with God. They would rule, and he would direct. And as he directed, he set limits for their actions. Adam and Eve were free to represent God in any way that was most natural to them. But God required that they depend on him for their ethical decisions. They could eat from any tree in the Garden, including the tree of life. However, with all this freedom came one restriction: they were not allowed to eat from the tree of the knowledge of good and evil. The boundary was not arbitrary. Rather, it gave a framework that would set them free to enjoy their relationship with God without an extra burden of responsibility.

Then the serpent offered them the fruit of the knowledge of good and evil, and told them that they would become like God if they consumed it. The tragedy of the Fall was that, although Adam and Eve had enjoyed an unmatched relationship with God, they chose to pull away from him and assert their independence[3]:

"The Lord God called to the man, 'Where are you?'" (Genesis 3:9)

God's poignant question resonates with a deep sense of loss—we can hear the dereliction in his voice. Why such a feeling of loss? Because his dearly loved children had chosen to determine their own lives rather than rely upon him. The "oneness" that was theirs had been lost, and the connection to him as their source of life was broken.

3: We can define sin as distance from God created by our desire for independence from him.

"He [Adam] answered, 'I heard you in the garden, and I was afraid because I was naked; so I hid.'" (Genesis 3:9-10)

Created in God's image, his first people had his imprint upon them. But as they pulled away, the impression made by this imprint was emptied, and they felt naked. In a futile attempt to feel covered, they sewed fig leaves together to clothe themselves. "Then the eyes of both of them were opened, and they realized they were naked; so they sewed fig leaves together and made coverings for themselves." (Genesis 3:7)

This freedom of choice was given as a sign of their relationship when God made them. He wanted them to choose partnership (being one with him), but they chose independence, self-determination and separation. Human beings continue to make this choice. But the consequence of this decision was not only separation from God. The consequence was even more serious. Because the connection to Life was severed, Adam and Eve began to die. And their broken relationship meant that they also surrendered their capacity to rule. In submitting to the temptation of the serpent, Adam and Eve lost their rightful place before God and surrendered their throne—making room for the accession of another, who would later be known as the devil.

And so the world fell under the influence of one who hated God, hated his creation and in particular hated that part of creation that bore God's image. All the maladies and miseries of the world originated here—all the sickness and suffering began here, with a wrongful ruler given power by our wrongdoing. In the darkness of his evil heart, the devil conceived a plan to oppose God's purposes by stealing the position designed for us.[4]

4: We may find this idea troubling, but the New Testament confirms the picture. The devil is known as the "god" of this world: the prince who rules in darkness. For example, "We know that we are children of God, and that the whole world is under the control of the evil one." (1 John 5:19) We'll look at this complex issue in more depth later.

HOPE OF RESTORATION

But God had a plan, one that would recover all the ground that was lost, remake the relationships that were broken and destroy the enemy that stood opposed to us all.

How would God do it? Not by the use of his overwhelming superiority or creative majesty, not by force or might, but by the use of one human being—another "Adam." God would give humanity a chance to reclaim what they had lost.[5] But it would require one who would live in perfect dependence on God: one who would live in a Covenant relationship with his Father and in the Kingdom responsibility that comes from the King of the universe. As we look at the unfolding story of Scripture, we see that in time the "second Adam" would be revealed.

However, we are given only hints of this in the first epic story of Genesis, a book that begins to reveal the depths of God's Covenant love and the scope of his Kingdom power.

5: By the end of the Bible, we see a glorious picture of the whole creation restored.

Chapter 2

After the Fall

"The Lord God made garments of skin for Adam and his wife and clothed them. And the Lord God said, 'The man has now become like one of us, knowing good and evil. He must not be allowed to reach out his hand and take also from the tree of life and eat, and live forever.' So the Lord God banished him from the Garden of Eden to work the ground from which he had been taken. After he drove the man out, he placed on the east side of the Garden of Eden cherubim and a flaming sword flashing back and forth to guard the way to the tree of life." (Genesis 3:21-24)

When we read these words, we are confronted with two quite different perspectives on God's character. We can see both tenderness and severity. Tenderness in the way that God made clothes for Adam and Eve. Severity in the way that he dealt with their rebellion by banishing them from his presence and cutting them off from the source of their eternal life with him. And so it will ever be: God is drawn toward us by his great love but simultaneously repelled by the ugliness of our sin.[1]

Incredibly, though, God's love is greater than his judgment—his impulse to embrace is greater than his impulse to reject. And so, in his great love, God began to unfold the plan that would make a way for us—a way back to the Garden and to the closeness of his presence that Adam and Eve once knew.

1: God's love for his lost children overcomes his repulsion of their sinfulness. His plan for a new relationship begins to unfold.

THE FLOOD OF JUDGMENT AND COVENANT PROMISE

When we lost our right to live in the Garden, we also lost some of our natural boundaries for good behavior. As the story continues, we see that humanity's separation from God led to increasingly extravagant sinfulness and a deepening depravity that caused God great pain.

"The Lord saw how great man's wickedness on the earth had become, and that every inclination of the thoughts of his heart was only evil all the time. The Lord was grieved that he had made man on the earth, and his heart was filled with pain." (Genesis 6:5-6)

God's decision (referred to as his "judgment") was to start again. He sent the flood to cleanse the world and give it a fresh start. But not all would be lost; Noah and his family would survive, in the safekeeping of the Ark.[2] When the rain had stopped, Noah released a dove, and when it did not return, he knew that the waters of judgment had subsided and that, somewhere, there was a safe place to start again. After the flood, God made a Covenant promise to Noah and all who came after him that the Lord would never again destroy the world with water. This promise was sealed with the symbol of the rainbow:

"And God said, 'This is the sign of the covenant I am making between me and you and every living creature with you, a covenant for all generations to come: I have set my rainbow in the clouds, and it will be the sign of the covenant between me and the earth. Whenever I bring the clouds over the earth and the rainbow appears in the clouds, I will remember my

2: See Genesis chapters 6 – 8

To unfold his plan, God decides to "start again."

14

covenant between me and you and all living creatures of every kind. Never again will the waters become a flood to destroy all life.'" (Genesis 9:12-15)

This "rainbow Covenant" was, to put it simply, an agreement between God and us that he would not destroy the world again by flood. Though more would be needed to put us fully right with God, he was taking a small but important step back toward a Covenant relationship.

Though God would have been justified in "unmaking" his creation so that it ceased to exist, he chose to preserve it with the knowledge that one day he would "remake" it when all his plans were fulfilled.

THE TOWER OF BABEL AND THE SCATTERING OF THE NATIONS

Even though humanity was not entirely destroyed in the flood, they were still lost and alienated from the Creator. This caused a deep longing. The empty space within them desired the presence of their Creator. The imprint left by his hand longed for the touch that would fill the emptiness.

"Then they said, 'Come, let us build ourselves a city, with a tower that reaches to the heavens.'" (Genesis 11:4)

Humanity's need for God was combined with self-assertiveness, and they decided to build a stairway to heaven. The worldview at this time was that God lived just beyond the

3: The Tower of Babel was probably a stepped pyramid like those built by many cultures around the world. Interestingly, when Jacob saw his "stairway to heaven," perhaps this is what he saw. (Genesis 28:11-17)

4: As created beings, we can achieve unity with one another only when we are one with the Creator. Paul picks up this emphasis in Galatians 3:28: "There is neither Jew nor Greek, slave nor free, male nor female, **for you are all one in Christ Jesus**." (emphasis mine)

visible sky. And so if they could build something that could break the clouds, then perhaps they could reach him also. If God would not come down and touch them, then they would build a tower and touch him![3]

God saw the presumption in their striving and confused their tongues, leading to the ethnic and national divisions that have separated humanity ever since. Since we had lost our close relationship with God, our relationships with one another were always susceptible to division. God wanted to build a secure foundation for the unity of humankind, and he would do this by creating a Covenant relationship with us. By making a Covenant and "being one" with us, he would enable us to "be one" with each another.[4]

Chapter 3

Abraham
Man of Covenant

"*T*he Lord had said to Abram, 'Leave your country, your people and your father's household and go to the land I will show you.'" (Genesis 12:1)

We meet Abram and his wife Sarai (later renamed Abraham and Sarah) as they travel in the household caravan of Abram's father Terah, migrating from the overcrowded plains of the Tigris and Euphrates rivers toward the Fertile Crescent of Canaan. Research into this period suggests that many others were making the same westward journey. But when Abram and Sarai came to Haran (only partway toward their destination), they settled. The Lord revealed himself to them and declared his intention to bless Abram and Sarai:

"I will make you into a great nation and I will bless you; I will make your name great, and you will be a blessing. I will bless those who bless you, and whoever curses you I will curse; and all the peoples on earth will be blessed through you." (Genesis 12:2-3)[1]

However, Haran was not the place of blessing, and so they had to move on. But like all of us, Abram inserts his own ideas into God's plan. Instead of leaving his "father's household" behind, Abram takes Lot, his nephew, along with the rest of his household.

"Now there was a famine in the land, and Abram went down to Egypt to live there for a while because the famine was severe." (Genesis 12:10)

Abram's whole family leaves Canaan for Egypt to escape starvation, and on their return, Abram and Lot choose to separate.

1: The new relationship begins with God taking an initiative. He chooses to bless Abram.

It would appear that their joint households were too numerous to use the same land and resources. Lot chose the fertile Jordan Rift Valley and the settled existence of urban life. Abram chose the nomadic existence of the "wandering Aramean."[2]

VITAL EARLY ALLIANCES

The relationship between Abram and Lot was tested further when land-hungry local chieftains went to war. After the attack on the place where Lot had chosen to settle, he and his household were carried off. When Abram heard of this, he took several hundred well-equipped men from his extended household, pursued the chieftains, fought them and rescued Lot and his family.[3]

These incidents and the record of the wanderings of Abram and Sarai (which can be so quickly passed over as we read through Genesis) reveal a world full of danger where alliances with local chieftains were the only means of securing peace and protection. It is difficult for us to comprehend how insecure the world was for them. In most places, there was no civil law— no protection of person or property. Without the presence of strong allies, individuals and their households, however numerous, would quickly fall prey to others. The only options for security were either to live in (or near) the newly emerging walled cities of the region or to make Covenants with others, ensuring mutual protection and support. Lot chose one alternative and Abram the other. For those who chose the wandering life, Covenant-making emerged as the best available thread to hold together the fragile fabric of society.[4]

Lot returned to his home in the city of Sodom. Abram began the process of forming a Covenant of friendship with Melchizedek, king of Salem. Melchizedek offered Abram a meal—always a sign of friendship in the world of the Bible—of bread and wine. Then, following the convention of the day in combining priesthood and Kingship, Melchizedek blessed Abram. Abram responded by giving one tenth of his property to Melchizedek.

In these actions, there was clearly a desire for friendship. Abram and Melchizedek shared food and exchanged blessings and gifts. Perhaps these actions were the first overtures of a Covenant relationship. However, we know a Covenant was much more than a simple friendship because a Covenant entailed two groups (families, households, tribes) actually becoming one. Having become one, the households then shared provision and protection. The benefits of a full Covenant relationship would last a lifetime. Perhaps this is why hospitality and the honoring of guests were, and continue to be, so important in Near Eastern culture. There was no knowing what good would result from a simple welcome!

As this part of the story concludes, the world for Abram and Sarai remains very uncertain. No doubt they often felt anxious and wondered where they might find the protection they needed. What a great relief it must have been to them when the Lord revealed his plan: he would be their protection.

5: The Covenant is formed.

THE LORD'S PROMISE TO ABRAM

"After this, the word of the Lord came to Abram in a vision: 'Do not be afraid, Abram. I am your shield, your very great reward.'" (Genesis 15:1)

The Lord offered himself as Abram's protection (shield) and provision (reward). Abram could rest in the confidence that he was protected and provided for.[5]

But there was much more than this hidden in God's promise to Abram. "Shield" and "sovereign" are the same word in Hebrew. By using this word, the Lord pointed to himself as the King of heaven, offering to bless Abram with a royal blessing. Abram had already received one such blessing, from an earthly king— Melchizedek. It was only natural for Abram to wonder what God's blessing might include. Could this be the answer to his and Sarai's longing for a son? Could this be the first overture of a hoped-for Covenant with God? Abram pursues the conversation and gently presses the Lord to see how far he might be prepared to go. Using the same word the Lord had used for himself, Abram replies:

"Oh sovereign Lord, what can you give me since I remain childless and the one who will inherit my estate is Eliezer of Damascus?" (Genesis 15:2)

Abram and his wife are old and well past the usual age for having children, so it is not surprising that we can hear the frustration in his voice.

"COUNT THE STARS" – GOD'S OUTRAGEOUS PROMISE

In response, the Lord takes Abram outside. God directs Abram's gaze toward the heavens. Remember, in Abram's mind, each luminous dot represented a member of God's royal court, the "heavenly host."

"Look up at the heavens and count the stars—if indeed you can count them . . . So shall your offspring be." (Genesis 15:5)[6]

Was God really saying that Abram's descendants would outnumber the multitudes that populated the sky? Could God truly be saying that Abram's household would be greater than the royal household of heaven? Surely this was impossible! Abram and his wife did not have a single child. And yet, somewhere in Abram's heart, he knew that it was enough that God had said it. Abram chose to believe God. In Abram's world, only the words of a Covenant partner could truly be trusted. However, Abram chose to trust God's words as if they were spoken by a Covenant partner. And so God related to Abram in exactly the same way.

The story so far in the book of Genesis makes it blatantly clear that humans could not come near to God by themselves. For Abram, God was unknown, far off and—in his understanding—of a completely different substance. God is holy; Abram was human. And Abram was alienated from God, like the rest of humanity. But God spoke to Abram, and Abram received what was spoken—and it became faith in his heart.[7] From a biblical point of view, faith to believe God comes from listening to God speak to us. Because of

23

6: God promises Abram's household will be as big as his.

"Abram believed the Lord, and he credited it to him as righteousness." (Genesis 15:6)

7: "Consequently, faith comes from hearing the message, and the message is heard through the word of Christ." (Romans 10:17)

his faith, God gave Abram the gift of a relationship with him. Literally, God gave Abram "righteousness"—or a "right relationship" where no "wrong" could spoil it. This had to be given by God as a gift—Abram could not have it by any right or effort of his own. God had extended an invitation to Abram: an invitation to a journey that would lead all the way back to the Garden of Eden.[8]

The two were no longer alienated. They would walk together always, and would know each other in the deep communion of Covenant.

The necessary acceptance and commitment had taken place within Abram's heart and mind, but God took what was hidden and revealed it. He confirmed it in blood and death.

THE COVENANT CONFIRMED IN BLOOD

"The Lord said . . . 'Bring me a heifer, a goat and a ram, each three years old, along with a dove and the young pigeon.'" (Genesis 15:9)

These were the words that Abram had been longing to hear! He had heard the promise; now he would have a Covenant. In common with most of us, Abram needed material evidence of spiritual truths. In the Bible, Covenants are always confirmed and represented in the external, physical world through the shedding of blood.

Only with difficulty can we imagine the scale of Abram's sheer joy and relief. No doubt his heart pounded and his pulse raced as he rushed to prepare the animals for the ritual:

"Abram brought all these to him, cut them in two and arranged the halves opposite each other." (Genesis 15:10)

Abram butchered the animals in the field, apparently laying open the creatures from head to tail so that their carcasses created a "corridor of blood." Having driven away the carrion birds, and exhausted from all his exertions, Abram fell into a deep sleep. The desert would already have been pitch black at night, but a supernatural darkness then descended on Abram.[9]

From the darkness and into Abram's sleep, God spoke. He spoke of the future, trial and difficulty, victory and freedom. But the Lord began with words Abram so needed to hear in his fragile and vulnerable world: "Know for certain." (Genesis 15:13) Relief flooded Abram's soul as he heard those words. There could be certainty at last. And to ratify the Covenant, God passed between the pieces.

"When the sun had set and darkness had fallen, a smoking fire pot with a blazing torch appeared and passed between the pieces. On that day the Lord made [literally "cut"] a covenant with Abram." (Genesis 15:17-18a)

Three physical signs of God's presence—a smoking firepot, a flaming torch and enveloping darkness—tell us everlasting truths about God. The Lord was both hidden (the darkness) and revealed (in the light). The Lord's presence, like fire, both attracts and repels. We draw near for warmth but must keep our distance, lest we be burned. God's love draws us toward him, but his holiness threatens to consume us as we come closer. In the end, it is our decision how close we come and how willing we are to risk being consumed.[10]

Notes

9: "As the sun was setting, Abram fell into a deep sleep, and a thick and dreadful darkness came over him." (Genesis 15:12)

10: In the New Testament, the book of Hebrews helps us understand this truth: "Let us draw near to God with a sincere heart in full assurance of faith, having our hearts sprinkled to cleanse us from a guilty conscience and having our bodies washed with pure water." (Hebrews 10:22) "Therefore, since we are receiving a kingdom that cannot be shaken, let us be thankful, and so worship God acceptably with reverence and awe, for our 'God is a consuming fire.'" (Hebrews 12:28-29)

TWO BECOMING ONE

We can appreciate the symbolism of fire, smoke and darkness, but why did the firepot and blazing torch "pass between the pieces"? Did this mean anything to Abram? To answer this, we need to use a little imagination. Let's picture two leaders—chieftains, representing their respective people—standing at either end of the "corridor of blood." As they each "pass between the pieces" of the sacrificed animals, the leaders move to take their new place, at the head of a new people. The leaders have exchanged places, and their actions state that "your people are now united with my people, and my people are united with yours." The two have become one. In Abram's case, this symbolic "becoming one" is visualized by God traveling from one end of the corridor of blood to the other. God clearly took the initiative in creating the Covenant by asking Abram to provide the animals, and as he laid them out, Abram passed between them himself. For a Covenant to work, both partners had to participate; both had to give up their old identities and start new lives.

Becoming one means taking on the identity of our Covenant partner.

BLOOD SACRIFICES IN ANCIENT CULTURE

To underline the importance and gravity of the Covenant, animals were sacrificed. And not just any animals; in Abram's case, it was precious three-year-old livestock, mature and capable of reproducing. When someone passed between the pieces of a butchered animal, the blood symbolized the surrender of the person's old life. It was a visualization of death. The bloody passageway could also be argued to represent the birth canal and the beginning of a new life.

This seems a strange ritual to us, but in the Bronze Age, Covenant-making culture, such things were quite normal. The world from which the Old Testament Scriptures arose was a society deeply familiar with the rituals of Covenant-making. Right up to the time of Jeremiah, many hundreds of years later, people were "walking between the pieces" to ratify a Covenant. In the book of Jeremiah, the people who had been enslaved by their fellow countrymen were set free into new lives by walking between the pieces of a butchered calf. The fact that in the books of Jeremiah and Genesis there is so little explanation given suggests that, to the original readers, these rituals were commonplace.[11]

Though Abram did not perhaps appreciate it, for him to embrace the death of his old identity meant that he left the curse of the Fall behind him. Incredibly, God was prepared to accept this symbolic "death" to give Abram a new life with a new identity.

The Lord took the initiative; but Abram was a willing participant, and the result was true "at-one-ment." Atonement means precisely what the word suggests. A Covenant sacrifice means that we "become one" with God. Because they had "cut a Covenant," the greater and stronger partner (the Lord) had conferred upon the lesser and weaker partners (Abram and Sarai) the right to be equal partners with him. Covenants with God always depend on the initiative of his grace.

11: Even in the time of Jeremiah, these rituals were so commonplace that they were mentioned with hardly any explanation: "The men who have violated my covenant and have not fulfilled the terms of the covenant they made before me, I will treat like the calf they cut in two and then walked between its pieces." (Jeremiah 34:18)

GOD'S ENDURING FAITHFULNESS

We have to assume that the full implications of the Covenant as we now understand it remained hidden from Abram and Sarai. Surely, they could not have imagined that one day God would fulfill the promise implicit in the Covenant and fully embrace their identity and become a human being. They could not have foreseen that their Covenant, sealed in the blood of animals, would point the way to a greater mystery, with the King of heaven leaving his home, taking our humanity, living a perfect life, giving up his own blood and his own life so that we could find new birth and everlasting life.

They could not have known.

In any case, next we read that they even tried to fulfill God's promise themselves, rather than waiting on God's timing. Following the conventional practice of the day, Abram slept with Sarai's servant girl Hagar to produce an heir, and she gave birth to Ishmael. But this was not God's plan, and he did not accept it as a solution. Abram and Sarai were trying to fix their childless state themselves, rather than depend on God. However, in his kindness, the Lord chose to bless them all anyway! Abram and Sarai were blessed and so were Hagar and her son.[12]

12: God's blessing included Hagar: "The angel added, 'I will so increase your descendants that they will be too numerous to count.' The angel of the Lord also said to her: 'you are now with child and you will have a son. You shall name him Ishmael, for the Lord has heard of your misery.'" (Genesis 16:10-11)

NEW NAME – NEW IDENTITY

As the story rolls forward, the Lord appeared again to Abram and reiterated his promise of children:

"I am the Lord Almighty, walk before me and be blameless. I will confirm my covenant between me and you and will greatly increase your numbers." (Genesis 17:2)

"Abram fell facedown as the Lord said to him, 'As for me, this is my covenant with you: you will be the father of many nations. No longer will you be called Abram [meaning "exalted father"]; your name will be Abraham ["father of nations"], for I have made you a father of many nations." (Genesis 17:1-5)

A new identity called for a new name. Both Abram and Sarai were "renamed" by God.[13] In giving them new names, the Lord did something extraordinary. He took letters from his own name—"Yahweh"—and gave one to each. In Hebrew, only the consonants are recorded, so Yahweh is written YHWH. (The vowels are added in speech as the text is read aloud.) God took his two "H's" and gave one each to Abram and Sarai so that their names became Abraham and Sarah. Abraham became the "father of many nations" and Sarah remained a "princess," but now her children would carry the mark of heaven's King. Covenant is about "two becoming one," and the identities of the partners are shared. God shows his amazing commitment to his Covenant partners in the gift of the letters of his name.

13: "God also said to Abraham, 'As for Sarai your wife, you are no longer to call her Sarai; her name will be Sarah. I will bless her and will surely give you a son by her. I will bless her so that she will be the mother of nations; kings of peoples will come from her.'" (Genesis 17:15-16)

Rabbinical teachers of the Old Testament such as Rabbi Abbahu (c. AD 300) taught that "And I will make your name great" (Genesis 12:2) means, "I will add the letter He to your name," thus reinforcing the idea of a shared identity in the Covenant that God was making. I thank my friend Dr. Crispin Fletcher-Louis, Principal of Westminster Theological Centre, for confirming this.

14: Being one with God means
reconnecting with his desire for
us—he wants us to be fruitful.

THE MARK OF COVENANT

The Lord was refashioning a relationship with human beings through Abraham and Sarah. The Lord chose a couple who were childless and spent as his partners, proving their new "oneness" with him through a new, clearly God-given, capacity to reproduce despite their age.[14] They fulfilled God's original desire for humanity to "be fruitful." The Lord's promise of children and his renewed commitment to them were signaled in a permanent, irrevocable sign—a scar.

"You and your descendants must keep my covenant; every male shall be circumcised." (Genesis 17:10)

Circumcision was not a public sign but, rather, a personal reminder of the Covenant that God had made with his people. Abraham and all his male descendants would bear a mark on their bodies to confirm that their old lives were gone (literally "rolled away") and new lives had begun.

Many Covenant-making cultures throughout history and around the world have used scars as a way to ratify agreements. We have some knowledge of the "blood brother" rituals of the Native American peoples and the Roman legionnaires. The physical reminder of a scar had an important role in underlining the significance of the relationship. In this case, the scar of circumcision makes a clear statement that the spiritual and physical are interlinked, not separate.

Interestingly, scars continue as important signs of the New Covenant in Jesus.

Remember, Covenant is a relationship of "oneness" and reciprocation. God asked Abraham to bear a scar in order to confirm their Covenant—but in the New Covenant, God himself chose to carry scars. The resurrected body of Jesus bears scars to this day.[15]

The New Testament tells us that today those who are in Covenant relationship with God through Jesus also bear a scar: "circumcision of the heart."[16] This hidden spiritual scar is produced by the operation of God's Spirit within us. As God fulfills his promise to be one with us, so we begin to sense the growth of inner confidence and self-worth. The presence of God's Spirit constantly reminds us that we are children of God—that we share his identity and he has shared ours:

"For you did not receive a spirit that makes you a slave again to fear, but you received the Spirit of sonship. And by him we cry, 'Abba Father.' The Spirit himself testifies with our spirit that we are God's children." (Romans 8:15-16)

These are amazing words, and this is an incredible truth. As we continue to journey through the Bible, we will see the truth deepen until we have a complete picture of the Covenant relationship.

ISAAC, THE LONG-AWAITED SON

The Lord kept his promise, and he announced its imminent arrival in a quite remarkable way.

"Abraham looked up and saw three men standing nearby . . .

Notes

15: After being resurrected, Jesus showed his scars to his disciples (Luke 24:40 and John 20:27) as evidence that he really was the same Jesus who had been publicly crucified a few days before and that he was more than an apparition—they could see and touch his scars! Of course, Abraham had no idea that his Covenant foreshadowed another.

16: "No, a man is a Jew if he is one inwardly; and circumcision is circumcision of the heart, by the Spirit, not by the written code. Such a man's praise is not from men, but from God." (Romans 2:29)

17: "Then the Lord said, 'The outcry against Sodom and Gomorrah is so great and their sin so grievous that I will go down and see if what they have done is as bad as the outcry that has reached me. If not, I will know.' The men turned away and went toward Sodom, but Abraham remained standing before the Lord." (Genesis 18:20-22)

18: See Genesis 18:23-33

19: Lot's wife, hankering for her past life, was caught in the moment of judgment and turned to salt.

20: See Genesis 19:1-29

The Lord said, 'I will surely return to you about this time next year, and Sarah your wife will have a son.'" (Genesis 18:1-10, extracted v. 2 and 10)

Flanked by two angels, members of his royal court, the Lord revealed himself and spoke to Abraham face-to-face. Not since the Garden had the Lord been in such close proximity—sitting, eating, walking and talking—with his creatures. During their conversation, framed within the welcoming rituals of the day, the Lord revealed that Sarah would become pregnant and have a son. His name would be "laughter" (Isaac), both because of the joy he would bring and the chuckle that Sarah let out as she listened to the Lord's promise from the other side of the tent curtain.

After the meal, the Lord and his companions rose to leave. Following established convention, Abraham accompanied them part of the way. The two angels, focused on a new task, moved ahead toward the cities of Sodom and Gomorrah. As the angels looked into the Jordan Rift Valley and toward the Dead Sea, the Lord engaged Abraham in discussion. God had decided to destroy the two cities because of their unbridled wickedness.[17] "Abraham, knowing that his nephew Lot lived there, sought mercy for those not caught up in the cities' sin."[18]

Abraham's boldness may seem surprising given that he was talking to the Creator bent on carrying out righteous judgment. However, Abraham's confidence came from the knowledge that his Covenant relationship was secure and any offense he might give would be forgiven or overlooked by his Covenant partner. In response to Abraham's plea, the angels rescued Lot and his family.[19] What of the cities of Sodom and Gomorrah? They were consumed by fire and would never rise again.[20]

Within a year, God duly gave Abraham and Sarah their promised son. The long-awaited child was born at last. The other part of the promise—ownership of the land of Canaan—would not be fulfilled for more than four hundred years, many generations after Abraham and Sarah's deaths. But Abraham and Sarah chose to trust God even though they had "no country of their own." They had Isaac—and that was enough.[21]

THE UNTHINKABLE SACRIFICE

Up to this point, God's Covenant with Abraham had been largely about confirming identity: an identity that comes from giving up an old life and starting a new one in union with God. But there is another vital component to a Covenant relationship, which is submission. This is described most commonly in Scripture as obedience. And this would be revealed as Abraham suffered the severest of tests.

"Then God said, 'Take your son, your only son Isaac, whom you love, and go to the region of Moriah. Sacrifice him there as a burnt offering on one of the mountains that I will tell you about.'" (Genesis 22:2)

Isaac had been given to Abraham as the physical manifestation of the promise of God. Isaac was the flesh and blood representation of Abraham's new name. Isaac was supposed to be the "father of many nations." He defined all Abraham's hopes and destiny. Yet now God wanted Isaac back!

21: This is beautifully explained in the New Testament book Hebrews: "By faith Abraham, even though he was past age—and Sarah herself was barren—was enabled to become a father because he considered him faithful who had made the promise. And so from this one man, and he as good as dead, came descendants as numerous as the stars in the sky and as countless as the sand on the seashore.

"All these people were still living by faith when they died. They did not receive the things promised; they only saw them and welcomed them from a distance. And they admitted that they were aliens and strangers on earth. People who say such things show that they are looking for a country of their own. If they had been thinking of the country they had left, they would have had opportunity to return. Instead, they were longing for a better country—a heavenly one. Therefore God is not ashamed to be called their God, for he has prepared a city for them." (Hebrews 11:11-16)

What follows is one of the great narratives of ancient literature. The story of Genesis has at times leapt through centuries, even millennia. Much of Abraham's story is light on detail. But now we have a story rich in texture, full of pace and poignancy.

Abraham, no doubt in a terrified daze, made preparations to leave. The servants were left behind, and Abraham carried the firepot.[22] The firepot was a symbol to Abraham of the Lord's presence, and the wood for the burnt offering was laid upon Isaac's shoulders. The father and son walked toward Moriah, among the hills where Abraham's friend Melchizedek lived, where King David would later establish a great city and Solomon would build a great temple. A hill where, one day in the future, another young man would carry the wood for his own sacrifice.

As they walked, Isaac asked, "Where is the lamb?" With a combination of tenderness and steely faith, Abraham replied, "God himself will provide the lamb for the burnt offering, my son." With growing tension, they walked on together.[23]

Now the story sweeps from their initial conversation to the moment where, with the altar built, the wood laid and Isaac bound, the boy is laid on the altar. It is as if the story takes a deep breath as with painful slowness it recounts Abraham taking the dagger, lifting it up and preparing to plunge it into the heart of his son. Into this most awful of moments, the Lord speaks:

"Do not lay a hand on the boy. Do not do anything to him. Now I know that you fear God, because you have not withheld from me your son, your only son." (Genesis 22:12)

Abraham's Covenant partner had tested the strength of their relationship, and it had proved unbreakable. Nothing had been

22: See Genesis 15:17

23: Abraham and Isaac's conversation reveals a son's curiosity and a father's faith.

"Isaac spoke up and said to his father Abraham, 'Father?'

Yes, my son?' Abraham replied.

'The fire and wood are here,' Isaac said, 'but where is the lamb for the burnt offering?' Abraham answered, 'God himself will provide the lamb for the burnt offering, my son.' And the two of them went on together." (Genesis 22:7-8)

held back by Abraham; and so nothing would now be withheld by the Lord. The floodgates of blessing were opened:

"I swear by myself, declares the Lord, that because you have done this and have not withheld your son, your only son, I will surely bless you and make your descendants as numerous as the stars in the sky and as the sand on the seashore. Your descendants will take possession of the cities of their enemies, and through your offspring all nations on earth will be blessed, because you have obeyed me." (Genesis 22:16-18)

There is no detailed account of their journey home. But I wonder, as Abraham walked back with Isaac to the waiting servants, what occupied his thoughts? Did he ask himself whether the Lord, his Covenant partner, would do the same for him?

We may wonder at Abraham's capacity to obey God in what seemed an impossible task. We may have wondered at his boldness, even rudeness, when interceding for Sodom and Gomorrah. Abraham's secret was his sense of security: God had chosen Abraham, and had given him a new identity—of oneness with himself. Because of this, Abraham knew what God was like, and so could trust the outcome of even the hardest trial. In our walk with God, our capacity for perseverance in difficulties, and the ability to obey will be determined by how secure we feel in our relationship with him. If we begin with our new identity, given to us in the Covenant we share with God, then we will have security; security will lead to confidence, and confidence to courage.

FINAL THOUGHTS ON THE FIRST COVENANT

As we come to the end of Abraham and Sarah's story, our journey through the Scriptures has only just begun. We have seen that a Covenant is about "becoming one," and so at its heart is about **identity**. We have come to understand that Covenant is about submitting what we have into the hands of our Covenant partner, and so our **obedience** is fundamental.

The Bible is a landscape, and as our journey through the Bible continues, these ideas will be deepened and refined so that we find ourselves more confidently traversing the mountains and valleys of Scripture. But (if you will allow me a swift switch of imagery) the Bible is also like an intricately woven fabric, and having identified the first thread (the "warp" of Covenant), we must now turn to examine the other—the "weft" of Kingdom.

Bloodthirsty Passages in the Bible

"They devoted the city (Jericho) to the Lord and destroyed with the sword every living thing in it – men and women, young and old, cattle, sheep and donkeys." (Joshua 6:21)

"Completely destroy them – the Hittites, Amorites, Canaanites, Perizzites, Hivites and Jebusites – as the Lord your God has commanded you." (Deuteronomy 20:17)

"Let burning coals fall upon them; may they be thrown into the fire, into miry pits, never to rise." (Psalms 140:10)

"Surely God will crush the heads of his enemies . . . that you may plunge your feet in the blood of your foes." (Psalms 68:21a and 23a)

There is no getting away from the fact that the Old Testament is filled with stories of a bloodthirsty nature, with God apparently cheering his people on as they kill their enemies and call down curses on them.[1] Perhaps the best way to understand such disturbing passages of Scripture is to remember the old adage, "the Old Testament is the New Testament concealed—the New Testament is the Old Testament revealed."

These stories were written in times that were very different from ours, when violent attacks could come from any corner at any time, and the Israelites would never have survived as a people for any period of time without defending themselves from their enemies. For us, these events should be understood as visual aids showing the gravity of the threat from (in our case, hidden) forces of evil and to help us understand how we should take up our positions in relation to that evil. When the writers of the Psalms ask for God's intervention and judgment on particular people, the writers are expressing the desire in all of us for simple justice.

In the New Testament, now that the people of God have become defined spiritually rather than ethnically, we discover that we are to leave such things in the hands of God, knowing that all injustices will be set right by him on the last day. Some theologians

---

1 See, for instance, 1 Samuel 18:25-27 or 1 Samuel 27:8-9.

have proposed the idea of a "just war"—one that is waged to bring justice and deliverance from oppression. This is quite different from any kind of "holy war," which is not sanctioned by Scripture when the whole of the Bible is taken into account. Of course, this has not stopped some people from drawing on religion to justify wars, massacres and atrocities down through the centuries—wrongs that sadly remain all too present today.

The New Testament makes it clear that the battle we now face is not meant to be principally with human beings but with the agents of evil (fallen angels called demons, controlled and overseen by their leader and master, the devil), and it is this enemy that we must gird ourselves to fight and defeat. Thus, as we read the Psalms today, we can read them with gusto, knowing that the adversaries we need to defeat are not human but the devil and his demonic hierarchy:

"For our struggle is not against flesh and blood, but against the rulers, against the authorities, against the powers of this dark world and against the spiritual forces of evil in the heavenly realms." (Ephesians 6:12)

These Old Testament passages, so graphic in their content, remind us that our life is not just like a battle but actually is a battle, and one we fight every day.

The last book of the Bible, Revelation, makes it clear that standing behind the brutality and sadness of the world is a mighty conflict between the Kingdom of God and the kingdom of darkness. The devil and his minions seek to extend their control through evil, pain and corruption, while God aims to extend his rule through his people as they imitate Jesus' life to overcome their mutual enemy. God will win, because he is the Creator of the universe and there is no one with comparative power. But he chooses to use human beings—Abraham, Joseph and others throughout the Old Testament, and then his Son, who became a man, and now us, as the people who have responded to his call.

The task of redeeming his creation from the occupying powers of evil is not straightforward, and there will be many twists and turns in the battle before victory is won. There will be many who suffer the assaults of the devil's arsenal of sin, pain and suffering, with no guarantee of earthly resolution before the final shout of victory is heard.

The result is certain, but the battle is real. The Bible is our visual aid intended to help us understand this truth.

Chapter 4

Joseph
Called to Kingdom Rule

*W*e have only just begun our journey through the Bible, and there will be many twists and turns before we reach our destination. To navigate the physical landscape effectively, we need coordinates of latitude and longitude. The first is found in the theme of Covenant, and the second is in Kingdom.

In Abraham, we saw how the Lord made a sovereign decision to win back humanity. He would remake a relationship with us, using a Covenant agreement as the basis. Symbolically, God and Abraham became one. As a token, animal substitutes shed their blood and died. As God and Abraham each walked the bloody pathway "between the pieces," they made a life-and-death commitment to one another and put an end to any separate existence.

With the story of Abraham and Sarah, Scripture introduces us to the governing principles behind Covenant. However, by the end of this first book of the Bible, the other great theme would also be developed. In the story of Joseph, we see the Kingdom—or "Kingship" of God—at work.

In the life of Joseph, we see for the first time something of what the "rule" of God would be like when working through a chosen representative.

In the same way that we saw God refashioning a relationship with humankind through Abraham, so in Joseph we see God relaunching his plan for human representation in the world.

> *Covenant refers to relationship.*
> *Kingdom refers to responsibility.*

We have already seen that Covenant means relationship. Now we discover that Kingdom reveals responsibility.

Covenant is about identity and obedience. Kingdom (Kingship) is about authority and power.

Of course, some may question the legitimacy of my approach here. They may suggest that Covenant is the principal theme of the Old Testament, and Kingdom of the New. It is true that when we read the New Testament we encounter a clear presentation of the Kingdom of God, and it was clearly fundamental to the message of Jesus. But what Jesus said and how he lived were consistent with the whole of Scripture from beginning to end. Yes, Jesus did teach the Kingdom of God with great clarity—as is especially recorded in the first three books of the New Testament. But in doing so he was building on the Old Testament stories and doctrine. God's Kingship is one of the undergirding themes of the Old Testament. It is represented in the human kings of Israel and is often beautifully expressed in the worship of God's people enshrined in the book of Psalms.[1]

1: For instance: "The Lord has established his throne in heaven, and his kingdom rules over all." (Psalms 103:19)
"They will tell of the glory of your kingdom and speak of your might." (Psalms 145:11)

REDEMPTION AND THE CALL TO RULE

In the story of Joseph, we see the beginnings of the unfolding revelation of God's Kingship expressed through human beings. God's desire to rule "through" people is demonstrated clearly in his life. When we read the Acts of the Apostles, we find that Stephen, one of the early church leaders, defended himself before a religious court, making this point as he gave a brief overview of Scripture:

"Because the patriarchs were jealous of Joseph, they sold him as a slave into Egypt. But God was with him and rescued him from all his troubles. He gave Joseph wisdom and enabled him to gain the goodwill of Pharaoh, King of Egypt, so he made him ruler over Egypt and all his palace." (Acts 7:9-10)

Being the "ruler" over Egypt was the unmistakable calling of Joseph's life. He was called to take on a role that God had prepared for him. Joseph's relationship to Pharaoh is symbolic of his (and our) relationship with God. There was, of course, only one King, but he chose to rule "through" Joseph. He was to become the governor of the greatest nation on the earth, and in this, he was likewise the empowered emissary of God in the world.[2]

But we learn that the path to this exalted place was not an easy one. It is a path marked by humility and weakness born out of suffering and difficulty. Joseph's story introduces the idea of us representing God in this world.

DESPISED BY HIS BROTHERS

"Now Israel (Jacob) loved Joseph more than any of his other sons, because he had been born to him in his old age; and he made a richly ornamented robe for him. When his brothers saw that their father loved him more than any of them, they hated him and could not speak a kind word to him." (Genesis 37:1-4)[3]

This remarkable young man was identified as the object of his father's special love and attention. Joseph was the favored one.

43

He was even given a coat with rich ornamentation and long sleeves such as might normally be given to the firstborn son, to indicate that he should not have to do any manual labor. Rather foolishly, by this Jacob declared to all his other sons that Joseph bore the responsibility of supervision. But God had not yet begun to shape Joseph's character, and so pride and naiveté informed his words and actions. His brothers hated him! To make matters worse, Joseph then decided to share his visions and dreams.

He said to them, "Listen to this dream I had: We were binding sheaves of grain out in the field when suddenly my sheaf rose and stood upright, while your sheaves gathered around mine and bowed down to it."

His brothers said to him, "Do you intend to reign over us? Will you actually rule us?" And they hated him all the more because of his dream and what he had said.

Then he had another dream, and he told it to his brothers. "Listen," he said, "I had another dream, and this time the sun and moon and eleven stars were bowing down to me." (Genesis 37:6-9)

THE FOOLISH PRIDE OF YOUTH

With no wisdom or training in how to share his revelations, Joseph just blurted them out, not thinking about the interpretation and application of his prophecies. He may have assumed he was the center of the universe, but he had no awareness of how others might feel about his making that assumption!

Joseph was seventeen years old, and many teenagers might identify with his feelings—why shouldn't the sun and moon and stars all revolve around him? His prophecy accurately foretold the future, but nobody knew that, and no one was endeared to him for sharing it. Jacob, Joseph's apparently preoccupied father, mildly rebuked his son for his pride. But his brothers responded with contempt: "Do you intend to rule over us?" Astonishingly, that was indeed God's plan. Joseph would govern the life of his brothers, but first he needed to learn the wisdom of humility.

"Jacob said: 'Go and see if all is well with your brothers and with the flocks, and bring word back to me.'[4] So Joseph went after his brothers and found them near Dothan. But they saw him in the distance, and before he reached them, they plotted to kill him. 'Here comes the dreamer!' They said to each other. 'Come now, let's kill him and throw him into one of these cisterns and say that a ferocious animal devoured him. Then we'll see what comes of his dreams.'" (Genesis 37:14, 17-20)

We can imagine a little of how this band of brothers may have behaved—quite likely petty bandits and bullies who had been terrorizing the neighborhood for years. But Jacob still saw fit to send his young favorite to supervise their work and report back. Jacob put his favored son in harm's way—and they both suffered the consequences for it. His brutal brothers beat Joseph up and threw him into a well. Only with the intervention of one of the less desensitized of his brothers did Joseph avoid death and instead was sold into slavery. Their distant cousins—the children of Ishmael—dragged him off to the slave market in Egypt, where he was bought by Potiphar, the chief jailer and what we might call head of security for Pharaoh, king of Egypt.[5]

45

4: Joseph was given the responsibility normally reserved for a firstborn son. His father Jacob asks Joseph to supervise his brothers.

5: Only the hated symbol of Jacob's favoritism was brought back to him by his wicked sons. See Genesis 37:31-33.

COVENANT BLESSINGS

"The Lord was with Joseph and he prospered, and he lived in the house of his Egyptian master. When his master saw that the Lord was with him and that the Lord gave him success in everything he did, Joseph found favor in his eyes and became his attendant. Potiphar put him in charge of his household and he entrusted to his care everything he owned.... The blessing of the Lord was on everything Potiphar had, both in the house and in the field." (Genesis 39:2-5)

Abraham's Covenant with God extended to the whole of his family, which now covered three generations. Joseph had been chosen by God, and therefore, the Lord's presence and blessing were assured. This was so evident that it overflowed into everything that Joseph's life touched. Of course, though the blessing was assured to the whole family, God brought his provision and protection to each by different circumstances. For Joseph, the circumstances of God's Covenant blessing suddenly became complicated.

"Now Joseph was well built and handsome, and after a while his master's wife took notice of Joseph and said, 'Come to bed with me!' But he refused." (Genesis 39:6b-8a)

Potiphar's lascivious wife fancied her chances with the young man. She was very direct with her proposal! Joseph resisted her advances, only to be falsely accused of assaulting her and put in prison.[6] It is clear that Potiphar probably did not believe that Joseph was guilty—normally, the allegation alone should have led to Joseph's death. Instead, he was placed in another part of the compound where Potiphar's household lived—the place where all Pharaoh's prisoners were held.[7]

6: See Genesis 39:11-19

7: See Genesis 39:20

46

PROSPERING IN PRISON

"But while Joseph was there in the prison, the Lord was with him; he showed him kindness and granted him favor in the eyes of the prison warden. So the warden put Joseph in charge of all those held in the prison, and he was made responsible for all that was done there. The warden paid no attention to anything under Joseph's care because the Lord was with Joseph and gave him success in whatever did." (Genesis 39:20-23)

Again God blessed Joseph, and he rose to be the chief of the prisoners. God's presence caused Joseph to prosper.[8] Despite Joseph's faults and these terrible circumstances, God proved faithful to his Covenant promise of provision and protection. God had given Joseph visions of greatness, and even though he was now in prison, he was on the threshold of their fulfillment:

"Sometime later, the cupbearer and the baker of the king of Egypt offended their master." (Genesis 40:1)

Joseph was joined in prison by Pharaoh's cupbearer and baker; for some reason, the king (Pharaoh) did not trust them—did he become ill after eating some food prepared by his baker or blame the cupbearer (chief taster) for a bad bottle of wine? In any event, the king feared a conspiracy to kill him, but there was no proof so he had both staff arrested until the matter could be settled. To us, this may seem like an enormous overreaction. But in those times, such threats were quite common, and when a monarch's continuing health secured peace for his country, such precautions can be understood.

8: The favor of God was with Joseph in every circumstance he faced: "The Lord was with Joseph and he prospered, and he lived in the house of his Egyptian master." (Genesis 39:2) "The Lord was with him; he showed him kindness and granted him favor in the eyes of the prison warden." (Genesis 39:21)

While in prison, both the butler (the cupbearer) and the baker had disturbing dreams.[9] The butler had a dream about grapes being squeezed into a cup, and the baker saw a vision of baskets of pastries on his head. When Joseph came to serve them at breakfast the next day, he noticed their troubled faces:

"'We both had dreams,' they answered, 'but there is no one to interpret them.' And Joseph said to them, 'do not interpretations belong to God? Tell **me** your dreams.'" (Genesis 40:8)

ON THE PATH TO HUMILITY

Joseph was twenty-eight years old. He had been a slave for about eleven years, during which time he had begun to learn some humility through his experience of suffering, isolation and injustice. Now the process was nearly complete. At the beginning of his story, Joseph saw himself at the center of the universe, interpreting his own dreams without reference to God. Now, with all that he has been through, he allows God to be at the center of his world: "Do not interpretations belong to God? Tell me your dreams."

Joseph gave interpretations that proved to be true—they were both "lifted up" as the story tells us.[10] The butler was reinstated to his former position, while the baker's head was lifted off his shoulders in summary execution.

When Joseph gave the interpretations to his fellow inmates, he had pleaded for their help in securing his freedom.[11] Given his circumstances, this seems reasonable, but God wanted Joseph utterly surrendered so that the Lord alone could bring the victory. The cupbearer forgot about Joseph.

Joseph had journeyed a long way, from the position of favored son to that of slave and then, even worse, the slave of prisoners. His heart had been partly transformed. He had become more open and more available to God. However, Joseph had not completely surrendered to God's purposes. Scripture often paints the picture of "victory" in the themes of Kingdom and ruling on God's behalf. But here is the Kingdom paradox: victory comes only when we surrender to the One who brings true Victory.

PHARAOH'S DREAMS

After two more years though (long, hard, tiresome years), the time was right for a breakthrough. Finally, the circumstances were ready for Joseph to fulfill his destiny. Enough had changed within him, and then something happened in Pharaoh's palace.

"Pharaoh had a dream: 'Out of the river there came seven cows, sleek and fat . . . After them seven other cows, ugly and gaunt . . . The ugly and gaunt cows ate up the seven sleek and fat cows . . .' He had a second dream: 'Seven heads of grain, healthy and good . . . After them seven heads of grain, thin and scorched . . . The thin heads of grain swallowed up the seven healthy, full heads.' Then Pharaoh woke up; it had been a dream. In the morning his mind was troubled, so he sent for the magicians and the wise men of Egypt. Pharaoh told them his

12: We can imagine the butler slapping his forehead and saying: "Then the chief cupbearer said to Pharaoh, 'Today I am reminded of my shortcomings. Pharaoh was once angry with his servants, and he imprisoned me and the chief baker in the house of the captain of the guard. Each of us had a dream the same night, and each dream had a meaning of its own. Now a young Hebrew was there with us, a servant of the captain of the guard. We told him our dreams, and he interpreted them for us, giving each man the interpretation of his dream. And things turned out exactly as he interpreted them to us: I was restored to my position, and the other man was hanged.'" (Genesis 41:9-13)

dreams, but no one could interpret them for him."
(Genesis 41:1-8)

In an era when dreams were considered to be an important perspective on reality, these strange images of cows and wheat devouring other cows and wheat, respectively, must have been deeply troubling for Pharaoh. He had no idea what it all meant, and none of his normal advisers could help him. At last, the butler remembered: there was someone in Egypt who could interpret dreams.[12] Joseph was sent for and made ready to meet the king.

"Pharaoh said to Joseph, 'I had a dream, and no one can interpret it. But I have heard it said of you that when you hear a dream you can interpret it.'" (Genesis 41:15)

FULL AND FINAL SURRENDER

Joseph here is on the brink of destiny. What would he say? Had he finally come to the point of humility? Could he now be used by God, or would Joseph have to continue on the hard road to fully surrender?

What follows is the most important statement of Joseph's life:

"**I cannot do it**," Joseph replied to Pharaoh, "**but God** will give Pharaoh the answer he desires." (Genesis 41:16)

His dreams had begun when he was seventeen years old, and now at last, at the age of thirty, his destiny was fulfilled. Joseph had finally come to a place of total surrender and put God at the center of his world. It had taken thirteen years of slavery and imprisonment.[13]

God was finally in a position where he could work through Joseph.

Only when God is at the center of our lives can he work through us in the way he intends to. God wants to rule through us, with divine authority and power, but to do this, he must know that he is on the throne of our hearts.

FROM PRIDE TO SUBMISSION

In the beginning, the devil used the lure of "becoming like God" to tempt us away from our intimate place of relationship with him. In other words, pride—wanting to be like God—got us into trouble in the first place. God has to deal with our pride if he is to repair the damage of the past and use us as his representatives again.

Joseph had been shown that he was called to rule over others—God had placed the vision in Joseph's heart when he was seventeen years old. But his vision could never be fulfilled while he was consumed with pride. His lack of humility had stopped him functioning with Kingdom authority. And so he was taken on a journey to submission—and, practically speaking, to the place and position where God needed him to be—through a deep valley of darkness and shadow, of rejection, betrayal, physical attack, slavery, false accusations and years as a prisoner. It was a long, hard road to reach the place where God could use him.[14]

Notes

13: Surrender is the essential preparation for being used by God.

14: One of the secrets to being used by God is revealed in the life of Joseph.

But by finally submitting to God (as shown by the admission "I cannot do it"), Joseph discovered that the Lord was prepared to entrust him with real authority. Joseph's humble surrender had cleared the way for the Lord to work through him. He had become a conduit through which God could release His power and authority. And so Joseph was given victory over his circumstances, and that Kingdom breakthrough touched every part of his life.

COMPLETE DEPENDENCE UPON GOD

What was it that God wanted to see in Joseph (and still seeks from us)? The answer is, humility. In the Garden, before the Fall, humility was expressed simply in these terms: "you will not eat from the tree of good and evil. Instead you will eat from the tree of life and all the other fruits that are found in the garden." (Genesis 2:16-17)

In other words, God was saying, "completely depend on me for your moral decisions." Pride does the opposite—it asserts our independence, our perceived right to self-determination. Pride tells God that we do not need him to rule in our lives.

As Pharaoh's representative (and God's), Joseph was to be the channel through which Kingship flowed, with authority and power, just like the rest of us, Joseph had to wrestle (with himself and his situation) to attain a position where he could act on God's behalf.

The path to fulfillment in God's Kingdom, as walked by Joseph, is traced many times in Scripture, and the destination is greatly to be prized. But the journey is hard and has been navigated to full completion by only one person—Jesus. Later in the Bible, the apostle Paul suggests that we pattern ourselves on the model of Jesus.[15] He "emptied himself even to death on a cross" so that he could take his rightful place and exercise the authority that God had planned for him. If we are to take Joseph's example and follow Jesus' lead, we will take the hard path. But we will have to empty ourselves.

And in the end, what is God's purpose? Joseph says it once, Jesus many times: God intends "the saving of many lives." "You intended to harm me, but God intended it for good to accomplish what is now being done, the saving of many lives." (Genesis 50:20)

JOSEPH'S KINGDOM PROMOTION

Although Joseph's world now changed for the better, the implications of Pharaoh's dreams were catastrophic for the nation of Egypt. As the events prophesied in the dreams unfolded, the geopolitical map was changed for generations to come.

Joseph, using his God-given wisdom and his new authority to speak on Pharaoh's behalf, offered a strategy to rescue the people of Egypt from the seven years of famine. His plan would save the lives of thousands, including those of his own family.

15: "Your attitude should be the same as that of Christ Jesus: Who, being in very nature God, did not consider equality with God something to be grasped, but made himself nothing, taking the very nature of a servant, being made in human likeness. And being found in appearance as a man, he humbled himself and became obedient to death—even death on a cross! Therefore God exalted him to the highest place and gave him the name that is above every name." (Philippians 2:5-9)

16: See Genesis 41:38, 41-43

Pharaoh recognized the divine origin of Joseph's abilities, asking his royal court, "Can we find anyone like this man, one in whom is the spirit of God?" . . . Pharaoh said to Joseph, "I hereby put you in charge of the whole land of Egypt." Then Pharaoh took his signet ring off his finger and put it on Joseph's. He dressed him in robes of fine linen and put a gold chain around his neck. He had him ride in a chariot as his second in command, and men went before him shouting, "Make way!" Thus he put him in charge of the whole land of Egypt.[16]

Joseph had traveled from the deepest depths to the highest of mountains in just a few moments. In a single day, he was transformed—from an imprisoned slave to prince regent of the greatest nation on earth!

Joseph now began his work in earnest. His God-given wisdom proved extremely effective in organizing the nation to face the coming crisis. After years of humbling culminating in his eventual surrender to God, finally Joseph had been elevated to rule, just as his teenage vision had predicted.

FORGIVENESS – THE ULTIMATE POWER

Having received authority from God to do the work for which he had been designed, Joseph learned the connection between power and authority. God's power may be expressed in many ways, but Joseph's story focuses on the most important—the power to forgive. He is given the choice to exact justice or to grant mercy to the very people who caused his years of hardship—his brothers. He has been given the power to extract maximum retribution from his family, but he knows he's called to take another path.

As the amazing story continues, famine swept through the whole region, extending as far as Jacob's household in Canaan. The brothers journeyed back and forth seeking food for their families, and finally ended up at the court of the Pharaoh, where they encountered Joseph, though his identity is hidden from them at first. With tales of hidden money in the bags of wheat, and the eldest brother being held as a guarantee of trustworthiness, the brothers are brought to a place of powerlessness in just the same way as Joseph had been at their hands, so long before.[17]

In an emotional scene, with their lives in his hands, Joseph revealed himself and offered his brothers complete forgiveness.[18]

His mercy had a much greater effect than any retribution could have managed. His brothers confessed and asked his forgiveness for all their past wrongs toward him, and the family was reconciled at last.

Joseph's contrite brothers finally brought Jacob to Egypt. Jacob's household was reunited, and Joseph was in every way established in the position of "eldest son." Jacob had foolishly accorded Joseph that kind of status at a time when he was unable to carry the responsibility. But now it was God's doing that the title was bestowed.

Notes

17: You might like to read Genesis chapters 42-45 at this point.

18: Joseph offers complete forgiveness to his wicked brothers: "Joseph said to his brothers, 'I am Joseph! Is my father still living?' But his brothers were not able to answer him, because they were terrified at his presence. Then Joseph said to his brothers, 'Come close to me.' When they had done so, he said, 'I am your brother Joseph, the one you sold into Egypt! And now, do not be distressed and do not be angry with yourselves for selling me here, because it was to save lives that God sent me ahead of you. For two years now there has been famine in the land, and for the next five years there will not be plowing and reaping. But God sent me ahead of you to preserve for you a remnant on earth and to save your lives by a great deliverance.'" (Genesis 45:3-7)

When we think of ourselves in relation to this story, we may ask, what are the obstacles that block us from fulfilling our God-given destiny? The answer is anything that takes us from a position of surrender and submission before God. We have already seen that pride can do this. What about unforgiveness?

Bitterness and a desire for revenge lead us into a position where we assume God's role in judgment. If we choose to judge others and withhold forgiveness, we are asserting our own authority rather than surrendering to God's.

The issue of submission had finally been settled for Joseph. He was willing to forgive even when faced with his brothers, confronted with the painful recollection of all he had suffered at their hands. Joseph may have agonized over forgiving his brothers, but the fundamental issue had already been settled: God was God, and he was not. Only God could judge and although Joseph presumably had to wrestle with this truth, nevertheless, the outcome was assured, because Joseph had already submitted to God.

The issue of submission was hugely important in enabling Joseph to be used to his full potential; so is it for us, and likewise it was also true for Jesus. Jesus became the portal through which heaven touched earth as he continuously offered himself to the Father in submission.[19]

Every sign, every wonder Jesus did was heaven's Kingdom touching earth's need through Jesus' surrendered life.

Jesus' absolute commitment to living a surrendered life took him to Calvary. He went to the Cross and died, still surrendering, in order to find the victory. After all his suffering

19: The example of Jesus is seen in passages such as this: "Jesus gave them this answer: 'I tell you the truth, the Son can do nothing by himself; he can do only what he sees his Father doing, because whatever the Father does the Son also does.'" (John 5:19)

and struggle, despite God's rejection of Jesus on our behalf, still he placed his life in the Father's hands, knowing that the place that the first Adam abandoned was a safe place. And in this great act of sacrifice and submission, heaven's forgiveness broke into a world of sin.

DOUBLE BLESSING

We know very little of what happened after Joseph's family migrated to Egypt to join him. Although we know that Joseph continued in his position as Pharaoh's royal representative, little more of the story is recorded. But we do know how it ended.

Jacob, on his deathbed, underlined Joseph's prime position by giving him the eldest son's "double portion."[20] Joseph's two sons, Ephraim and Manasseh, were given the full status of Jacob's own sons. Unlike all of the other brothers, Joseph's tribe became two, ensuring that his influence would be doubled for generations to come.

With Jacob's death, though, Joseph's brothers grew troubled, concerned that he would turn on them without the restraining influence of Jacob's presence. But with a wonderful grasp of God's grace, Joseph assured his brothers of his continuing love for them. His forgiveness was full and final.[21]

20: In the end, Joseph receives the blessing of the firstborn son.

21: Joseph reiterates his forgiveness after his father's death: "His brothers then came and threw themselves down before him. 'We are your slaves,' they said. But Joseph said to them, 'don't be afraid. Am I in the place of God? You intended to harm me, but God intended it for good to accomplish what is now being done, the saving of many lives. So then, don't be afraid. I will provide for you and your children.' And he reassured them and spoke kindly to them." (Genesis 50:18-21)

PURE KINGDOM VISION

We are moving rapidly to the conclusion of the first book of the Bible, but I am compelled to touch on one final subject—vision. When you or I pursue a vision, what is it that we are aiming for?

Joseph had a God-given vision ("to rule"), but at the beginning, his own self-centeredness was mingled in the revelation. Make no mistake; some of the vision that beats in your heart is also in the heart of God. It's a vision of God's future, and we are right to pray for it by saying, "Your Kingdom come: Your will be done on earth as it is in heaven." (Matthew 6:10)

Any vision, however noble, has both human and divine elements within it. For Joseph, he received very clear visions from God—but his humanity betrayed him in his understanding of them. For us, we may not have the same clarity of vision from God, but the visions we pursue in the light of God's guidance and our own hearts also need to be considered. Do you long for your loved ones' hearts to be so moved by the overwhelming grace of God that their lives are transformed? Do you long for greater numbers of people to be touched by the healing presence of God? Do you long for the principalities and powers that grip your nation to be brought down, so that people's chains can be broken and they set free? Do you long for peace and justice?

Then you are longing for the Kingdom of God, albeit no doubt mixing your own aspirations with your God-given desires.

For God's Kingdom to be revealed, we need to move beyond our merely human aspirations. So if the distinction is to be made, what is required? The answer is expressed in the life of Joseph and more perfectly portrayed in the life of Christ. There needs to be both death and resurrection. Our feelings of self-importance, and our belief that we are the "center of the universe," have to die, so that God can be enthroned as the King of our circumstances and his vision for our life can live.

This is a deep mystery, a profound paradox. How did we see it in Joseph's story?

JOSEPH'S DREAM EXTINGUISHED

As Joseph lay shaking at the bottom of the well, fearing for his life, his visions and dreams were the last things of which he would have thought. By the time he had been sold into slavery, wrongly accused of assault and abandoned in prison, his youthful expectations for his life had almost certainly died. Languishing in prison, he must have been pleading for God to do something, hoping against hope. But God was waiting for Joseph—waiting for his expectations to die. God was waiting for the human part of Joseph's vision to be extinguished. Every personal vision includes human and divine elements. God may have to allow the human part to die before his part can be fulfilled. This will often bring us to a "breaking" experience—this is dying to our self. But genuine Kingdom breakthrough is seen only through personal brokenness.[22]

Only God—the King of heaven—can reveal the Kingdom of heaven here on earth.

22: Retracing the steps of Joseph's life to ensure we understand the meaning of his story.

Did you have a vision? Do you feel as though it has failed? Do your circumstances tell you that you have wasted your time, energy and money on a fruitless adventure? My advice is: hold on! Not to the self-centered elements of your vision, which lie in ashes, but to the part of the vision that expresses God's Kingdom. Did Joseph remember the sheaves of wheat bowing down to him, the sun, moon and stars all revolving around him as he lay in prison? I doubt it! If he did, it can only have been to mourn that those hopes were all but extinguished, especially in those last two years when the butler had forgotten him.

THE KINGDOM BREAKS THROUGH

When Jesus' disciples were under severe pressure, he gave them an amazing promise: "Fear not little flock, your Father is pleased to give you the Kingdom." (Luke 12:32) Just when they were at the point of desperation, God was at the point of intervention! In other words, he was saying, "Hold on!" At your moment of greatest despair, God is ready to step in.

The Kingdom (Kingship) of God is a reality just beyond our perception, much like "tomorrow." By the time we get to the New Testament, the Bible tells us that one day "tomorrow" will be "today." But while we wait for that day, we earnestly look for the evidence of God's Kingdom today. The problem is that placing ourselves in the middle of the picture and trying to fulfill the vision in our own strength will only cause the picture to elude our grasp.

If we strive in our human strength to "make it happen," then God will resist even our best efforts. If we surrender to him, we will see his Kingdom breaking in.

We may not see the complete fulfillment of all our hopes in the "here and now." But if we walk in submission and weakness, we will come to know his authority and power. In time, this will lead to a greater confidence in the present and greater courage for the future.[23]

The life of Joseph tells us that there is a Kingdom, and a call and a vision for us to represent the Lord. He actually wants to express his Kingdom and extend his rule through us. His eyes are forever casting about the earth, looking for hearts that are prepared and ready—surrendered, choosing the path of obedience.[24] And when he finds those hearts? Then the Kingdom pours through, because the Lord has found the channel through which he can release his blessing.

My friends, even though you struggle, choose the path of surrender. Stay on that path even though your heart has been broken by a vision that appears to have died. Lift your disappointment to him, knowing that in this you will find his touch of mercy, and in his time, fulfillment.

THE CLOSE OF GENESIS

As the first book of the Bible closes, the two great themes of Scripture have been introduced.

Abraham received the Covenant and surrendered to his Covenant partner.

Joseph submitted to the King and received great authority and power to represent him.

Introduced to us in this way, these two themes, similar to the warp and weft of a rich fabric, will now be woven together in the lives of the characters that follow. Next we see how one of the greatest of all, Moses, lived out the confidence of the Covenant and the conviction of the Kingdom.

Esther

"For if you remain silent at this time, relief and deliverance for the Jews will arise from another place, but you and your father's family will perish. And who knows but that you have come to royal position for such a time as this?"[1]

The story of Esther is a story of Covenant relationship and the responsibilities that come with God's Kingdom rule.

Although God's name is never mentioned throughout the entire book, Esther's identity as a Jew lies at the heart of the narrative. She and her uncle and mentor Mordecai, along with all of the other Jews who had been carried off into exile by the invading Medes and Persians, were still God's Covenant people, even though they were suffering the consequences of their rebellion. The terms of the Covenant still applied: God had committed himself to provide for and protect them. Esther became an illustration of how God remains faithful to his promise, provided there is a reciprocal faithfulness from his Covenant partners. Similar to Joseph and Daniel before her, she was prospered by the Lord in unexpected ways. Esther won a competition to become the next queen of Persia, replacing Vashti, who appeared to have tired of being used as an object of pleasure by the king and his court. After a rather unpleasantly superficial beauty contest, Esther was promoted to a position of unimaginable influence for a young woman of her background.

Haman, an Amalekite—ancient enemies of the people of Israel—and the king's counselor, was the villain. Using his position of power, he manipulated King Xerxes to pass a decree requiring the extermination of all the Jews. Mordecai, a particular object of Haman's hatred, enlisted Esther's support in the cause of her people. Through a series of wily interventions, Esther and Mordecai reversed the circumstances of the Jews in the Persian Empire and vanquished their foes.

---

1 Esther 4:14

The story of Esther deals with the main elements of Covenant relationship, which are **identity** and **obedience**. Mordecai reminds Esther of her identity, and calls her to obedient action to save her people. He also revealed the call to represent the Lord as the true King of the world. Esther took her responsibility seriously, and God acted through her with authority and power. Living consistently within her Covenant relationship and representing God's Kingship within her circumstances, Esther was used to bring about an extraordinary act of deliverance by God.[2]

---

2 Purim—the celebration of God's deliverance through Esther—was established from this time as one of the great festivities of the Jewish people.

Chapter 5

Moses
Priest and Prince

The double helix of the DNA of Scripture is beginning to spiral through every page. As each theme emerges, we see that the Bible at its heart is about relationship and responsibility.

From the life of Abraham, we see that in Covenant (the call to a relationship), we surrender our separate existence and become "one" with God. A Covenant relationship depends upon identity and obedience. This new identity is found in a new relationship where we are united with our Covenant partner and we receive a new name that expresses this new identity. Obedience is defined by submission to God, our Covenant partner. In a Covenant, both partners jointly own everything. Each has the same rights and freedoms, and either can ask the other for anything.

The life of Joseph exposed the power of God's Kingdom—the call to represent God and take responsibility for our relationship with him. We learned that representing God's Kingship means functioning with the authority and power that he gives us. We saw in Joseph's life that authority is found when we learn humility, as we recognize the appropriate posture before God. We saw that God wants us to exercise the power of forgiveness before all else.

In the life of Moses (and later in David), we can see what happens when Covenant and Kingdom combine.

David, the great king of Israel, finally conquered the peoples who inhabited the land that God had given to his children. David was the one who united the twelve tribes under a single monarchy, established the beginnings of a relative

A brief overview of the story so far.

"superpower" and built the nation a capital. His life was lived in the full reality of Covenant and Kingdom, and in his lifetime, the promise that God had given to Abraham was finally fulfilled—prosperity, peace and protection for all of God's people.

But we must begin with Moses. His life was the first to fully unite both themes. He was the first to weave together the threads of Covenant relationship and those of Kingdom responsibility.

Moses, the first person to fully integrate Covenant and Kingdom in his life.

Moses was a remarkable man—one of the greatest characters not only of biblical history but of all human history as well. He led his people on the road of freedom to their final destiny.

FROM PRINCE TO FUGITIVE

Moses began life being snatched from the waters of the Nile—rescued as a baby to be raised in Pharaoh's palace as a prince.[1] After a privileged childhood and a prince's education, when he left the protective confines of the royal court, he was confronted by the suffering of his enslaved people. Enraged at their oppression, Moses killed the Egyptian guard whose mistreatment he witnessed—but was then forced to flee the country himself.[2]

This is where we pick up the story: Moses has escaped justice in Egypt and is living as a fugitive in the land of Midian.

1: See Exodus 2:1-10

2: See Exodus 2:11-25

DESERT SHEPHERD

"Now Moses was tending the flock of Jethro his father-in-law, the priest of Midian, and he led the flock to the far side of the desert and came to Horeb, the mountain of God." (Exodus 3:1)

It was a lifetime since he had lived in Egypt. Indeed, it had been forty years—a whole generation. In those palace days, raised as a royal prince, he had known the power and the privilege of living in Pharaoh's household. Now he knew the responsibility of attending to the daily needs of his father-in-law's flock.

Sheep rarely move anywhere at high speed, certainly not in the strength-sapping heat of the desert. So who knows how long it took for Moses to lead his flock to the "far side of the desert"? And they need constant care and the watchful eye of an attentive shepherd. At the end of each day, he gathered and counted his sheep, checking them for wounds and parasites, sending one of his helpers, perhaps a son or a hired hand, ahead to survey the area. They were looking for indications of water—Moses could lead his flock only to where he found the water to sustain them. River beds, despite being dried up, provided shelter in the heat of the day, because there the trees and desert vegetation multiplied. Water could perhaps be found somewhere under the surface in extreme circumstances, but rather than digging new wells, the main task of each day was to identify and then traverse the distance to the next well and waterhole before considering the next day's journey with equal care.

This meticulous rhythmic pattern, leading the sheep through the sparse vegetation from one supply of water to another,

Moses encounters God in the desert.

inevitably led to the destination that Moses had in his heart. He wanted to get to the "far side of the desert." He had come to the desert to escape, a fugitive from Pharaoh's law. And rather than pining away, dwelling on all that he had lost, Moses chose to embrace his circumstance and not just exist in the desert, but thrive there: taking a wife, starting a family and traveling through its heart from one side to the other.

A FIRE IN THE DESERT

"The angel of the Lord appeared to him (Moses) in flames of fire from within a bush."

Moses saw that though the bush was on fire it did not burn up. So Moses thought:

"I will go over and see this strange sight—why the bush does not burn up." (Exodus 3:2-3)

It is important to remember these events take place in a desert, where each day is very much like all the others. Temperatures in the desert increase in the summer, but rain and cloudy skies were rare. Seasonal variation was not great. Monotony would have been an ever-present companion. Such circumstances tend to lead people in one of two directions—acquiescence to the monotony, often leading to depression and hopelessness, or an intense attention to the nuanced changes in the environment—enabling continued interest and personal engagement. Moses lasted forty years, so we can safely assume that he chose the latter. He would notice the lizard on the rock, the changing pattern of shadows as the sun moved

Moses begins his journey to freedom.

through the sky, the small changes in temperature indicating the presence of water below the surface, the birds of prey circling overhead and the rustling of leaves on the desert trees.

The desert is a study in stillness, interspersed with sudden movement. The snake is immobile until it strikes. The bird on a branch is still until it darts to devour an insect. After forty years, Moses' life began to reflect his environment. He had the capacity to notice the smallest changes in his surroundings.

A bush was on fire. Had it been struck by lightning? Had other travelers left a fire unattended? Or was it that most mysterious of events, spontaneous combustion? Seeing a fire was not particularly remarkable. All desert plants burn; many rely on fire for germination. But this fire was unusual, because the flames were not consuming the bush on which they burned. The twigs were not becoming blackened; the leaves were not being devoured by the flames. The bush was alight, but somehow it was not being burned up.

The Lord had come to reveal himself "in flames of fire." Fire burns and repels. The Lord is transcendent—holy, mysterious and unapproachable. Fire warms, too, and it attracts. The Lord is immanent—present, involved and responsive. Fire is the symbol of God's presence.

The Lord intended to get Moses' attention; but he wanted to give a deeper revelation. So as Moses drew closer to take in this marvel, the Lord spoke. Moses heard the voice of God for the first time in his life—and he would never be the same again.

"When the Lord saw that he had gone over to look, God called to him from within the bush, 'Moses! Moses!' And Moses said,

Moses meets God in fire.

'Here I am.' 'Do not come any closer,' God said. 'Take off your sandals, for the place where you are standing is holy ground.' Then he said, 'I am the God of your father, the God of Abraham, the God of Isaac and the God of Jacob.'" (Exodus 3:4-6a)

When Moses heard God speak, he immediately understood something deep and profound about God and himself. God knew Moses' name and his heritage. The Lord knew his identity. It was as though the Lord had said, "I know who you are; you belong to me."[3]

"At this, Moses hid his face, because he was afraid to look at God." (Exodus 3:6b)

STRUGGLING WITH IDENTITY

I imagine we would all be afraid if we were so directly confronted by the Creator of the universe! But something else is revealed about Moses as he spoke with God. He had a deep sense of personal insecurity. When someone is sure in his identity, he tends to live out a certain measure of self-confidence. In this area of life, Moses apparently struggled. He had been saved from death as a baby, but the privileges of the royal court—which should have given him tremendous self-assurance—in fact brought a crippling separation from his natural family. Although miraculously his mother had been employed as his nanny, being raised in Pharaoh's palace had alienated Moses from his enslaved people. This was underlined by the events that had led to him becoming a fugitive.

3: In the unfolding revelation of Covenant throughout Scripture, it is clear that Abraham, Isaac and Jacob were "fathers" because they started the nation of Israel and because they were in Covenant (and thus shared in the identity) of "the Father" in heaven.

Only a free man can set others at liberty. God has to release Moses from his past.

In defense of a Hebrew slave, Moses had killed an Egyptian guard. Perhaps emboldened by this, Moses had attempted to break up a fight between two of his kinsman. He certainly did not expect the reaction he got. I am sure he could still hear the words of the men he had tried to separate as they fought: "Who made you ruler and judge over us? Are you thinking of killing me as you killed the Egyptian?" (Exodus 2:14) The story was out, and he had to run to escape justice at the hands of Pharaoh.

Moses' lifelong social separation and insecurity would be compounded by his isolation and guilt as he fled his home and his people into the Midian desert.

But something had stirred deep within the heart of God. His great love would result in a truly special relationship with Moses and the people of Israel. God's fiery determination would achieve the great goal of rescuing his people.

Coming together in Moses, God's love and determination would launch a world-changing mission through him. But for Moses to fulfill this mission and to live in the reality of God's love and all-encompassing Kingship, he would have to address the issue of his insecurity.

"Moses, Moses . . . I am the God of your father Abraham." (Exodus 3:4-6a)

Naturally, God had the answer to the problem. He would give Moses an identity on which he could stand and from which his confidence would grow. God would help Moses realize that he had a Covenant with the King of the universe—and that makes all the difference!

4: Moses is God's Covenant partner who is now commissioned to do God's Kingdom work.

Perhaps the wounds of exile had healed in Moses, but the scars remained. His anger, guilt and sense of loss may have subsided, but the underlying anxiety and insecurity caused by his disconnection from his blood family and heritage continued. However, God knew Moses' name and now addressed him as one with a heritage going back to Abraham. The Lord was saying: "this is who you are and this is how I will relate to you." Hearing this began to bring healing to Moses' soul.

Identity is always given from the outside before it becomes reality on the inside. Moses heard God confirm his identity. In time, his confidence grew, and his long-dormant capacity to lead emerged.

THE CALL AND DESTINY OF MOSES

"The Lord said, 'I have indeed seen the misery of my people in Egypt. I have heard them crying out because of their slave drivers, and I am concerned about their suffering. So I have come down to rescue them from the hand of the Egyptians and to bring them up out of that land into a good and spacious land, a land flowing with milk and honey . . . So now, go. I am sending you to Pharaoh to bring my people the Israelites out of Egypt.'" (Exodus 3:7-8a, 10)[4]

The promise of Covenant always includes protection and provision. Both parties may be called on for help by the other in times of need. The Lord had heard the call for help and would keep his end of the bargain by rescuing his people and giving them a new land, the land he had promised to Abraham and

Sarah. He called upon Moses to respond to this by fulfilling his obligations. Moses had a destiny, a calling, and God had now revealed it to him.

But Moses' response revealed what was going on inside. He still had a long way to go. He was uncertain, diffident and tentative, lacking the confidence necessary to lead his people. He wanted the Lord to send someone else, believing that anyone would be better than him:

"'Who am I, that I should go to Pharaoh and bring the Israelites out of Egypt?' And God said, 'I will be with you. And this will be the sign to you that it is I who have sent you: when you have brought the people out of Egypt, you will worship God on this mountain.'" (Exodus 3:11-12)

For Moses, the internal struggle continued:

"Suppose I go to the Israelites and say to them, 'the God of your fathers has sent me to you,' and they ask me, 'what is his name?' Then what shall I tell them?" (Exodus 3:13)[5]

To this, the Lord responded by giving himself a name that revealed he was both eternal and all-powerful:

"I AM WHO I AM. This is what you are to say to the Israelites: 'I AM has sent me to you.'" (Exodus 3:14)[6]

With this astonishing revelation, God revealed more of himself to Moses than the Lord had to anyone since Adam. However, God had come to do more than reveal himself to Moses. God had come to commit himself to Moses—and in time, Moses came to understand that this was all he needed.

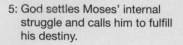

5: God settles Moses' internal struggle and calls him to fulfill his destiny.

6: "I AM" also means "I WILL BE." God is revealing to Moses both a present and future truth.

"'So now, go. I am sending you to Pharaoh to bring my people the Israelites out of Egypt.' . . . And God said, 'I will be with you. And this will be the sign to you that it is I who have sent you: when you have brought the people out of Egypt, you will worship God on this mountain.'" (Exodus 3:10, 12)

But, of course, this meant that Moses had to confront Pharaoh, the most powerful man in the world, and all the powers that stood behind him!

PREPARATION FOR THE BLESSING

So—he had been prepared. The first phase of Moses' life in Pharaoh's court had built him up, humanly speaking at least; the second phase in the desert had broken him down. Now Moses would be used as a great blessing. This pattern of building, breaking and blessing is seen in all the great characters of biblical history. God wants to use us, but we are not fully usable until we have surrendered ourselves completely into his hands.

We may ask why brokenness is so often a prelude to the surrender that God seeks, and for the answer, we need to go back again to the Garden. It was there that our human nature was forged. Our natural tendency is always to assert our independence, and seek to determine our own destiny. As we have seen, the consequences of this are grave. God in his wisdom will allow events that will curb our headlong dash for independence. Inevitably, the failure and disappointment of these events will lead to personal brokenness. God chooses not to leave us there, but to draw us back into his presence with his loving kindness, so that he might remake and start to really use us.[7]

His desire is for a relationship that will lead to the possibility of us truly representing him in this fallen world. God is working to reveal both his Covenant and his Kingdom in us.

This is what he wanted for Moses, but as for many of us, the final surrender was the most difficult. For Moses, embracing his identity was one thing; living with the consequences of his destiny was quite another.

He would have preferred simply to enjoy God's presence—the blessings of a Covenant relationship. But for God, it had to be relationship *and* representation. It was Covenant *and* Kingdom.

And so the Lord continued to press Moses. God wanted to bring about the response that would launch Moses into his Kingdom calling.

THE STRUGGLE TO SURRENDER

We can see the struggle in Moses' heart as he wrestled with God and the consequences of this final surrender:

"What if they do not believe me or listen to me and say, 'The Lord did not appear to you?' The Lord said, 'Throw it (your staff) on the ground' and it became a snake. 'This is so that they may believe that the Lord has appeared to you.' 'O Lord, I have never been eloquent, neither in the past nor since you

8: We can see our own lives
reflected in Moses' internal
struggles.

have spoken to your servant. I am slow of speech and tongue.'
The Lord said to him, 'Who gave man his mouth? . . . Now go;
I will help you speak and will teach you what to say.'"
(Exodus 4:1-10 extracts)[8]

Each anguished question from Moses was answered with a
demonstration of power and an explanation of the authority in
which he was being sent. But Moses continued to agonize,
resisting the inevitable. He grew desperate:

"O Lord, please send someone else to do it." (Exodus 4:13)

Moses was getting perilously close to crossing the line! It was a
tremendous thing to stand before a burning bush speaking to
the Lord, Moses' Covenant partner, like a friend. But it was
presumptuous to suggest to God that his plan was not perfect.
However, even in his anger, the Lord revealed a pattern that we
see throughout Scripture.[9] He gave Moses mercy and grace to
hear and obey his call:

"What about your brother, Aaron the Levite? I know he can
speak well. He is already on his way to meet you, and his heart
will be glad when he sees you. You shall speak to him and put
words in his mouth; I will help both of you speak and will teach
you what to do. He will speak to the people for you, and it will
be as if he were your mouth and as if you were God to him."
(Exodus 4:14-17 extracts)

This illustrates how God chooses to treat us with understanding
and kindness alongside his firm knowledge of what is best for
us. The Lord wanted Moses to take responsibility for his calling.
But God wanted Moses to receive that responsibility with the
confidence that comes from a deep and loving relationship.

The Lord had come "in fire" to Moses—but not to destroy him. God's burning presence had come to consume the bonds that bound Moses' heart. As Moses received his calling and heard the Lord set out his destiny, the chains of failure and insecurity fell away. And as Moses took his first faltering steps toward true freedom, his spirit, long bowed down by years of guilt and separation, began to wake up and respond to the call. Free at last! Now he could bring freedom to his people. Only those who are free can set others free.

We may wonder if there is any purpose in the "broken" times of our life, times when we have suffered failure, loss or disappointment. The life of Moses tells us that these hurts are like instruments that God can use to shape our lives. Difficulty rather than ease fashions our character and gives us "depth." Moses embraced the conditions of his life and "went to the far side of the desert."[10] He may have thought he was escaping only his difficult circumstances, but in fact, Moses gave God the opportunity to shape him into the man that he would become. We must do the same if we are to achieve all that God has for us.

10: See Exodus 3:1

RETURNING TO EGYPT AS A FREE MAN

"So Moses took his wife and sons, put them on a donkey and started back to Egypt. And he took the staff of God in his hand." (Exodus 4:20)

Covenant and Kingdom had come together in Moses' life. He was a man remade. Abraham had known Covenant friendship with the Lord while Joseph had known Kingdom authority to lead and to forgive. Moses returned to Egypt as the Lord's friend, with the authority to lead and to defeat the powers that resisted God's will for his people.

In Moses, God intended to confront the pantheon of false gods standing behind the earthly rule of Pharaoh. He intended to systematically dismantle the devil's capacity to hold God's people captive. The clash of Kingdoms was about to begin, and God would be victorious.

CLASH OF KINGDOMS

"Moses and Aaron went to Pharaoh and said, 'This is what the Lord, the God of Israel, says: 'Let my people go . . .'" (Exodus 5:1)

Moses returned to Egypt, taking his brother Aaron as spokesman. Moses confronted Pharaoh with the call of God to allow his people to worship him in the desert—and incredible things began to happen. Moses had been raised as a prince in Pharaoh's palace, but nothing compared with this. Acting with newfound authority, Moses discovered that God, his true King, was able to unleash unimaginable power.[11]

Unsurprisingly, Pharaoh showed little enthusiasm for releasing his Hebrew slaves. Why should he? Asserting his authority, the Egyptian king "upped the stakes" and made the work of the slaves even more difficult—they had to make bricks without straw. But in his stubborn refusal, Pharaoh had challenged God's authority and in doing so engaged in a conflict the king could never win.

THE TEN PLAGUES

God's Kingship, represented in Moses and manifested in awesome miracles, would humble Pharaoh and systematically dismantle the infrastructure standing behind his throne. From a New Testament point of view, we can see that these Egyptian "gods" opened the world's most powerful empire to demonic influence. Each of the ten plagues underlined the superiority of the Kingdom of God over the kingdom of darkness. The Egyptian pantheon was exposed for what it was: a pale and futile imitation of the Creator's power.

As the Lord battled to set his people free (through Moses), he began by demonstrating his power over the gods of the earth. The Egyptian pantheon was somewhat complex—it appears to have been ruled by the male sky deity, or "Sun god"—Ra. The female earth deity, thought to inhabit the River Nile (later known as Isis), was perhaps the second in importance, and all the other gods, represented in animal forms, were subordinate to

Notes

11: The confrontation between the Kingdom of God and the kingdom of Egypt begins. See Exodus 5.

In the battle between the Kingdom of God and Pharaoh's kingdom, God's supremacy is revealed as he dismantles his enemy's infrastructure.

12: "Moses and Aaron did just as
the Lord had commanded. He
raised his staff in the presence
of Pharaoh and his officials and
struck the water of the Nile,
and all the water was changed
into blood." (Exodus 7:20)

13: See Exodus 8 and 9

14: See Exodus 9 and 10

See Exodus 11 and 12

these principal deities. Moses raised his staff and touched the waters of the Nile.[12] The mighty river, vital to the fertility of the land, was struck a deadly blow and appeared to bleed to death. All the creatures dependent upon the Nile were affected—all the fish died, and the water was undrinkable.

After a plague of frogs that left the land covered in their dead rotting carcasses, plagues of gnats (some kind of biting insects) and flies followed. Perhaps these plagues led directly to the next plagues—the decimation of Egyptian livestock and boils on all living things.[13]

Pharaoh wavered repeatedly, but did not relent. The evil powers that stood behind him would not easily release their grip. And so the Lord turned his attention from the earth to the heavens, the realm of the male god Ra, who was believed to control weather and rainfall. In response to Moses' command, there were hail storms, and then locusts swept in on unexpected winds. Finally, the sun—the physical representation of Ra in the heavens—was darkened.[14]

Each successive plague brought Pharaoh's heart to the brink of repentance, but then his heart hardened again. His recalcitrance brought him and his nation to a point of terrible loss.

THE FINAL PLAGUE

Pharaoh's name was Ramses, meaning "son of Ra." In Egyptian thought, the king of the gods was incarnate in

Pharaoh and his firstborn son. In the final confrontation between Moses and Pharaoh, the Lord claimed the life of Pharaoh's son and that of the firstborn son of every Egyptian household. Pharaoh's pride, reflective of the arrogance in the evil powers that he served, had brought him to that point. He was learning the cost of resisting the Lord's purposes.

There was a force more powerful than the gods of the Egyptians, an angel of death called "the destroyer" whose power only God himself could restrain. When the Egyptians lost their firstborn to "the destroyer," it was because the Lord did not extend his hand of protection over them. But the Israelites had a different fate. The Lord had said to Moses: "I have heard the groaning of the Israelites, whom the Egyptians are enslaving, and I have remembered my Covenant."[15] God was committed to their protection and provision.

THE FIRST PASSOVER

As the angel of death was released over Egypt, the angel was prevented from striking anyone protected under the sign of God's Covenant protection. The sign was an apt reminder of Covenant sacrifice—the blood of a lamb smeared on the doorposts of every Israelite house. The angel's grisly assignment did not include them—he was told that he must "pass over" them.

They killed a lamb, painting its blood on the posts and the lintels of their doors.[16] The journey that had begun for Abraham in a pathway of blood had brought them now to this door, and through the bloodstained doorway, they passed from death to life. Once safely inside, they ate the roasted lamb, gorging themselves to take on enough fuel for the long journey. The bitter herbs cooked with the meat represented the sour experience of slavery, and the unleavened bread reminded them that their flight was made in haste.

And when the night had passed and the angel of death had gone, they plundered their neighbors, who were only too willing to surrender their treasures to rid Egypt of the Israelite slaves whose God was so powerful.

The events of that night have been enshrined as the principal celebration of Israel's identity. That night stood as a permanent testimony to God's Covenant faithfulness. God gave instructions through Moses that the people should prepare for their "exodus" from the land of Egypt, dressed for the journey and fed for the long march, with the symbols of life and death, slavery and freedom resonating in their hearts.

The Israelites returned to this scene every year in their hearts and minds, recalling how God had rescued them. But, more importantly, as the Israelites reenacted the "Passover," they remembered to whom they belonged. They were "the people of God," and that was the most important fact of their existence.

Many years later, picking up the theme of remembrance, Jesus told his disciples that they should eat the bread and drink the wine of the Passover meal "in remembrance" of him. And so as his disciples ate the bread and drank the wine they identified with him, enacting the central truth of Covenant—that they were "one" with their Covenant partner Jesus.[17]

84

LOUD WAILING IN EGYPT

The angel of death swept over the nation of Egypt, and the last, most terrible plague struck. The Egyptians were devastated.

"Pharaoh and all his officials and all the Egyptians got up during the night, and there was loud wailing in Egypt, for there was not a house without someone dead."[18]

Pharaoh and his court and all his people now desperately wanted the Israelites to leave—as quickly as possible.

Moses led his people out of the land of their captivity toward their appointed meeting place with the Lord.[19] As they walked unscathed through their blood-daubed doors, the Lord appeared in cloud and fire. A "pillar of cloud" by day evoked the smoking firepot, and a "pillar of fire" by night pointed to the blazing torch that had revealed God's presence to Abraham. With the symbols of God's presence before them, God guided his people first through the Red Sea and then through the desert.

In revenge and hardness of heart though, Pharaoh changed his mind yet again. Foolishly, he chose to pursue the Israelites, not wanting to lose such vital resources in his economy. When the people of Israel saw the Egyptian army of horses and chariots pursuing, the Israelites panicked. Moses assured them that the Lord had come to fight on their behalf:

"Moses answered the people, 'Do not be afraid. Stand firm and you will see the deliverance the Lord will bring you today. The Egyptians you see today you will never see again. The Lord will fight for you; you need only to be still.'" (Exodus 14:13-14)

Notes

18: See Exodus 12:30

19: The presence of God is revealed to the Israelites as he leads them out of captivity.

20: See Psalms 77:16-20 and Psalms 78:13.

21: In the New Testament, Paul suggests that this passage through the Red Sea marked the baptism into a new life for the whole nation of Israel. We could see the bloodied doorposts as the beginning of their new life in God and the parting of the chaotic forces of the Red Sea the completion: "For I do not want you to be ignorant of the fact, brothers, that our forefathers were all under the cloud and that they all passed through the sea. They were all baptized into Moses in the cloud and in the sea. They all ate the same spiritual food and drank the same spiritual drink; for they drank from the spiritual rock that accompanied them, and that rock was Christ. Nevertheless, God was not pleased with most of them; their bodies were scattered over the desert." (1 Corinthians 10:1-5)

22: See Exodus 15:2-5

Moses was a changed man. No longer the diffident shepherd, now he was full of confidence.

And as they watched, the Israelites saw the Lord come between them and their enemies. The pillar of fire and cloud held back Pharaoh's army, and when Moses lifted his staff, God parted the waters of the Red Sea.

In the culture of Old Testament people, this was a hugely significant event. To them, the sea was a mighty force, untamed and unpredictable, that resisted God's authority.[20] The sea represented the powers of chaos lurking at the margins of creation, waiting for any opportunity to wreak havoc. God demonstrated his power over the forces of chaos, and with a single breath, he created a highway for his people to walk on.[21]

A NATION IS FORGED

As Moses and the Israelites reached safety on the other side, they celebrated. Nothing could stand in the way of God's power—he was their mighty warrior King!

"The Lord is my strength and my song; he has become my salvation. He is my God, and I will praise him, my father's God, and I will exalt him. The Lord is a warrior; the Lord is his name. Pharaoh's chariots and his army he has hurled into the sea. The best of Pharaoh's officers are drowned in the Red Sea. The deep waters have covered them; they sank to the depths like a stone."[22]

God's people were free. Now they could live the life that the Lord had prepared for them. As they made their way toward Mount Sinai (the mountain of God), the children of Israel encountered more of God's provision and protection. He gave them water from a rock and food from the skies. He defeated the powerful Amalekites when they attacked, and helped the Israelites function as a society, showing his care for practical details as he guided them to a greater level of organization.[23]

As Moses followed the Lord, so the Lord forged a nation. This group of slaves, dislocated from their past and alienated from their destiny, became a people whom the other nations could recognize as set apart—the Lord's people.

CARRIED ON EAGLES' WINGS

The Israelites moved as one to Mount Sinai, the place where God had first met with Moses and commissioned him to liberate his people. Moses listened on behalf of the people as the Lord said:

"This is what you are to say to the house of Jacob and what you are to tell the people of Israel: 'You yourselves have seen what I did to Egypt, and how I carried you on eagles' wings and brought you to myself. Now if you obey me fully and keep my Covenant, then out of all nations you will be my treasured possession. Although the whole earth is mine, you will be for me a Kingdom of priests and a holy nation.'" (Exodus 19:3b-6a)

The Lord had carried his people "on eagles' wings." If they remained faithful to him, they would become his "treasured

23: See Exodus 15:22-25; 16:4-26; 17:5-6; 17:8-13; 18:17-26.

The Israelites go to the mountain where God revealed himself to Moses.

possession"; he would make them the crown of his creation. This sounds like a big "if"! But remember the context in which God spoke these words. The Lord had set his people free as a gift. Into that gift of freedom, he now placed a simple framework—the Ten Commandments. These defined the thoughts and behaviors that would help the children of Israel stay faithful.

IDENTITY COMES BEFORE OBEDIENCE

The Commandments begin with how to prioritize our relationship with God and conclude with how to guard our thoughts toward other people.[24] The Commandments were intended to be like a "baby harness" that holds a child close to its parent's heart. But in time, insecurity led the people to turn the harness into a straitjacket, holding them away from God rather than to him. Why did this happen? It happened because the people of Israel placed obedience before identity. In a Covenant relationship, obedience should always flow out of identity. This was true for Moses, and it is true for us. Like Moses, we have to settle our identity before we can ever hope to obey.

If we try to relate to God through obedience first, we will always be striving for his approval, immobilized by constant insecurity.[25] We will be held away from God rather than to him.

Our good works and best intentions can never be good enough to pave the way toward a holy God, and the struggle to obey will in itself lead to separation.

24: See Exodus 20:1-17.

25: We cannot approach God through obedience; we must approach him first through knowing that we are "his."

The Israelites were to be "a Kingdom of priests." They were to be Kingdom warriors and Covenant worshippers. The Tabernacle, Israel's portable temple in the desert, would attest to this truth. The Tabernacle resembled the tent of a king in the midst of his army. The pillar of cloud by day and of fire by night hovered above the Tabernacle. When the cloud moved, the people moved, because where the king went, his army must follow, challenging any who opposed him. The Tabernacle was the battlefield residence of the King, and he was Israel's Covenant partner. It was full of glorious gold-covered furnishings to indicate the presence of a king. But there was also a bloodstained altar as the symbol of Covenant. Overshadowing all this was the pillar of fire and cloud, revealing the presence of God.

THE BENEFITS AND BLESSINGS OF THE COVENANT

Moses' forty years of guiding the Israelites through the wilderness probably marks him as one of the greatest leaders of all time. His story is marked by incredible perseverance and faithfulness in the face of considerable highs and lows. The glorious revelation of the Ten Commandments on Mount Sinai was followed quickly by the disastrous idolatry of the golden calf.

The stories of Moses and the children of Israel are extensively covered in the four books of Exodus, Leviticus, Numbers and Deuteronomy.

There are tales of battle and forbearance: of struggle against powerful enemies[26] and making peace with the ancient family of Abraham.[27]

26: See Exodus 17:8-16

27: See Numbers 20:14-21

Notes

28: See Numbers 13-14.

29: "Nevertheless, in their presumption they went up toward the high hill country, though neither Moses nor the ark of the Lord's covenant moved from the camp. Then the Amalekites and Canaanites who lived in that hill country came down and attacked them and beat them down all the way to Hormah." (Numbers 14:44-45)

There are tales of rebellion and repentance, too. In the book of Numbers,[28] we see how the Lord instructed Moses to send spies into the land of Canaan. A reconnaissance team, one spy from each of the twelve tribes, was responsible for bringing back vital intelligence for the campaign to occupy the Promised Land. But only two spies (Joshua and Caleb) were confident about victory, and the rest gave a resounding "no," overwhelmed by the enemy. After an initial complete refusal, then much dissent and grumbling, the people finally changed their minds. But it was too late; God's moment had passed. When they tried to put it right and attacked the people in the land, the tribes went without the Lord's protection and were defeated.[29]

In many ways, this story expresses the heart of the issue for the people of God in the wilderness, and the challenges facing Moses as a leader. Would they choose to live in the benefits and blessings of the Covenant, confident that God was committed to their provision and protection?

The Israelites who said "no" died in the desert. Only their children, led by Joshua and Caleb, entered the Promised Land. A whole generation missed an amazing opportunity. The promises that God had made about the Promised Land echoed the blessings of the long-lost paradise that he had shared with his first children Adam and Eve. The Israelites had come within touching distance of a near-Eden, and had lost it again. Surely with Moses at the helm, they should have been able to conquer the land and bring a swift end to their wandering. But it was not to be.

These early Old Testament stories are also tales of spiritual intimacy and psalmody: of speaking to God "face-to-face" as a friend[30] and framing the long march through the wilderness with song. Songs marked the beginning and the end of the wilderness journey. We saw Moses in Exodus 15 rejoicing in God's rescue from captivity, and in Deuteronomy 32 with stunning poetry, preparing the people (a new generation of Israelites) to enter the Promised Land. God, who had fought for his people as "a mighty warrior" and had found them "in a barren and howling waste" was now "stirring up his nest," "carrying them on his pinions"—causing his fledgling people to fly toward their promised home. At last, the people would be able to rest.[31]

MOSES – A WOVEN IDENTITY

The Bible is about Covenant and Kingdom. Abraham defined Covenant, and Joseph defined Kingdom. But when we come to Moses, we see something new. For the first time, both realities are forged together in one person's life. Moses came to know and understand his Covenant identity, and he grasped that he had the backing of the King of heaven.

The process of combining Covenant and Kingdom, of bringing together the warp and weft of Scripture's fabric, begins in the life of one man, Moses.

Next we turn to David, the other giant of Old Testament history. His call was to establish a pattern of kingly rule that would truly honor God and complete the conquest of the land God had given his people. David did all of this—living out the realities of Covenant and Kingdom—as a worshipper and a warrior.

Notes

30: "The Lord would speak to Moses face to face, as a man speaks with his friend. Then Moses would return to the camp." (Exodus 33:11a)

31: "The Lord is a warrior; the Lord is his name." (Exodus 15:3) "In a desert land he found him, in a barren and howling waste. He shielded him and cared for him; he guarded him as the apple of his eye, like an eagle that stirs up its nest and hovers over its young, that spreads its wings to catch them and carries them on its pinions." (Deuteronomy 32:10-11)

Ruth

"But Ruth replied, 'Don't urge me to leave you or to turn back from you. Where you go I will go, and where you stay I will stay. Your people will be my people and your God my God. Where you die I will die, and there I will be buried. May the Lord deal with me be it ever so severely, if anything but death separates you and me.'" (Ruth 1:16-17)

In the book of Ruth, we have one of the great stories of the Hebrew narrative tradition, a beautifully balanced story full of tension and drama that explores the ancestry of Israel's greatest king, David.

Ruth, a Moabitess, married the son of an Israelite woman, but he, his brother and his father all died. Though Ruth's sister-in-law chose to remain in Moab, Ruth elected to go back to Israel with her mother-in-law Naomi. Ruth chose to find her identity in a Covenant relationship with Naomi and to walk with Naomi's God. Ruth's selfless love for Naomi precisely expresses what the Old Testament describes as a life of obedience.

Together, they returned to Bethlehem, Naomi's hometown. There they hoped that the ancient traditions built upon Israel's Covenant history would save them from destitution. The nearest male relative—Naomi's "kinsman-redeemer"—should take responsibility for their protection and provision, reflecting God's commitment in the Covenant. But Boaz, another close relative, having fallen in love with Ruth, asked for the responsibilities of the kinsman-redeemer to pass to him so that he might marry Ruth and care for Naomi.

The book of Ruth beautifully reminds us how our relationships should reflect God's Covenant love for us. The Lord's commitment to sacrificial generosity in his Covenant is poignantly expressed in the words and actions of Ruth, who chose faithfulness to Naomi over self-preservation. In similar fashion, the actions of Boaz, conveyed with such depth of integrity, echo the character of God in his dealings with his people. The Covenant message is that we should be as faithful to one another as God is to us.

Interestingly, having revolved so clearly around the issue of relationship and Covenant, the book then points us toward the Kingdom of God. Boaz and Ruth were the great-grandparents of King David, the great warrior and worshipper whose life so fully expressed Covenant and Kingdom.

Chapter 6

David
Worshipper and Warrior

*T*he exact chronology is uncertain, but we know that by the time David came to prominence, more than four hundred years had passed since the time of Moses. Joshua and Caleb, with their families, were the only members of the generation that left Egypt who entered the Promised Land. The others, because of their "hardness of heart," were not trusted by God to conquer and settle Canaan. They died in the desert.[1]

Joshua led the people to victory in their God-given land, but although Joshua enjoyed peace in his lifetime, the peoples who were already there were never fully driven out. In time, this would lead to trouble for the people of Israel as they began to adopt the lifestyles, habits and even the fertility religions of the native population.[2]

A REPEATING PATTERN

The story from Joshua to David is the period of biblical history dominated by the judges, and it was a spiritual roller-coaster ride. A repeating pattern swiftly emerged that went something like this:

- The people would forget the Lord and their Covenant relationship.
- Their authority and power to maintain control of the Land would be diminished.
- Competing nations around them would move into their territory or
- resident people groups would put the Israelites under pressure.

Notes

From Moses to David

1: "The Lord replied, 'I have forgiven them, as you asked. Nevertheless, as surely as I live and as surely as the glory of the Lord fills the whole earth, not one of the men who saw my glory and the miraculous signs I performed in Egypt and in the desert but who disobeyed me and tested me ten times- not one of them will ever see the land I promised on oath to their forefathers. No one who has treated me with contempt will ever see it.'" (Numbers 14:20-23)

2: Various Canaanite tribes were already there, and the Philistines arrived at the same time as the Israelites, leading to a continuous conflict between them for the land of Canaan. Once the Canaanite tribes were subjugated, the real contest was between the Israelites and the Philistines.

- The Lord would raise up a judge who would rescue them.
- The Lord would call them to return to their Covenant relationship.
- The judge would rule Israel for his or her lifetime.
- The cycle would begin again.

ISRAEL DEMANDS AN EARTHLY KING

The judges were men or women who walked closely with God and (despite their human failings) understood something of the nature of Covenant relationship and Kingdom representation. The last and greatest of these was the prophet Samuel (known at that time as a "seer"). He oversaw the transition from the governorship of the judges to the rule of kings.

When the people of Israel came to Samuel and demanded that they be given a king, he was crestfallen. He rightly believed that the Lord alone was King. In Samuel's distress, he inquired of the Lord, and the Lord said:

"Listen to all that the people are saying to you; it is not you they have rejected, but they have rejected me as their king. As they have done from the day I brought them up out of Egypt until this day forsaking me and serving other gods, so they are doing to you. Now listen to them; but warn them solemnly and let them know what the king who will reign over them will do."
(1 Samuel 8:7-9)

So Samuel spoke to the elders of Israel and warned them of all the negative consequences of taking a human king. But they would not listen. They wanted to be like all the other nations and have a king, a visible figurehead to look to in times of trial. Samuel was still sure that he should not meet their request—but the Lord urged him to agree:

"Listen to them and give them a king." (1 Samuel 8:22a)[3]

Thus, at God's command, Samuel anointed Saul, the tallest man in Israel, to be their king. He was "head and shoulders" above any other candidate! But though he began well, he quickly wandered from the Lord and the safety of Samuel's counsel. Samuel had to respond to Saul's waywardness:

"'You acted foolishly,' Samuel said. 'You have not kept the command the Lord your God gave you; if you had, he would have established your kingdom over Israel for all time. But now your kingdom will not endure; the Lord has sought out a man after his own heart and appointed him leader of his people, because you have not kept the Lord's command.'" (1 Samuel 13:13-14)[4]

Samuel was deeply saddened by the turn of events, but the Lord had another job for him:

"How long will you mourn for Saul, since I have rejected him as king over Israel? Fill your horn with oil and be on your way; I am sending you to Jesse in Bethlehem. I have chosen one of his sons to be king." (1 Samuel 16:1)

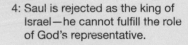

JESSE'S YOUNGEST SON

God had rejected Saul as King, and so Samuel began the search for a new one. The Lord directed Samuel to Jesse's household in Bethlehem to find a replacement. Although Samuel asked the Lord about each of David's brothers as they were brought before him, none was chosen. The Lord indicated another, and so Samuel pushed to see the last and youngest brother.

David was in the fields, oblivious to the great events shaping the life of his nation. One of the hired men ran breathlessly to bring David the message that the prophet had come to the homestead and was asking for him. As the youngest, he had been given the most menial of tasks, and when Samuel arrived, David was taking care of the sheep as usual. We can only imagine how the news was greeted—to the people of Israel, Samuel must have been like a combination of Winston Churchill and Billy Graham!

When Samuel saw the youngest brother, the prophet knew that David was the one who would shepherd God's people, and it was his heart for God that had opened the door to him being used. Young as he was, Samuel anointed David as the future king of Israel. As the oil was poured upon his head, the power of the Holy Spirit came upon David, equipping him for his task, but similar to Joseph, David would have to wait for God's timing before he could fulfill his destiny. (1 Samuel 16:1-13)[5]

5: God finds one who can represent him.

DAVID THE WORSHIPPER

Being a shepherd was tedious and monotonous work, especially for a teenager. But to David, it presented only opportunity. Using his time well, he drew close to God and practiced the harp until he became one of the most accomplished musicians in Israel. He also mastered the shepherd's weaponry—the sling and the stone. He clearly had talent, but it requires much practice and discipline to get that good—we can safely assume that it took him many hundreds, even thousands, of hours. In time, his abilities shone through, and one of the king's attendants noticed David.

Saul's growing distance from the Lord had led him into spiritual jeopardy. His divine protection had been removed, and an evil spirit was troubling him. On the advice of some of his counselors, he sought out a gifted musician whose worship could usher in the presence of the Lord and drive the evil spirit away. A national search was conducted, and David was chosen. A royal attendant reported—"I have seen a son of Jesse of Bethlehem who knows how to play the harp. He is a brave man and a warrior. He speaks well and is a fine looking man. And the Lord is with him." (1 Samuel 16:18) Suddenly David was thrust into the limelight as a musician serving in the court of the king.[6]

We don't know all the songs that David sang for Saul and the tunes that David used are lost to antiquity. But some of his incredible lyrics, recorded throughout his life and enshrined in the book of Psalms, have touched the lives of millions. His songs came from a deep walk with the Lord, and they reveal "a man after God's own heart."[7]

6: For David (called to be king), worship was his first desire.

7: "the Lord has sought out a man after his own heart and appointed him leader of his people." (1 Samuel 13:14)

THE SHEPHERD'S PSALM

One of David's greatest achievements is now known to us as Psalm 23—the shepherd's song. Like all great worship, this song touches the heart of God but is earthed in ordinary human experience. Surely, the song began life in the years of David's service as a shepherd:

> The Lord is my shepherd,
> I shall not be in want.
> He makes me lie down in green pastures,
> He leads me beside quiet waters,
> He restores my soul.
> He guides me in paths of righteousness for his name's sake.
> Even though I walk through the valley of the shadow of death,
> I will fear no evil,
> For you are with me;
> Your rod and your staff, they comfort me.
> You prepare a table before me in the presence of my enemies.
> You anoint my head with oil;
> My cup overflows.
> Surely goodness and love will follow me all the days of my life,
> And I will dwell in the house of the Lord forever. (Psalm 23)[8]

8: Phillip Keller's *A Shepherd Looks at Psalm 23* is a fascinating read.

Perhaps at the waterhole, where the flocks mingled, he imagined that he heard one of his sheep comparing shepherds. Many times, David would have been with his corralled sheep through the winter, waiting for the lambing season. He knew that unless he made the ewes "lie down in green pastures" they would stand anxiously, ready to run and thus not ready to give birth. He knew he needed to provide good food and be near water, to help them with the exertions of giving birth. And once spring had come, he would lead them again toward the summer meadows in the hills.[9]

For David, this was all part of the cycle of life, and it was deeply connected to his own intimate walk with the Lord. He knew what it was like to be led by him. He knew how God provided for his deepest needs, and David knew that if he was going to reach the mountaintop, he would have to go through "the valley of the shadow of death," where the predators lived.[10] In the valley, the sheep drew closer to the shepherd. They could smell the jackals and wolves everywhere, in every crag and gully, while the disorientating presence of running water caused some to fall into the streams and drown.

At this point in the Psalm, David stops talking about the Lord and starts talking to him. The Psalm moves from third-person descriptions of God taking action, to talking to the Lord himself about how his care affects him: "your rod and staff they comfort me."[11] The shepherd uses his staff to pull the wayward sheep out of the ravine or from under the thorn bush. He uses his rod to protect them from the attacks of enemies and to discipline the ones that go astray.[12]

The second half addresses the Lord directly, and though there remains an underlay of metaphor, the human elements come more and more to the fore as David expresses his love for his God and his thankfulness for his loving care.

9: See Psalms 23:2-3

10: See Psalms 23:4a

11: See Psalms 23:4b

12: Sadly, we do not have space to study all the Psalms within this book, but I encourage you to read them regularly and discover the call to the Covenant relationship and the commission to represent the King.

FROM WORSHIP TO WAR

As a psalmist, David is unsurpassed in Scripture, but this is explained only partly by his remarkable skill with words and music. Mostly it was his heart, the very quality that the Lord saw in David, that equipped him for the great heights of worship that he achieved.

David's heart was fashioned in the light of a Covenant relationship with the Lord. This was the rich resource in David's songwriting and the solid foundation on which he built a life of purpose. The security that came from his walk with God bred first confidence and then an incredible courage as David sought to extend the Lord's kingly rule.

DAVID THE WARRIOR

David's Covenant confidence and Kingdom courage could be seen even at an early age.

Goliath stood on the other side of the valley, a terrifying sight to the menfolk of Israel. Shouting his usual challenge, he offered a way for the inevitable mass bloodshed to be minimized. He proposed single combat between a champion drawn from the ranks of Israel and himself, the champion of the Philistines.[13] Perhaps he intended to take on (or at least to goad) King Saul, the tallest man in Israel. Whatever Goliath's intent, he bellowed the same challenge across the valley morning and evening for almost six weeks.[14]

13: See 1 Samuel 17

14: For David (called to be king), warfare was a continuous part of life.

104

David had been sent by his father Jesse to see how his brothers were doing. They were in Saul's army, and like everyone else, they were petrified by the Philistine champion. David saw the desperate situation and heard the call to act. He went to Saul and asked for permission to represent him and his army.[15]

THE KING WAS NOT VERY KEEN

"Saul replied, 'you are not able to go out against this Philistine and fight him; you are only a boy and he has been a fighting man from his youth.'" (1 Samuel 17:33)

The king knew David as a court musician but not his prowess as a warrior. David described his exploits as a shepherd, killing bears and lions, and eventually convinced Saul to let him go.[16] Saul offered David his armor, but after trying it on, the young man refused. It was too heavy and cumbersome, and it did not belong to him.

In his mind, David had three major combat advantages:

1. One-on-one, he was much quicker. Goliath was enormous (over nine feet tall) and incredibly powerful, but he was slow, ponderous and dangerous only within range of his enormous reach.
2. Using his sling, David could strike the giant from a distance. Although Goliath could throw his iron-tipped javelin, thick as a weaver's rod, David would see that coming and could easily dodge it.
3. But David had something else, a hidden advantage that

Notes

15: "David said to Saul, 'let no one lose heart on account of this Philistine; your servant will go and fight him.'" (1 Samuel 17:32)

16: "But David said to Saul, 'Your servant has been keeping his father's sheep. When a lion or a bear came and carried off a sheep from the flock, I went after it, struck it and rescued the sheep from its mouth. When it turned on me, I seized it by its hair, struck it and killed it. Your servant has killed both the lion and the bear; this uncircumcised Philistine will be like one of them, because he has defied the armies of the living God. The Lord who delivered me from the paw of the lion and the paw of the bear will deliver me from the hand of this Philistine.' Saul said to David, 'Go, and the Lord be with you.'" (1 Samuel 17:34-37)

gave him enormous confidence in the fight. He was protected under the Covenant of God. Just as all the men of Israel, David bore the mark of that Covenant relationship in his flesh, but Goliath—an "uncircumcised Philistine"—was unprotected.[17]

Similar to all great warriors, David no doubt enjoyed the feelings associated with the fight: the rush of adrenalin, the raised heart rate, the nervous energy transmuting into preternatural calm as he focused all his energy on taking one, clear shot. As David was an expert with his sling (well able to take a bird in flight), Goliath made an easy target as he stood there still as a sentinel. David just had to hit Goliath's face hard enough to knock him down. David had done it before with bears and lions, striking hard and fast at the most vulnerable part of his target.[18]

Reaching the bottom of the valley, David put his hand down into the waters of the cool stream and found five smooth stones. He put four into his shepherd's pouch and placed one in his sling, testing the stone's weight, swinging it in his hand.

Goliath did not sound impressed:

"He said to David, 'Am I a dog that you come at me with sticks?' And the Philistine cursed David by his gods. 'Come here,' he said, 'and I'll give your flesh to the birds of the air and the beasts of the field!'" (1 Samuel 17:43-44)

Perhaps it was the mention of the Philistine gods, so insignificant compared to the Lord, but something happened in David's heart, and the warrior in him replied:

"You come against me with sword and spear and javelin, but I come against you in the name of the Lord Almighty, the God of the armies of Israel, whom you have defied. This day the Lord will hand you over to me, and I'll strike you down and cut off your head. Today I will give the carcasses of the Philistine army to the birds of the air and the beasts of the earth, and the whole world will know that there is a God in Israel. All those gathered here will know that it is not by sword or spear that the Lord saves; for the battle is the Lord's and he will give all of you into our hands." (1 Samuel 17:45b-47)

The sneering remarks of the giant continued despite David's amazing statement of faith as the boy moved toward a combat position. Although young, David was a honed fighting man, a formidable opponent. Whirling the sling above his head until it sang, David moved against his foe and released the stone. The smooth-sided pebble struck Goliath on the bridge of the nose and sank into his forehead. Dropping his weapons, the Philistine champion fell face forward, like a tree with an axe at its roots. His armor bearer offered no resistance as David took the champion's sword, hefted it skyward and cut off the giant's head. The greatest enemy of Israel lay dead, his head severed with his own sword.[19]

There was silence in the ranks of the Philistines. For the Israelites' part, after a stunned pause, all was noise and dust as they broke into ecstatic cheering and charged. The Philistine soldiers began to retreat, and then to run. The rout was soon complete and victory assured.

After the battle, David, boyishly carrying Goliath's head in one hand, reentered the king's tent to claim the prizes of victory—

What does the enemy come against me with?

19: "So David triumphed over the Philistine with a sling and a stone; without a sword in his hand he struck down the Philistine and killed him." (1 Samuel 17:50) tax exemptions for his father and the king's daughter in marriage. A hero was born.

As we reflect on this well-known story, we can ask ourselves some simple questions. Do we have the Covenant confidence that David showed, as we face the giants in our lives? Are we able to stand on the security God gives us, or do we cower among the crowd, hoping for others to offer us help and protection? Are we tempted to wear someone else's armor? When we look to anyone other than God for our protection, we may find safety in the short term, but our confidence to stand never grows. We might also ask what we can carry in our pocket that could bring down a giant.[20]

COVENANT BROTHERS

In the midst of this amazing day, a special friendship blossomed:

"Jonathan became one in spirit with David, and he loved him as himself . . . And Jonathan made a Covenant with David because he loved him as himself." (1 Samuel 18:1, 3)

Immediately after the defeat of Goliath and the Philistine army, the text tells us that David and Jonathan "cut" a Covenant. The blood of animals would have been involved in this ritual, and probably a scar in the flesh would have been created.[21]

Jonathan then gave David personal items that would be particularly identified with him.[22] He was a prince of Israel, a man of wealth and status, wearing a distinctive royal robe and

20: David used a small stone to topple his giant; Jesus used the verses of Scripture to defeat his. See Luke 4:1-12.

21: The suggestion that this relationship was homosexual borders on the ridiculous. Covenant friendships between young male warriors were not uncommon. This can be seen in Greek, Roman, Mongol, North American Indian and West African cultures. In some circumstances, a "blood brother" Covenant is still a common social device to ensure the protection of honor and the loyalty of those involved.

22: "Jonathan took off the robe he was wearing and gave it to David, along with his tunic, and even his sword, his bow and his belt." (1 Samuel 18:4)

108

one of the few to carry a sword.[23] Known as a great bowman, he would have been particularly identified with this weapon. So when people saw David wearing Jonathan's robe and carrying his bow and sword, David could be mistaken for Jonathan. The two had become as one. They were Covenant brothers.

Both men would stay faithful to their Covenant relationship throughout their lives. In fact, when David became king and Saul and Jonathan were dead, David sought out the one remaining son of Jonathan—crippled Mephibosheth—and adopted him as his own.

TWO KINDS OF KINGS: THE FIRST KIND – SAUL, THE SPEAR THROWER

As they returned home, the women's ecstatic welcome, "Saul has slain his thousands, David his tens of thousands," (1 Samuel 18:7) rang out among the returning warriors. King Saul was a big man on the outside, but deeply insecure within, and he began to view David as a rival rather than as a loyal subject. Thus, the pattern for their future relationship was set.

Taking the opportunity afforded by Saul's insecurity, the evil spirit that had troubled him caused his mood to darken further. As David played music, murderous thoughts emerged in Saul's mind. He threw his spear (a symbol of his kingship) at David; and with it, Saul threw away his kingdom. He was lashing out from the pain of his inner conflict, but the target of his rage was the channel of God's blessing![24]

Notes

23: See 1 Samuel 13:19-21

24: Saul uses the symbol of his kingship—his spear—to try to kill David: "and he hurled it, saying to himself, 'I'll pin David to the wall.' But David eluded him twice." (1 Samuel 18:11)

David eluded Saul's spear but stayed at court to continue in service. This suited Saul, because he was afraid of David's hero status among the people. Saul never allowed David to return to his father's home again. Instead, the king kept David at court in the unusual and yet strangely appropriate dual roles of warrior and worshipper. Sometimes David played for Saul, and sometimes Saul sent David out to battle. Saul wanted David either where the king could see the shepherd or on the battlefield, where the king could put David in harm's way. Capriciously, Saul had decided that David needed to die—and what better way than at the hands of their enemies the Philistines? The intrigue increased as Saul drew his attendants into the plot. Together, they ensured that David was given the most difficult military assignments that the king and his attendants hoped would result in the shepherd's downfall. But David always won, and his reputation grew among the people.

At this point, David's position at court had become more dangerous. Saul had not been successful with indirect attacks so he had decided that a more direct approach was necessary. Fortunately, David had supporters in the king's family, and Jonathan, David's Covenant friend and the king's eldest son, often spoke on David's behalf. Michal, Saul's daughter and David's wife, cleverly intervened with delaying tactics when the king sent his soldiers to kill David in his own bed.[25]

He had been unjustly treated, but there was no way for David to regain his position at this point. He was forced to flee, and could not return to the Israelite community while Saul was alive. This was a great loss to David and led to thirteen years of difficulty and struggle. He ended up living an outlaw's life in a cave in the Judean desert.

25: Perhaps it was this very situation that caused David to write: "Deliver me from my enemies, O God; protect me from those who rise up against me. Deliver me from evildoers and save me from bloodthirsty men . . . I have done no wrong, yet they are ready to attack me. Arise to help me; look on my plight! . . . They return at evening, snarling like dogs, and prowl about the city." (Psalms 59:1-2, 4, 6)

SAUL'S DOWNFALL

For Saul, this was the beginning of the end. David had lost his home—but Saul would lose his kingdom. Samuel had told Saul from the start that his willfulness had caused God to reject him as the rightful king of Israel.[26] But Saul had not learned. God was not looking for a clever king, just one whose heart was surrendered to the Lord. Saul had tried to take his own approach to Kingship rather than the path of simple obedience. Racked by insecurity, instead of cultivating his relationship with God, Saul tried to maintain his position by controlling his circumstances. It had the opposite effect. It only led him away from God's protective hand—and into the dark embrace of the devil. He couldn't even control his own mood.

Saul never fully surrendered his heart to God, and so never knew the confidence in the Lord that David enjoyed. From Saul's high position on the throne of Israel, he had no competitors; and yet to the king, David felt like a threat. But in attacking David, Saul had lifted his hand against the Lord. And though the path was long and at times tortuous for David, the conclusion was assured: Saul was certain to lose his throne, and David would be given Saul's kingdom.

The story of Saul is one of the great tragedies of Scripture. His deepening madness and paranoia even led him to seek the help of the "Witch of Endor."[27] By this time, Samuel was dead, and so Saul foolishly decided to consult Samuel using the "art" of a necromancer. It was a desperate attempt to seek the wisdom that Saul needed from his long-deceased advisor.[28] Saul fell fast and sadly took Jonathan with him.

26: "But Samuel replied: 'Does the Lord delight in burnt offerings and sacrifices as much as in obeying the voice of the Lord? To obey is better than sacrifice, and to heed is better than the fat of rams.'" (1 Samuel 15:22)

"He who is the Glory of Israel does not lie or change his mind; for he is not a man, that he should change his mind." (1 Samuel 15:29).

27: Saul's willful rebellion places him in a dire position with God.

28: See 1 Samuel 28

29: See 1 Samuel 31

In the final scene of the tragedy, Saul and Jonathan made their last desperate stand together. The Philistines surrounded the two. Jonathan—a good man to the last—died at their hands and reaped the consequences of being caught up in his father's failure. Saul fell on his sword and died by his own hand, receiving the just penalty for his foolishness and sin.[29]

In the end, Saul found himself facing an opponent he could not defeat: not the Philistines baying for his blood but the Lord. Because Saul had not humbled himself before the Lord, he rescinded Saul's Kingship and gave it to David. The tragedy of this final chapter and the lives needlessly lost were recorded in the melancholic requiem that David sang: "How the mighty are fallen!"

> "Your glory, O Israel, lies slain on your heights. How the mighty have fallen! O mountains of Gilboa, may you have neither dew nor rain, nor fields that yield offerings of grain. For there the shield of the mighty was defiled, the shield of Saul . . . Saul and Jonathan – in life they were loved and gracious, and in death they were not parted. They were swifter than eagles; they were stronger than lions . . . How the mighty have fallen in battle! Jonathan lies slain on your heights. I grieve for you, Jonathan my brother." (2 Samuel 1:19, 21, 23, 25-26a)

TWO KINDS OF KINGS:
THE SECOND KIND – DAVID THE SHEPHERD

After Saul and Jonathan's deaths, David and his "mighty men" were free to return. Of course, there were "mopping up" operations to be carried out against the house of Saul, but in due course, David was proclaimed king at Hebron. The people affirmed their common Covenant identity: "we are your own flesh and blood,"[30] and they recalled how the Lord had called David to be the shepherd king of Israel:

"The Lord said to you, 'you will shepherd my people Israel, and you will become their ruler.'" (2 Samuel 5:2)

As we reflect on the different outcomes of the lives of Saul and David, we might wonder about our own leadership. Are we spear-throwers, driven by insecurity to push others away, or are we shepherds, secure in the knowledge that we are loved by God with nothing to lose when we share that love with others?

Within seven years, David conquered Jerusalem and moved his family and court there. By the time he was in his mid-thirties, David was established as the undisputed king of Israel and the ruler of all the people who lived in the "Land." After his long wait, David was at last "settled in his palace and the Lord had given him rest from all his enemies around him."[31] As a man of Covenant, David had received progressively more Kingdom authority and power. He had reached the goal prophesied by Samuel years before.

Notes

30: David is established as the king of Israel: "All the tribes of Israel came to David at Hebron and said, 'We are your own flesh and blood.'" (2 Samuel 5:1)

31: See 2 Samuel 7:1

However, the path to this place in David's life had been marked by many battles. <u>What David revealed in his life was that even though God makes a Covenant promise, we still have to engage in Kingdom warfare to possess the promise.</u> God had promised the land of Israel to Abraham, and although Joshua and Caleb had led and fought well, at the end of their lives, the job remained incomplete. It needed David's total determination to secure final possession of what had been promised.

<u>Jesus revealed similar determination as he brought healing, deliverance, justice for the oppressed and mercy for the abused</u>. <u>If we are to follow Jesus, we will have to fight for these things.</u> <u>The New Testament makes it clear that the kind of physical battles that David engaged in foreshadowed the spiritual battles that are ours</u>:

"For our struggle is not against flesh and blood, but against the rulers against the authorities against the powers of this dark world and against the spiritual forces of evil in the heavenly realms."[32]

Our battle is not with human beings but with the agents of evil,[33] and this enemy is the one against which we must equip ourselves to fight and defeat. As we come to Scripture with a New Testament understanding, we can see that Scripture does not support or endorse the various "holy wars," genocides, ethnic cleansing and torture-ridden regimes that we have seen down through the centuries and are sadly all too present in our contemporary world. We must instead use the biblical history of armed conflict as a graphic illustration of how we should fight for what is right and good. The struggle is nonetheless real for us, but it is spiritual rather than physical.[34]

David provides a pattern for future Kingdom representatives.

32: See Ephesians 6:12

33: "Agents of evil" are fallen angels called demons, controlled and overseen by their leader, the devil.

34: See also page 37, "Bloodthirsty Passages in the Bible."

114

Jesus came as the champion of our struggle, and our warrior king. He was a descendant of David and confronted our spiritual enemies with the same level of determination that David he did in his day. By the end of the Bible, the decisive battle had been won on the Cross, and victory is assured for those who still fight on.

THE TEMPLE

Confident that the need for warfare in establishing and building his kingdom was coming to an end, David the worshipper began to imagine what it would be like to build a permanent home to worship the Lord and house the Ark of the Covenant, the beautifully crafted box that contained the Ten Commandments on tablets and was carried into battle by the Levites.[35] The Ark represented the presence of God, the heavenly King of Israel, going into battle at the head of his people. In times of peace, the Ark was contained within the royal tent, the portable temple called the Tabernacle. Now that all the battles were over, David naturally assumed that the Lord, similar to the king, should have his own permanent residence.

DAVID SAID:

"Here I am, living in a palace of cedar, while the Ark of God remains in a tent."[36]

35: See Exodus 25:10-16

36: See 2 Samuel 7:2

115

But the Lord saw it differently:

"I will provide a place for my people Israel and will plant them so that they can have a home of their own and no longer be disturbed. Wicked people will not oppress them any more as they did in the beginning and have done ever since the time I appointed leaders over my people Israel." (2 Samuel 7:10-11)

It was more important to the Lord that he made "a place" for his people than that he had a "house" built for himself. And he wanted to do the same for David as well:

"I will give you rest from your enemies . . . I will establish a house for you: when your days are over and you rest with your fathers, I will raise up your offspring to succeed you, who will come from your body and I will establish his kingdom. He is the one who will build a house for my Name, and I will establish the throne of his kingdom forever. I will be his father and he will be my son." (2 Samuel 7:4-14 extracts)

David was overwhelmed. The Lord had promised him something he had never expected. He was extending the terms of the Covenant of Abraham and Moses—which David already enjoyed—to include a special and everlasting inheritance for David. The journey to this place had been long and hard, though he was still young. But the battles were now over and the future secure. For David, there was only one response—worship.

He entered the Tabernacle, sat before the Ark and wondered:

"Who am I, O sovereign Lord, and what is my family, that you have brought me this far." (2 Samuel 7:18)

David's kingly authority emerged from his Covenant identity.

David's role as worshipper and warrior king did not include building the temple. That would be the responsibility of his son Solomon.

116

Covenant and Kingdom, at their simplest, are about "being" and "doing," respectively. At a practical level, David knew who he was (his identity and relationship with God) and what he had to do (his responsibility to represent the living God).

Sadly, Saul did not know who to "be" and so could never know what to "do." And his lack of confidence resulted in an inability to make sound or lasting decisions. He lost his Kingship because he never made a Covenant connection with God. That would have brought Samuel the sense of identity and security that he longed for. In contrast, even as a teenager facing Goliath, David knew who he was and that he needed only the Lord's presence to succeed in what he was called to do. For David, to worship was to "be," and to make war on God's behalf was what he was called to "do."

Of course, there were many difficult times. David had had to fight for survival in his "desert years." When he was separated from his home and his people, his confidence in God was tested to the limit. But David's deep faith in God meant that David did not try to make things happen for himself. Confidence in God's promises meant that David had waited for God to do things in his time. When Saul was placed at David's mercy as the king relieved himself in a cave, David knew that he must not kill his enemy the king. Despite extreme provocation, David knew it was not the way that the Lord wanted to do things.

David learned to "be" and to "do."

David learned the "not yet" of the Kingdom and the "not you" of his calling.

WORSHIP AND WARFARE

David experienced the tensions of living out God's kingly authority here on earth in at least two ways. In the early part of David's life, he learned the "not yet" of the Kingdom—he was anointed and selected but had to wait until the appointed time to receive the authority and power of the throne. In learning submission in that way, he was ready to hear God's "not yet" and "not you" in relation to the Temple. David's desire to establish the Temple was noble, but another had been chosen for the task. The Temple would be built but not in his lifetime. His son Solomon was given that task.

The fabric of David's inner life was woven together with Covenant and Kingdom—a deep relationship with God and a recognition that he was called to represent God. Together, these strands fashioned David's identity and purpose, which was to worship God and extend the boundaries of his recognized Kingship.

Worship was David's intimate expression of Covenant relationship—the connecting of his heart to God.

Warfare, on the other hand, was the ultimate expression of Kingdom authority and power, resulting in David taking possession of what God had promised.

POINTING TOWARD THE NEW TESTAMENT

"He chose David his servant and took him from the sheep pens; from tending the sheep he brought him to be the shepherd of his people Jacob, of Israel his inheritance. And David shepherded them with integrity of heart; with skillful hands he led them." (Psalms 78:70-72)

We are coming to the conclusion of David's life, and have looked at its major themes, but there has been space to touch on only some stories from the rich and detailed narrative. His "integrity of heart" fitted David for God's purpose. Within David's heart, the great themes of Scripture were fully integrated, and so his life was lived in harmony with God's promises.

Our journey through the Bible has brought us halfway through the two thousand years from Abraham to Jesus, and with David, we have reached a balance point. Of all the characters in the Old Testament, David exhibits the most complete picture of Covenant and Kingdom.

This model of life is of huge significance—it is the pattern Jesus adopted in his own ministry and forms the basis of the more developed understanding of Covenant and Kingdom in the New Testament. Its writers clearly teach that the Covenant promise is the basis for our Kingdom fight. In the New Testament, Covenant is expressed in the intimate terms of loving worship, and Kingdom is understood in terms of "spiritual warfare" as Jesus and his followers fight to retake possession of what was lost.

David is a "picture" of a King who was yet to come.

When Covenant and Kingdom work together in this way, we begin to see the truths of Scripture take on flesh to change the world.

Kingdom courage flows from Covenant confidence.

Old Testament Prophets

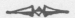

Isaiah – Jeremiah – Ezekiel – Daniel – Hosea – Joel – Amos – Obadiah – Jonah – Micah – Nahum – Habakkuk – Zephaniah – Haggai – Zechariah – Malachi

Both themes, Covenant and Kingdom, are present in all the books of the prophets, whether they are pigeonholed by us as "major" or "minor."[1] And yet there is particular emphasis in each of these writings, if we are willing to look intently. It is much easier to understand these sometimes obscure books if we appreciate the principal theme of each.

One clue to understanding which theme might dominate can be found in any passage that describes the calling of the particular prophet. For instance, the prophet **Isaiah** recounts his calling thus:

"I saw the Lord seated on a throne, high and exalted, and the train of his robe filled the temple . . . then I heard the voice of the Lord, saying, 'Whom shall I send? And who will go for us?' and I said, 'Here I am. Send me!'"[2]

Isaiah was sent on a royal errand representing his Lord with a message to share. Clearly, this is a "Kingdom" passage. The earthly king Uzziah was dead, but the Lord Almighty lived forever, and so Isaiah looked to the heavenly King for the answers his people needed. Throughout the book of Isaiah,[3] the Kingdom theme is preeminent. The calling of the prophet here defines the content of the prophecy.

For **Jeremiah**, the context of calling was quite different, although he, too, was sent with God's word upon his lips, commissioned with a special task:

---

1 The "major" prophets are Isaiah, Jeremiah, Ezekiel and Daniel. "Minor" prophets are all the rest!
2 Isaiah 6:1b,8
3 Some view the whole book as authored by him, others partly by his disciples, but this element is consistent throughout.

"Before I formed you in the womb I knew you, before you were born I set you apart."[4]

This intimate relationship with God, initiated by the Lord while Jeremiah was in his mother's womb, was the basis of his calling. From this initial revelation of relationship, Jeremiah continuously called God's people back to their Covenant. Although Kingdom is certainly present as a theme in Jeremiah, Covenant is the central thrust of the book. When Jeremiah foresaw the future, his vision was of a new Covenant written in people's hearts.[5]

Of course, the other major and minor prophets contain similar emphasis, but each appears to lean one way or the other. **Daniel** appears more Kingdom-oriented.[6] Though earthly kings recognized the Kingship of God in Daniel, there was an even greater insight about God's greater Kingdom. God's rule was advancing not only on earth, in circumstances that can be observed, but in the spiritual world—the heavenly places— where God's Kingdom advance was resisted by other beings of great power.[7]

Both Daniel and Ezekiel, along with other prophets, use apocalyptic writing in their prophesies. These highly symbolic passages point to 'another world' beyond the physical realm, which defy normal language as the prophets try to describe them.

Ezekiel is chiefly a book of Covenant,[8] whereas Joel foresees a world of Kingdom advance. He prophesies a Kingdom of peace that follows a great struggle and a final day of judgment.[9]

---

4 Jeremiah 1:5a

5 "'The time is coming,' declares the Lord, 'when I will make a new covenant with the house of Israel and with the house of Judah . . . 'I will put my law in their minds and write it on their hearts. I will be their God, and they will be my people. No longer will a man teach his neighbor, or a man his brother, saying, 'Know the Lord,' because they will all know me, from the least of them to the greatest,' declares the Lord. 'For I will forgive their wickedness and will remember their sins no more.'" (Jeremiah 31:31, 33b-34)

6 "How great are his signs, how mighty his wonders! His kingdom is an eternal kingdom; his dominion endures from generation to generation." (Daniel 4:3, or read Daniel 6:25-27)

7 See Daniel 9:20-11:1

8 "I myself will tend my sheep and have them lie down, declares the Sovereign Lord. I will search for the lost and bring back the strays. I will bind up the injured and strengthen the weak, but the sleek and the strong I will destroy. I will shepherd the flock with justice." (Ezekiel 34:16)

9 "Proclaim this among the nations: Prepare for war! Rouse the warriors! Let all the fighting men draw near and attack. Beat your plowshares into swords and your pruning hooks into spears. Let the weakling say, 'I am strong!' Come quickly, all you nations from every side, and assemble there. Bring down your warriors, O Lord!" (Joel 3:9-11; see also Joel 2:1-5, 31-32)

Hosea contains some of the richest and most beautiful descriptions of Covenant relationship. Hosea is called to marry an unfaithful wife, who represents the waywardness of Israel. Although God's anger is stirred, his compassion triumphs.[10]

Once we understand these Covenant and Kingdom themes provide us with an interpretive lens through which we can understand the Scriptures, the interpretation of even the most difficult prophetic passages becomes much more straightforward.

---

10 "When Israel was a child, I loved him, and out of Egypt I called my son." (Hosea 11:1) "How can I give you up, Ephraim? How can I hand you over, Israel? . . . My heart is changed within me; all my compassion is aroused." (Hosea 11:8)

The Journey So Far
Summary of Covenant and Kingdom in the Old Testament

We have reached an important point in our study of the Scriptures. By now, I trust we are getting more familiar with the themes of Covenant and Kingdom. As the Bible moves on, our journey will begin to head toward Jesus.

In any journey, in addition to the destination, the most important decision we make is picking the route. As we have traversed the landscape of the Old Testament, our path has followed the lives of four great characters: Abraham, Joseph, Moses and David. The route set by these narratives has allowed us only the briefest of pauses to look at the stories of others such as Esther and Ruth. We have taken long-distance views of the other portions of the Old Testament. Sadly, within the confines of this book, we will be unable to do any more. However, what we have found in the lives of these heroes equips us to take other journeys across this landscape at our leisure. We have discovered the coordinates that help to orient any effective study of the Bible. We have found the latitude and longitude of biblical revelation in Covenant and Kingdom.

Now we must move on. We need to set out for the high lands of biblical revelation—we must reach the story of Jesus. But before we do that, perhaps a brief look back across the territory that we have traveled will help us all.

SUMMARY OF COVENANT IN THE OLD TESTAMENT

Covenant is the way in which the Bible describes and defines relationship: first our relationship with God and then our relationship with everyone else.

In the beginning, when we lived in perfect union with God, the only thing necessary was to maintain the "oneness" that God had already created. After the Fall and the commensurate alienation from God, we see him time and again making a gracious initiative toward us. We could never make our own way back to God (the way was blocked), but he could build a bridge to us. And so beginning with Abraham, God rebuilt a Covenant connection with humankind.

FATHER

Although God is recognized as a Father to his people in the Old Testament, the revelation of the fatherhood of God is incomplete and is largely located in the fathers of the nation: Abraham, Isaac and Jacob.[1] They were the first recipients of God's Covenant call, and the nation's connection to them reminded the people that they were one with God. In Jesus, the revelation is completed. It is not a human father that we need; it is a heavenly Father.

IDENTITY

Identity flows from Covenant relationship. Among the people of the Old Testament, this identity was one of nationhood, but in this identity, a genuine heart connection with God was invited. From this relationship flowed the necessary security that is the foundation for a successful and productive life. When the people of Israel understood their Covenant connection, they were able to grasp the security of their identity.

OBEDIENCE

Obedience was always intended to flow from identity. It is not possible to behave in the right way without knowing first who you are. So the law as a framework for behavior came after the call to be God's people.

The problem for Israel was that the people placed obedience before identity. Before long, this led to one of three things: a decadent disregard of laws that could not be kept, a bondage to performance or an incapacitation caused by continuous failure.

---

1 "See, I have given you this land. Go in and take possession of the land that the Lord swore he would give to your fathers—to Abraham, Isaac and Jacob—and to their descendants after them." (Deuteronomy 1:8)

By the time we reach the New Testament, three elements of Covenant have emerged. The three corners of a triangle might help us to portray these three elements. The corner pointing upward refers to God as Father, the corner on the right-hand side points to us and our identity and the third corner points toward our response in obedience:

SUMMARY OF KINGDOM IN THE OLD TESTAMENT

With the loss of relationship in the Garden, human beings lost their ability to represent God as his royal emissaries. With the restoration of relationship through Abraham, the process of rebuilding our capacity to rule was begun.

Joseph was the first exponent of the Kingdom, but we have seen that others such as Moses, David and Esther similarly expressed God's Kingship in their day. Though often conscious of their frailty and weakness, these heroes regularly revealed the three key elements of Kingdom life.

KING

Throughout Scripture, even during the days of an active monarchy in Israel, God was seen as the king of his people. More than this, he was the king of the universe, enthroned among his starry host, first creating and then directing the destiny of humankind. David was the archetypal exponent of human Kingship in the Old Testament. In him, we see God ruling through a human being, but not until Jesus are the obstacles of human frailty removed and we see God's rule as he intends it to be.

AUTHORITY

From Joseph on, the authority that God wants to reveal in and through us is found in the lessons of humility. Authority gives us the freedom to act on God's behalf. As this works out through us, God intends that we represent him in such a way that people see him. David, Esther, Daniel, Deborah and many others operated with God's regal authority.

POWER

Power is exercised as a direct result of having authority. The nature of this power requires a level of personal surrender that prevents people being the object of others' praise. It could be the power given to Joseph to forgive, the power to lead for David or the power to rescue, as seen in the life of Esther. Occasionally in the Old Testament story, the miraculous intervention of God's power changes the circumstances of the people involved. This was seen particularly in the ministry of Moses, Elijah and Elisha. But, of course, it is not until Jesus that we see the power of God released and revealed in its full measure.

Again, using a triangle to portray the three main elements of Kingdom, we see that the top corner points to God as king, the right-hand corner to his authority in us and the third corner to his power flowing to us and through us:

It is good to note that power always flows from authority. Authority is about placing ourselves in the right place before God. As we humbly recognize his and our position, he authorizes us to exercise power on his behalf.

Soon we will plunge headlong into the story of Jesus and the New Testament, but before we do this, we should pause to connect the Old and New Testaments.

Chapter 7

Connecting
The Old and New Testaments

*T*here are a thousand years between David and Jesus. We want to explore the two main themes woven in the lives of the great biblical characters, rather than taking a dry historical survey of the Bible. But a thousand years is too long to skip over! There are centuries filled with kings and royal intrigues, prophets and their declarations of judgment and the people of God declining in significance until they were taken into exile and captivity. How does the era of David connect with the time of Jesus?

Solomon inherited the Kingdom of Israel from his father David.[1] David also left Solomon plans for the Temple in Jerusalem and enough wealth to accomplish all he wished.[2] Though Solomon started well, by the end of his life, he had allowed his many wives to draw his heart away from the Lord.[3] By doing this, he squandered his father's most important legacy. Solomon's Covenant with God was compromised, and so the relational unity of his people suffered. On Solomon's death, deep fissures emerged among the people. The result was that the Davidic kingdom was divided into the kingdoms of Israel and Judah— Israel to the north, Judah to the south.[4]

With the monarchy divided, the two kingdoms never regained the glories of their past. Solomon had taken a step away from the Lord. The kings of the divided kingdom began first to walk and then to run away from God. Without a Covenant relationship, they had progressively less authority to represent God as the king. There were a few notable exceptions, such as King Josiah of Judah,[5] but in general, the Kingship of God was no longer represented by men who knew him. Things went from bad to worse.

As we read the Old Testament, there is a growing feeling of inevitability as the Lord's people lose their way, come under his chastening hand and fall prey to their enemies. An air of resigned sadness sets in over the later centuries of Old Testament history.

Lacking God's protection, Israel and Judah were attacked by newly emerged great empires, greedy to gobble up as much territory as possible. Israel and Judah were too vulnerable and too weak to resist, and thus, they were brutally subjugated. Following the imperial practices of the day, successive waves of Israelites were taken into captivity and exile and resettled in foreign lands.

Through the prophets and other godly men and women, the Lord continued to reveal his desire for a Covenant relationship with his people.

"I have loved you with an everlasting love; I have drawn you with loving kindness. I will build you up again and you will be rebuilt." (Jeremiah 31:3b-4a)

God made it clear that he still wanted to be their king:

"This is what the Lord says—Israel's King and Redeemer, the Lord Almighty: I am the first and I am the last; apart from me there is no God." (Isaiah 44:6)

Most of God's people ignored his call.

But some responded and made the experience of judgment and exile less bleak for the people. Heroes such as Daniel and Esther stood tall as great examples of godliness in their day. And, in time, outstanding leaders such as Ezra and Nehemiah emerged to lead the exiles home.

Once home, they began to rebuild Jerusalem with the Temple at its heart. But they rarely experienced the peace and prosperity of their early years.

Occupying the strategically important trade routes from north to south and east to west, Israel and Judah continued to claim the attention of successive empires: first the Hellenistic rulers who were heirs to Alexander the Great, and eventually the greatest empire of them all. The people of God came under the heel of mighty Rome, which dominated the region for more than four hundred years.

These circumstances caused a deep longing to rise in the heart of God's people. They knew that the Lord had rescued them and had set things right before. They knew that he had promised through the prophets that one like David would come and establish an everlasting Kingdom. But when would it happen? They cried out to the Lord:

My soul is in anguish.

How long, O Lord, how long?

Will you forget me forever?

How long will you hide your face from me?[6]

6: Psalms 6:3 and 13:1. A major theme in the Israelites' worship and reflected in many Psalms is that the Lord was the King to whom the people of God should bring their complaints and requests for justice. This appears to have been particularly important during the Exile and in the Intertestamental period (the time between the last book of the Old Testament and the birth of Jesus).

Chapter 8

—◆—

Jesus
Son of God and Son of Man

*O*ur journey through Scripture so far has been an odyssey of amazing individuals and great heroes of faith. Now we come to the greatest of them all, Jesus.

As we approach his story, we enter a territory much traveled and extensively explored. But as we traverse this landscape, we will not examine the complex vistas of New Testament scholarship or the easy paths of our Sunday school journeys, though we may look at some of their features as we pass. Rather, we will trace the footsteps of the Savior and pause to reflect on the great events of his life. As we look again at the significant moments of Jesus' life, we will perceive more deeply as we look through the two "lenses" of Covenant and Kingdom.

These two great themes of the Bible find their fullest expression in Jesus. Only when we look at him are we able to grasp their complete meaning.

For example, in the Gospels, Jesus is given many titles, but perhaps the two most important are Son of God and Son of Man. Son of Man is the most common title that Jesus uses for himself, one that no one else uses about him. Son of God, though acknowledged by Jesus of himself, is more often the way in which others described him.[1] The Father's voice identifies Jesus as his son at the baptism in the Jordan, the devil seeks to undermine this claim in the temptations and Peter affirms the title in his confession.

When Jesus is referred to as the "Son of God," it is his Covenant identity with God the Father that is being revealed. "This is the Son of God." (John 1: 34) The "Son of God" is fully identified with God and shares his nature. The Son of God has the same spiritual DNA as the Father.

137

Notes

We begin the next stage of our journey as we walk with Jesus.

1: "They all asked, 'Are you then the Son of God?' He replied, 'You are right in saying I am.'" (Luke 22:70)

When Jesus describes himself as the "Son of Man," he appears to be referring to his role as the representative of God's Kingship in the world. "At that time men will see the Son of Man coming in clouds with great power and glory." (Mark 13:26) <u>"Son of Man" indicates that Jesus has come to restore humanity's role, as one of us, to rule on behalf of God.</u>[2]

COVENANT AND KINGDOM IN THE GOSPELS

Naturally, the two themes are woven throughout the Gospels, although each writer has different emphasis.

The Gospels of Matthew, Mark and Luke focus on how the Kingdom of God invades our lives in the person of Jesus. They emphasize his ministry to the crowds in Galilee. They record his call to the disciples to represent the King. He offers hope to the masses as he preaches and proves that the king of heaven is among them.

John's Gospel focuses on the Covenant and becoming one with God. The Gospel records how Jesus taught his followers to enter a Covenant relationship with him so that they could become one with their Father. John's account deals mostly with the work and teaching of Jesus in Jerusalem, often at the great Jewish festivals. At these events, designed to remind the Jewish people of their history, Jesus taught the pilgrims how their Covenant identity could be found only in him.

Although these strong emphases differentiate the Gospels, both themes are clearly revealed in all four, especially in the defining events[3] of Jesus' life and in his encounters[4] with individuals and small groups.

2: "Son of Man" is used in the prophetic books of the Old Testament to address the prophets in their role as God's representatives or to indicate the intervention of God in the world as he sends a heavenly representative of his kingly power. For example, see Ezekiel 2:1 and Daniel 7:13-14.

Different emphasis of Covenant and Kingdom for different Gospel writers.

3: I refer to "events" such as his baptism, death and resurrection.

4: "Encounters with individuals and small groups" refers to times when Covenant and Kingdom were brought together—for example, at the confession of Peter at Caesarea Philippi (Matthew 16:13-20) and at the Last Supper in the Synoptic Gospels (Luke 22:14-31). Or where Jesus speaks to Nathaniel (John 1:43-51), Nicodemus (John 3:1-21) and Pontius Pilate (John 18:33-38).

Two of the Gospels record the birth of Jesus. Matthew speaks of the newborn king attracting visitors from around the world. Just as Solomon's kingdom was so glorious that it drew the adulation of the nations around,[5] so Jesus—"David's greater son"—drew the adoration of the Magi.[6] In Luke's gospel, Jesus' birth as a humble King is presented as good news to the poor and alienated. Mary's Song speaks eloquently of this truth,[7] and the visitation of the shepherds—a despised underclass – reveals that the King has come for everyone.[8] Both Matthew and Luke make it absolutely clear that Jesus was born to a virgin and that his conception was miraculous.

Little is known of Jesus' childhood. We do know that he had a natural development, and by the time he was thirty (the age when Israelite priests entered their calling and Joseph and David accepted their call to rule), Jesus was ready.

In the narratives that surround Jesus' baptism and resurrection, we see the introduction and fulfillment of these great themes. But we see the deepest revelation of these mysteries at the Cross.

On the Cross, Jesus reconnected the Kingdom of heaven with the people of earth. On the Cross, God stretched wide his arms to embrace us all. Kingdom and Covenant are here writ large. The banner headline above Jesus' head proclaimed that he was the king and the blood that flowed from his wounds indicated the sacrifice necessary to make a Covenant possible.

As the vertical and horizontal bars of the Cross were bound together to form an instrument of execution and torture, so both threads of Scripture were captured in time. The vast sweep of the story of God and the immeasurable depth of his love found their focus here, definitively expressed.

Notes

The birth and "early years" narratives found in Matthew and Luke speak clearly of the King, the long-expected descendant of David born among us. He was also born to rule—the Son of God born of a virgin come to live among us as a man. Mark's gospel, without any reference to his birth, still speaks of Jesus as both the King and the Son (Mark 1:1), and John in turn builds a clear case for Jesus as the divine Son of God who is also heaven's chosen King.

5: See 2 Chronicles 9:1-8

6: See Matthew 2:1-12

7: See Luke 1:46-55

8: See Luke 2:8-20

And so we begin our journey through the life of Jesus. It is appropriate that we have already glanced at our destination. Calvary is its highest peak; at the bloodstained Cross and empty grave, we find the most important feature in this wondrous landscape.

As we walk together through the Gospels, I trust that I will prove to be a faithful guide and that you will see more deeply into the life of Jesus than you have seen before. When we understand who Jesus was and what he did, we understand fully who we can be and what he calls us to do.

Chapter 9

Jesus' Baptism

"*I*n those days John the Baptist came, preaching in the Desert of Judea." (Matthew 3:1)

John the Baptist strode onto the stage of history as "a voice of one calling in the desert."[1] His message was simple: God wanted a relationship with his people again. If they would only return to their Covenant, they would be prepared to welcome Israel's new King. One like David was coming, and he would defeat their enemies, give them peace and establish a Kingdom that would never end.

The baptism John offered symbolized the washing away of the sins that separated the people from God. But there was a less obvious symbolism present, too: the voluntary giving up of one life to receive another. Being immersed below the waters was like death, and reemerging was embracing the new life of a Covenant relationship with God.[2]

IN THE WATERS OF THE JORDAN

The crowds had gathered at the water's edge. Some had strayed into the river, standing ankle-deep. Many more were finding shelter from the desert sun under the trees that gathered along the banks. These people were pilgrims on their way to Jerusalem. From the desert, they would travel through the mountains of Judea by way of Jericho to the Holy City.

Notes

John the Baptist

1: See Luke 3:1-20

Preparation for the King's arrival.

2: Later, the apostle Paul confirmed that baptism was a death and rebirth, a similar experience to Moses and the Israelites walking through the Red Sea. "They were all baptized into Moses in the cloud and in the sea" (1 Corinthians 10:2). As we are immersed in the waters, so we die in our old life; as we emerge from the waters, so we rise to the new life of a Covenant with Jesus. "Or don't you know that all of us who were baptized into Christ Jesus were baptized into his death? We were therefore buried with him through baptism into death in order that, just as Christ was raised from the dead through the glory of the Father, we too may live a new life." (Romans 6:3-4)

Notes

As John stood in the water, he preached his message of repentance from the prophet Isaiah, calling the people to turn from their sinful ways and prepare for the King who was coming:

"Repent, for the Kingdom of Heaven is near." This is he who was spoken of through the prophet Isaiah: "A voice of one calling in the desert, 'Prepare the way for the Lord, make straight paths for him.'" (Matthew 3:1-3)

John had obviously been touched by God. As he preached, all eyes were fixed on the Baptist. Some in the crowd wept over their sins while others resisted his call and stood aloof, dismissive of the rustic preacher. Then out of the crowd, without invitation, stepped a single figure who waded out toward the prophet. John knew who the man was: Jesus, John's kinsman. John's own sense of unworthiness rose up within him:

"I need to be baptized by you, and do you come to me?"

Holding his gaze, Jesus replied:

"Let it be so now; it is proper for us to do this to fulfill all righteousness."[3]

As Jesus went down into the water and then emerged, he and John and the whole crowd gazed up toward an incredible sight. The sky was being torn apart. Awed into silence, they watched as a bird flew from the other realm.

A dove descending, just as long ago one had been released from Noah's Ark to seek hope for humanity and a safe haven for those in the flood. This time, a dove was released from heaven across the floods of human rebellion and sin to find a "rock"

3: See Matthew 3:14-15

The sky is torn, and the Father testifies.

144

where all could find safe haven and rescue. The dove, symbolizing the Holy Spirit, settled and remained on Jesus.[4]

THE CONDUIT OF THE KINGDOM

In the waters of the River Jordan, the baton was passed from John to Jesus—from messenger to Messiah. The one who prepared the way welcomed the one who would lead the people into a new kind of Kingdom.

The heavens were rent and the two worlds were connected as the Holy Spirit descended and remained on Jesus. The Holy Spirit had connected this world with the world to come as in that moment Jesus became the portal of the Kingdom of heaven.

He was identified as the perfect representation of God's kingly authority and power. From this point on, wherever Jesus was found, the King was present.

All that was present in heaven was now available through him— forgiveness for sin, healing for sickness, deliverance from demonic bondage, freedom from all captivity such as the stultifying effects of poverty and injustice. With the heavens opened above him, Jesus was able to reach out with God's loving power and touch the broken, the hopeless, the hungry and the alienated.

In that moment, Jesus was established as the conduit of God's Kingship on earth. Anyone who came to Jesus would be able to receive the everlasting life of the Kingdom because it was flowing through him.

145

Notes

4: John made a particular note of the fact that the Holy Spirit "remained" on Jesus. Until then, the Holy Spirit had not found a person to remain on. The great characters of the Old Testament had known the Spirit to come and go. However, Jesus was quite different; as Jesus was the Son of God, the Holy Spirit always found a resting place with him. This was evidence that the Son of God had come among them, that Jesus had the Spirit "without measure" and therefore was able to baptize people with the Holy Spirit. (John 1:32-34, 3:34 and Matthew 3:11)

The work of the Holy Spirit in the life of Jesus.

THE COVENANT BAPTISM

Amazingly, there was even more than just a revelation of the Kingdom. Beyond the ragged edges of the earthly heavens, from the world beyond and the Kingdom to come, a voice was heard loud enough for all to hear:

"This is my son, whom I love; with him I am well pleased." (Matthew 3:17)[5]

5: The Father loves his son and is very proud of him.

As the voice of the Father boomed out, the message was clear: the Son of God is among you! And the Son of God was able to do something no one else could—reconnect us to the Father.

But this required a Covenant where both parties would agree to give up their old lives—in death—and become one in a new life. Jesus—both human and divine—represented both parties in himself. But the Covenant still required a death.

Jesus understood this and had already begun the task by being baptized. As he went down into the waters and reemerged, he committed himself to going the full distance on our behalf. He said to it was to "fulfill all righteousness"—literally, to create a "right relationship" based upon a Covenant agreement. In his baptism, Jesus promised to take the path of death on our behalf and offered to raise us to new life as we live with him in Covenant unity.

In submitting to baptism, Jesus was offering to represent us in the Covenant exchange. He was prepared to embrace our estranged condition and its full consequence of death. He would walk the path of death, fully identifying with us. He would give up his life and blood so that we could live.

Previously, in Old Testament revelations of Covenant, the "death" of the Covenant partners was represented in the blood of animals. Now there was a perfect representative who was both God and man. When Jesus died, the Covenant would no longer be symbolized in the death of animals but would be fully realized in the death of the Son.[6]

To underline this truth, John cried out:

"Look, the lamb of God, who takes away the sin of the world!" (John 1:29)

HEAVEN AND EARTH CONNECTED

At the beginning of Jesus' public ministry, we have seen how the themes of Covenant and Kingdom were woven together in his baptism. At the River Jordan, heaven opened to connect the future that we long for with a present that we live in. At his baptism, Jesus identified with us, and the Father identified himself with Jesus by declaring that he was his Son.

This is tremendously important to us. Jesus expected all his disciples to be baptized and to be involved in the calling of others to be part of the baptized community. Thus, he was defining our spiritual life.[7]

Our life of discipleship begins in Covenant and Kingdom of which baptism is the first sign. Thereafter, we should expect that the heavens are open above us and that the Kingship of God flows through our lives. And we should live in the full confidence that we are sons and daughters of the King whom we know intimately as Father.

147

6: The writer to the Hebrews makes this point very clearly: "How much more, then, will the blood of Christ, who through the eternal Spirit offered himself unblemished to God, cleanse our consciences from acts that lead to death, so that we may serve the living God!" (Hebrews 9:14) See also Hebrews 10.1-10.

7: "Then Jesus came to them and said, 'All authority in heaven and on earth has been given to me. Therefore go and make disciples of all nations, **baptizing** them in the name of the Father and of the Son and of the Holy Spirit, and teaching them to obey everything I have commanded you. And surely I am with you always, to the very end of the age.'" (Matthew 28:18-20)

Covenant Parables of the Lost Son and The Vine

"The younger son got together all he had, set off for a distant country and there squandered his wealth in wild living . . . when he came to his senses, he said, 'How many of my father's hired men have food to spare, and here I am starving to death! I will set out and go back to my father and say to him: Father, I have sinned against heaven and against you.' But while he was still a long way off, his father saw him and was filled with compassion for him; he ran to his son, threw his arms around him and kissed him."[1]

Often in the study of the parables of Jesus, the Kingdom is emphasized to the exclusion of the Covenant. However, in the stories that Jesus told and the analogies he drew, the Covenant is clearly present. One example is perhaps the best-known parable of all—that of the "Lost Son." Here, the Lord is portrayed as the father of two boys. The younger asks his father for his inheritance and promptly leaves to have fun with it.[2] His prodigal lifestyle comes to an end when he is destitute and forced to do something that a Jew would never do—earn his living caring for pigs.

On his return, the father embraces his son and welcomes him home, but the elder son, who has a "slave mentality,"[3] cannot bring himself to celebrate. Jesus is clearly telling this story to explain why he spent so much time "among sinners."[4] The Pharisees to whom he told the story realized that Jesus was saying that the Covenant relationship with God was not only for them, but as guardians of the Covenant,[5] they should reflect the Father's heart and welcome home the lost.

---

1 Luke 15:11-32
2 In those days, this would have been one third of the total value of the father's estate, and the eldest son's portion was always two-thirds.
3 Luke 15:29
4 Luke 15:29
5 Luke 15:2

"I am the true vine, and my Father is the gardener. He cuts off every branch in me that bears no fruit, while every branch that does bear fruit he prunes so that it will be even more fruitful . . . Remain in me, and I will remain in you. No branch can bear fruit by itself; it must remain in the vine."[6]

As Jesus was walking through the streets of Jerusalem toward the Garden of Gethsemane, having left the Upper Room and the scene of the Last Supper, he paints a remarkable picture of the new Covenant. He says that as he and his disciples flourish under the care of their Father, the Covenant unity between Jesus and his followers will always produce new disciples. The relationship will sometimes feel "pruned" (cut back), especially after times of great harvest. Pruning is given by the gardener so that the branch ceases to concentrate on itself and focuses on the source of its life. The pruned-back branch is much more aware of its need to remain connected to the vine. The natural consequence of remaining connected to Jesus is that we produce fruit:

"If you remain in me and I remain in you, ask whatever you wish, and it will be given you. This is to my Father's glory, that you bear much fruit, showing yourselves to be my disciples."[7]

When Jesus tells us to ask for whatever we wish, he is not suggesting that we pray with selfish motives or for symbols of prosperity. Rather, he points out that the vine has a purpose established by the gardener to bear fruit. When we remain in him, his words speak to us, and his love flows through us so that we will always fulfill our purpose, which is to multiply the life of Jesus into the lives of others. The purpose of the vine is to bear fruit. The purpose of the followers of Jesus is to make more disciples.

6 John 15:1-17
7 John 15:7-8

Chapter 10

Tempted in the Desert

$\mathcal{T}$he temptation of Jesus was his first engagement with the devil. As God's chosen kingly representative, Jesus sought to establish a "bridgehead" from which he could extend the frontiers of the Kingdom of God. To do this, Jesus would have to defeat his enemy on his own ground. If Jesus won there, then he would have a foothold, and he would be able to push out into all of the territory occupied by the kingdom of darkness. However, for this, he needed all the power of heaven, and he found it in the desert.

Jesus engages the enemy in his first battle.

CHALLENGE TO JESUS' IDENTITY

Luke tells us that Jesus went into the wilderness "full of the Holy Spirit" (Luke 4:1) and came out "in the power of the Spirit." (Luke 4:14) There appears to be a connection between the temptations Jesus resisted in the desert and the power he later exercised.

For Jesus to exercise the power of the Kingdom, he needed the authority of the King. This was established when the Father stated clearly that Jesus was his Son. Jesus' identity and therefore his authority to wield heavenly power were established in his baptism. Jesus was the heir to heaven's throne, and so all the authority and power of God were resident within the Son.[1]

The only chance the devil had was to somehow stop Jesus functioning in the knowledge of who he was. After forty days of fasting, Jesus was in a weakened physical state, and the devil

1: Jesus is the King among us.

153

3: Jesus uses the Bible as his only weapon against the devil. For example:

"Jesus answered, 'It is written: 'Man does not live on bread alone, but on every word that comes from the mouth of God.'" (Matthew 4:4)

"Jesus answered him, 'It is also written: Do not put the Lord your God to the test.'" (Matthew 4:7)

took full advantage. He said, "If you are the Son of God." The attack was aimed at Jesus' identity.[2] The devil hoped that if he could shake Jesus' confidence in who he was, then the devil could resist the Lord and maintain his position as the "ruler" of the world. Unwittingly, he was playing into God's hands. Every time Jesus resisted an attack on his identity, his authority became more certain and his power more complete.

Sending his Son as a human being was a huge risk for God—if Jesus failed, everything would be lost. The devil sought to exploit this situation. But the Father chose to trust Jesus, knowing that with each successive victory over the devil's attacks God's plan for redemption would gain momentum.

When the devil questioned Jesus' identity, he resisted the temptation to "prove" himself, choosing to trust in the truth rather than react to the insinuation. His Father had said that he was "the Son," and that was enough for him. He fired back at his assailant with God's word, quoting Deuteronomy.[3] Interestingly, that was the book in the Bible that recorded how God had prepared his people to leave "the desert" and conquer the territory he had given them.

Having failed with the first assault, the devil tried again. He had defeated human beings before, and he believed that he could do it again. Pride had worked with the first humans so he tried that method of attack. "Then the devil took him to the holy city and had him stand on the highest point of the temple. 'If you are the Son of God,' he said, 'throw yourself down. For it is written: He will command his angels concerning you, and they will lift you up in their hands, so that you will not strike your foot against a stone.'" (Matthew 4:5-6) But again, Jesus resisted the devil.

The devil had failed twice—he tried one more approach. Having taken Adam and Eve's abandoned position of rulership in the world, the devil was confident to assert his sovereignty. Showing Jesus "all the kingdoms of the world and their splendor," the devil offered Jesus an apparently easier way to extend his influence. "All this I will give you," he said, "if you will bow down and worship me." (Matthew 4:9) Jesus was unequivocal—"Away from me, Satan!" (Matthew 4:10) Jesus knew the truth—the devil had usurped the throne of the world, and Jesus had come to win it back.[4]

Unlike the devil, Jesus' claim to the throne was based on inheritance. He was the Son, and so the Crown was his. The first battle was intense, but Jesus won.

It is clear, that as Jesus wrestled with his enemy in the desert, there was a battle for his very identity. God the Father had affirmed his family Covenant with Jesus as he spoke over his Son at his baptism. This was the basis of all of Jesus' work. He was the Son of God, fully identified with the Father and sharing his divine nature. Jesus was the Son of Man—fully identified with us and sharing our nature. Jesus was the perfect Covenant representative because in him God and humanity were "made one." This was revealed in Jesus' baptism and confirmed by his temptations. Functioning as a real "flesh and blood" human being, Jesus settled his identity in the desert and strode into his task with great confidence.

Jesus was the Son of the King of heaven, and thus, he was the heir to the throne and the rightful recipient of the Crown. But his Kingdom was occupied by an enemy force led by the devil himself. And so the Son came to fight for his inheritance. As he took more ground with each successive victory, he released the

155

Notes

4: Jesus had come to reclaim the rulership of the world

Jesus is the Son of God and the Son of Man.

captives held in the kingdom of darkness. Jesus came to force his enemy from the throne and to destroy his instruments of slavery, forged over generations of tyranny. Jesus was the good King the world had been waiting for. He was our champion, and as he entered the fray on our behalf, he won our freedom and established goodness as the means by which he rules. All these things began in the desert. The first foothold for the Kingdom of God had been won, and next, Jesus looked for followers to help him in his cause.

WE ARE PORTALS OF POWER

We are representatives of the King, and we, too, should expect to be portals through which his loving power is poured out. We know the devil will use precisely the same tactics with us to prevent us from functioning in God's authority. He will seek to undermine our identity as children of God. Just as Jesus, we need to use the truth of God's word, which tells us that we are children of God:

"For you did not receive a spirit that makes you a slave again to fear, but you received the Spirit of sonship. And by him we cry, 'Abba, Father.' The Spirit himself testifies with our spirit that we are God's children. Now if we are children, then we are heirs -- heirs of God and co-heirs with Christ, if indeed we share his sufferings in order that we may also share in his glory."
(Romans 8:15-17)

Incredibly, our Covenant with God in Jesus means that we get to share "all things" with him.

Kingdom Parables of the Talents and the Foolish Virgins

Jesus used many parables to teach about the Kingdom of God, and much has been written about them. Toward the end of his ministry, Jesus taught some parables that prepared his followers for the time between his return to heaven and his second coming in triumph to the earth. He wanted his disciples to realize their responsibilities. As all parables of the Kingdom, these stories reveal the tension that exists as God's Kingdom purposes are worked out. Sometimes the King is present, and sometimes he is absent. At others times in the parables, we are told the King is returning, but his return seems delayed.

"At that time the kingdom of heaven will be like ten virgins who took their lamps and went out to meet the bridegroom. Five of them were foolish and five were wise . . . the bridegroom was a long time in coming, and they all became drowsy and fell asleep . . . Therefore keep watch, because you do not know the day or the hour."[1]

In the parable of the virgins, Jesus is clearly saying that, as we await his return, our task is to maintain an alertness that will prepare us for that day. The security of the knowledge that we are loved by God is not an excuse for laziness or a lack of focus on his Kingdom purpose.

"To one he gave five talents of money, to another two talents and another one talent, each according to his ability . . . His master replied, 'Well done, good and faithful servant!' . . . Then the man who had received the one talent came . . . 'I was afraid and hid your talent in the ground.' His master replied, 'you wicked, lazy servant . . . take the talent from him and give it to the one who has the ten talents.'"[2]

1 Matthew 25:1-13
2 Matthew 25:14-30, Mark 12:1-11

Jesus revealed what can be achieved when we have an attitude of active anticipation of his return. In this parable, he portrayed himself as the master of three servants who receive large—though differing—amounts of money. The master expected that these gifts would be put to work and invested wisely so that at his homecoming he would receive a return on his investment. The servants who received the gift as a gracious opportunity produced the most, but the third servant—frozen by the fear of the responsibility—allowed the gift to languish and produced nothing. <u>The call of the Kingdom representative is to take whatever the King puts into our lives and, by investing it in the lives of others, give him a return on the master's gift.</u>

Chapter 11

Jesus' Ministry Begins

*W*ith his identity asserted and his authority established, Jesus came out of his desert battlefield with a staggering level of power. The Holy Spirit was flowing through him—he was the Son and the heir to the Kingdom of heaven! Armed with this certainty, he began his ministry.

His plan was to travel to Galilee and to his home in Nazareth. There he would begin. However, before that, he had an appointment to keep. In the little town of Cana, to the north of Nazareth, he had been invited to a wedding.

Apparently with some reluctance, Jesus performed his first miracle here.[1] He turned the water used for Jewish ritual handwashing into wine when the supplies ran out. The simplest explanation, and the one to which John's gospel seems to point, is that this was a visual demonstration of the "New Covenant." The "Old Covenant"—first made with Abraham and Sarah—had lost its power because the Covenant had become trapped in the rituals of Jewish religious observance. A slavish obedience to the law had replaced the confidence and security of the Covenant. Instead of living in the knowledge that the Jewish people were one with God and that he was one with them, they tried to prove their value to him by living by a code of behavior they could never keep. Obedience should flow from identity, but by then, the Jewish people were trying to do the opposite, in attempting to find their identity through obedience.

When Jesus turned the water into wine, he was showing that he was taking all of the "Old" and making something deeper, richer and much more satisfying in the "New." Although the "New" would contain all the elements of the "Old," it would be far better. The "master of the banquet" expressed it perfectly:

Notes

Jesus begins his ministry: the New Covenant.

1: "On the third day a wedding took place at Cana in Galilee. Jesus' mother was there, and Jesus and his disciples had also been invited to the wedding. When the wine was gone, Jesus' mother said to him, 'They have no more wine.' 'Dear woman, why do you involve me?' Jesus replied, 'My time has not yet come.' His mother said to the servants, 'Do whatever he tells you.' (John 2:1-5)

"Everyone brings out the choice wine first and then the cheaper wine after the guests have had too much to drink, but you have saved the best till now." (John 2:10)

The Old Covenant formed with Abraham and reconfirmed in the lives of people such as Moses and David always pointed toward Jesus. As both Son of God and Son of Man, Jesus represented both parties in himself. Aptly, all this took place at a wedding—a celebration of human Covenant-making—as if to underline the meaning of the miracle.

DECLARATION OF THE KINGDOM

In Cana, Jesus had given a sign of the New Covenant. From here, he moved the short distance to his hometown of Nazareth, where he began to declare the manifesto of the Kingdom he had come to bring. In his local synagogue where as a child he would have been instructed in the Scriptures, Jesus used the words of the prophet Isaiah to proclaim:

"The Spirit of the Lord is on me, because he has anointed me to preach good news to the poor. He has sent me to proclaim freedom for the prisoners and recovery of sight for the blind, to release the oppressed, to proclaim the year of the Lord's favor." (Luke 4:18-19, compare Isaiah 61:1-2)[2]

This must have appeared outrageous to the local residents of Nazareth. They did not understand—they rejected him and tried to take his life.[3]

2: Jesus proclaims his manifesto: "the Kingdom of God has come to earth.'"

3: "All the people in the synagogue were furious when they heard this. They got up, drove him out of the town, and took him to the brow of the hill on which the town was built, in order to throw him down the cliff. But he walked right through the crowd and went on his way." (Luke 4:28-30)

Disappointed, but unsurprised, Jesus went to Capernaum, where he gathered his first disciples and made his headquarters at the home of Peter and Andrew. This period was Jesus' greatest popularity and breakthrough. As he began his ministry, his first proclamations sound like a declaration of war:

"The time has come. The Kingdom of God is near. Repent and believe the good news!" (Mark 1:15)

In Capernaum, Jesus taught by the lake and in the synagogue. He demonstrated his authority over the devil by casting out his demons. And at Peter's home, Jesus healed his mother-in-law, and all the crowds gathered at the door.[4] He even healed a paralyzed man after first forgiving his sins.[5]

Jesus was a sensation! He was the channel of God's Kingship.

Jesus' incredible authority, amazing power and relentless determination were thoroughly captivating, and people hung on his every word. Through him, all the power of the Kingdom of heaven poured out and touched those he encountered. All that humanity longed for in heaven was revealed on earth in Jesus.

But Jesus knew he had to build on the breakthrough.[6] He moved on from Capernaum and preached the message of the Kingdom in all the towns and villages of Galilee. Wherever he went, the miraculous accompanied him.[7]

He clearly intended for these events to be understood as a foretaste of a future world where he would reign as King.[8] They were a signpost to a destination, an invitation to a world that would surely come.

Notes

4: Mark 1:29-34

5: "A few days later, when Jesus again entered Capernaum, the people heard that he had come home. So many gathered that there was no room left, not even outside the door, and he preached the word to them. Some men came, bringing to him a paralytic, carried by four of them. Since they could not get him to Jesus because of the crowd, they made an opening in the roof above Jesus and, after digging through it, lowered the mat the paralyzed man was lying on. When Jesus saw their faith, he said to the paralytic, 'Son, your sins are forgiven.'" (Mark 2:1-5)

6: "Jesus replied, 'Let us go somewhere else—to the nearby villages—so I can preach there also. That is why I have come.' So he traveled throughout Galilee, preaching in their synagogues and driving out demons." (Mark 1:38-39)

7: "News about him spread all over Syria, and people brought to him all who were ill with various diseases, those suffering severe pain, the demon-possessed, those having seizures, and the paralyzed, and he healed them. Large crowds from Galilee, the Decapolis, Jerusalem, Judea and the region across the Jordan followed him." (Matthew 4:24-25)

8: "But if I drive out demons by the Spirit of God, then the kingdom of God has come upon you." (Matthew 12:28)

In heaven there is no sickness, and so Jesus healed the sick.

In heaven there is no hunger, and so Jesus fed the crowds.

In heaven there is no death, and so Jesus raised the dead.

Understandably, Jesus enlisted many followers. They quickly became conversant with his message and methods, and so he gave them a chance to try it for themselves. Having identified the leaders among his disciples, he sent first the twelve and then the seventy-two on local missions. They were to go with his authority and power to preach, heal, deliver and cleanse.[9] This was "all-out war," and Jesus wanted to conscript as many as possible in the struggle. Around this time, he said:

9: See Matthew 10, Mark 6 and Luke 9 and 10.

"From the days of John the Baptist until now, the kingdom of heaven has been forcefully advancing, and forceful men lay hold of it." (Matthew 11:12)

Warriors

MIRACLES AND KINGDOM ADVANCES

A little time later, the kingdom of darkness mounted a counter-offensive. First John the Baptist was executed in prison, and then the institutional leadership of Israel came out against Jesus.[10] Popularity turned to opposition, and Jesus decided to make a tactical retreat. In addition, the disciples, returning breathless and awed from their mission trip, were close to burnout. Jesus said:

10: "When Jesus left there, the Pharisees and the teachers of the law began to oppose him fiercely and to besiege him with questions, waiting to catch him in something he might say." (Luke 11:53-54)

"Come to me, all you who are weary and burdened and I will give you rest."

"Come with me by yourselves to a quiet place and get some rest."[11]

11: See Matthew 11:28-30 and Mark 6:31.

Hmmm

But they had to fight hard to find rest. The crowd anticipated their escape route across the lake and met them at Bethesda. Out of kindness, Jesus taught and miraculously fed the five thousand families that had gathered.[12]

Again Jesus had captured the imagination of the masses. Free food in a world of need was very popular! Jesus sensed that things were getting out of hand. He realized that the crowd might make him King by force. And so he sent his disciples ahead of him, dismissed the crowd, spent time in prayer and caught up with them by walking on the water.[13]

Perhaps Jesus and the disciples thought that finally they had escaped the crowds. But when they got back to Capernaum, the people found them again. Jesus decided to ramp up his call to commitment. He gathered many of the crowd into the synagogue at Capernaum and told them:

"I am the bread of life. He who comes to me will never go hungry, and he who believes in me will never be thirsty."

"No one can come to me unless the Father who sent me draws him, and I will raise him up at the last day."

"I tell you the truth, unless you eat the flesh of the Son of Man and drink his blood, you have no life in you."
(John 6:35, 44, 53)

Taken literally, these words were repulsive to his Jewish audience. But Jesus was speaking metaphorically of the New Covenant. If they were to enter into a relationship with God, they needed to "assimilate" him into their lives. If they wanted to live the new life of the New Covenant on offer in him, they would have to live according to the terms that he offered. They

Notes

12: See Matthew 14:13-21, Mark 6:30-44, Luke 9:10-17 and John 6:1-15.

13: See Matthew 14:22-33

would have to take him into their lives. If they did, then their souls would be nourished, and they would live forever.

Perhaps Jesus was making specific reference to Passover.[14] At Passover, the lamb was killed and consumed, and the "Angel of Death"—perhaps an early name for the personality we now refer to as the devil—could not touch them but had to "pass over." Jesus was saying that he was the Passover lamb. Of course, later all of this would be beautifully represented in the New Covenant meal of the Last Supper.

COVENANT INVITATION

The ministry of Jesus in Galilee presented its own "invitation" and "challenge."

First, there was the invitation to a Covenant relationship with Jesus. In Cana, Jesus revealed that the New Covenant contained the essential elements of the Old. When he turned the water into wine, it still contained the water.[15]

15: Jesus develops the process of
   discipling others through
   invitation and challenge.

In the stories of the Old Testament characters, we have seen that the Old Covenant was essentially about identity and obedience. The New Covenant is also about identity and obedience. But because Jesus was the perfect representative of both humanity and God, the New Covenant is therefore perfect and complete. The Old Covenant pointed to the New, and the New has fulfilled the Old.

In the synagogue at Capernaum, Jesus explained how this worked. Now our Covenant relationship has an identity that is defined by

Jesus. In the New Covenant, we "become one" with Jesus. We take him into ourselves as we would take in food.[16] Covenant is about sharing identity. In the New Covenant, Jesus becomes part of us—fully integrated into the fabric of our being. Amazing!

KINGDOM CHALLENGE

There is also the challenge to participate in the work of the Kingdom. The first disciples were arrested by Jesus' bold proclamation: "the Kingdom of God is near." (Mark 1:15) Then as now, those who heard him hoped God was near to them. They hoped that God was good and that he had good things stored up for them. Jesus understood this and revealed the future that they all longed for. Heaven's future was seen to be present in his life as he healed the sick, delivered the oppressed, cleansed alienated lepers and raised the dead.

Jesus called his first disciples to participate in this work of revealing the Kingship of God. Jesus sent them out to do all that they had seen him do.[17]

Surely, the challenge for us who are disciples today is no different. We have already seen that the New Covenant means that we are one with Jesus. Therefore, we must have the same message and ministry as him! His challenge to us is to reveal God's future in our lives.

We are to declare that the "King is among us," and we are to heal the sick, deliver the oppressed, cleanse the alienated and even raise the dead!

Notes

16: See John 6:35-54

17: See John 6:35-54

Healing

"And the people all tried to touch him, because power was coming from him and healing them all."[1]

Then as now, Jesus sends his disciples to heal. But Jesus had a vastly different experience of success in healing than we usually do![2] How do we explain the fact that so often we pray for healing and don't see an answer to our prayers?

This is much more easily answered if we apply what we are learning about Covenant and Kingdom to the question. As children, we come to our Father expecting that he wants us, and all his children, to be well. Jesus compared our heavenly Father to our earthly father on several occasions, suggesting that if we who are flawed want good things for our children, so will our heavenly Father also want these good things—only more so.[3]

So from the point of view of the Covenant, we always approach our prayers with great confidence, knowing that it is not so much about saying the right things but speaking to the right person. However, sickness, like sin and all other forms of suffering, entered the world under the rulership of the devil. Sickness is one of the main instruments he uses for the control of humanity. When Jesus heals the sick, he is forcing back the frontier of the kingdom of darkness and extending the Kingdom of light. This means that our bodies will sometimes become the battlefield for the struggle between good and evil. The battle may shape us and perfect our character, but this does not mean that God has sent the sickness for our personal improvement. It is a misrepresentation to suggest anything else.

---

1 Luke 6:19

2 "When Jesus had called the Twelve together, he gave them power and authority to drive out all demons and to cure diseases, and he sent them out to preach the kingdom of God and to heal the sick." (Luke 9:1-2) "Heal the sick who are there and tell them, 'The kingdom of God is near you.'" (Luke 10:9)

3 "Which of you fathers, if your son asks for a fish, will give him a snake instead? Or if he asks for an egg, will give him a scorpion? If you then, though you are evil, know how to give good gifts to your children, how much more will your Father in heaven give the Holy Spirit to those who ask him!" (Luke 11:11-13)

When we are healed, it is a sign to everyone of the future that awaits us. The healing "says" that heaven has no sickness in it. When we are not healed, we continue to fight against the assault that the sickness brings, knowing that as we persevere and stand firm, the enemy has no foothold to claim in our life. Therefore, in our prayer for Kingdom healing, we are either a sign of what will be or a soldier in the King's army. Even though we may not be healed, we never surrender to the sickness or the one who seeks to wield it as a weapon against us. And if we should die sick, we will die to the applause of our comrades in arms and will receive a hero's welcome in heaven.

It is clear from the life of Jesus that our Father wants us well—the Lord healed everyone who came to him. It is clear from our experience that not all are healed in this life. They have to wait for the next. An understanding of the Covenant gives us confidence to pray knowing our Father wants the best for us. An understanding of the Kingdom gives us courage to fight on knowing that victory will be declared one day.

Chapter 12

Retreat and Revelation

*A*mid the clamor of the crowds, Jesus and his disciples barely had time to eat. It took a great deal of effort to separate themselves from the crowds and take a pause. Jesus decided that he and his disciples needed some time to reflect, as well as to give some distance from the growing opposition of the religious establishment. This retreat was both tactical and spiritual.[1]

They had tried to get away by traveling to the eastern side of the Sea of Galilee, but the people simply followed Jesus and his disciples, and he had to feed another enormous host—four thousand families this time.[2] So Jesus took his disciples north outside Israel to the territory of Tyre and Sidon. After this, they went to the far northeast to the region around Caesarea Philippi.[3]

PETER PROCLAIMS JESUS AS MESSIAH

Having the time to retreat, the disciples began to reflect on the incredible events they had seen, and they slowly grew clearer about who they were following. Jesus was the long and expected King promised by the prophets long ago. Peter spoke for all the disciples when he said:

"You are the Christ (Messiah), the Son of the living God." (Matthew 16:16)

Peter declared that Jesus was both the long-awaited Messiah and the Son of the God who gave all things life. "Messiah" represented the King, and the "Son" related to the Father. Representation and relationship—Kingdom and Covenant— intersected in Peter's first "confession."

173

Notes

1: Jesus made time for retreat, reflection and revelation.

2: See Matthew 15:32-39 and Mark 8:1-9.

3: See Matthew 16:13

Peter announces who he believes Jesus is.

Jesus knew that Peter could have known his identity and title only by divine revelation:

"Blessed are you, Simon son of Jonah, for this was not revealed to you by men, but by my Father in heaven." (Matthew 16:17)

Identity is so central to an understanding of a Covenant relationship that Jesus naturally assumed the Father wanted him and Peter to share in a Covenant relationship and become one. So Jesus gave his new Covenant brother one of his names and access to his inheritance:

"And I tell you that you are Peter, and on this rock I will build my church, and the gates of Hades will not overcome it. I will give you the keys of the Kingdom of heaven; whatever you bind on earth will be bound in heaven and whatever you loose on earth will be loosed in heaven." (Matthew 16:18-19)

A NEW COVENANT NAME

The name Peter means "rock." Whether this was already a nickname for the disciple, we do not know. But Jesus took this name and gave it fresh significance.

Jesus had already identified himself with the name "rock" at the end of the Sermon on the Mount.[4] "Rock" is a common way to describe the Lord in the Old Testament, especially in the Psalms.[5] Essentially, Peter was given one of Jesus' names— they had "become one" in Covenant. By implication, this also meant that Peter and Jesus shared the same identity. Therefore, Peter had all the benefits of a Covenant connection

Peter "becomes one" with Jesus.

4: "Therefore everyone who hears these words of mine and puts them into practice is like a wise man who built his house on the rock." (Matthew 7:24)

5: "The Lord is my rock, my fortress and my deliverer; my God is my rock, in whom I take refuge." (Psalms 18:2a)

with the one from whom Jesus derived his identity—God the Father. Jesus as the Son of God was sharing his identity, and that meant Peter was now part of the family.[6]

Of course, a change of name is very common in Covenant-making and often continues in the marriage Covenant to this day. The Covenant made in marriage usually means that the couple shares all their resources and have all things in common. The same was true for Jesus and Peter. When Jesus gave Peter his name, Jesus also gave Peter the "keys of the Kingdom of Heaven." In other words, Jesus gave Peter access to all that belonged to him as the Son of the King.

For Peter, this was one of the great moments of his life, defining how he understood the work of Christ. After Pentecost when he was defending himself before the Sanhedrin (the governing body of the Jewish people), he quoted Psalms 118:22 and spoke of Jesus as the "stone rejected" becoming the "capstone."[7] The imagery of stones and rocks was clearly very much alive in Peter's mind as he considered why his own people had rejected Jesus.

The Covenant-making moment at Caesarea Philippi had an enormous impact on Peter. We see this again when toward the end of his life he made similar use of the same biblical metaphors and passages in his letters, describing Jesus again as a "stone" and a "rock."[8] But Peter clearly did not see his Covenant with Jesus as exclusive—Peter described all Christians as "living stones" who have come to Jesus, the original "living stone."[9] Peter also said that together with him we are being built into "a spiritual house"—in other words, "a temple." Similar to Peter, all Christians have a Covenant with Jesus. We all share his identity and carry his name.

175

DEEPER REVELATION – THE TRANSFIGURATION

10: See Matthew 17:1-13

11: "We ourselves heard this voice that came from heaven when we were with him on the sacred mountain." (2 Peter 1:17-19)

12: "They spoke about his departure, which he was about to bring to fulfillment at Jerusalem." (Luke 9:31)

To confirm this new revelation, Jesus led his "inner circle" "up a high mountain by themselves."[10] This may appear a rather exclusive gesture. But it seems that Jesus took Peter, James and John with him because they had all reached the same conclusion about Jesus' identity and therefore had the same relationship with him.

On the mountain that Peter later describes as "the sacred mountain,"[11] a cloud, similar to the one indicating God's presence above the tabernacle in the wilderness, came down upon the mountain. Jesus shone like the sun, and Moses and Elijah appeared and talked with the Son of God about the next stage of his ministry.[12] From within the cloud, the voice of God spoke:

"This is my son, whom I love. Listen to him!" (Mark 9:7b)

With Moses, Elijah and Jesus all together within the glorious presence of God, Peter naturally assumes that this is what they have all been working toward.

"'Rabbi, it is good for us to be here. Let us put up three shelters— one for you, one for Moses and one for Elijah.' (He did not know what to say, they were so frightened.)" (Mark 9:5-6)

But as the cloud lifted, Moses and Elijah disappeared, and Jesus looked just the same as before. The Transfiguration was not intended as the high point of the mission but rather the balance point. The revelation of the divine sonship of Jesus to the three disciples was the fulcrum from which Jesus' ministry began to tilt toward Jerusalem.

As he went down the mountain, Jesus and the others encountered a powerful demon destroying the life of a desperate child. It was a presage of things to come. The enemy was going to harass and oppose Jesus and his disciples every step of the way. From this point on, Jesus avoided the crowds wherever possible. He resolutely pressed on toward his goal. He "set his face toward Jerusalem" and his "last stand" on a hill outside that ancient city.[13]

JESUS' INVITATION AND CHALLENGE

We have seen in the early ministry of Jesus in Capernaum and Galilee that invitation and challenge were deeply embedded in the way he related to his disciples. Jesus gave an invitation to Covenant relationship and a challenge to take responsibility for Kingdom representation.

In the retreat at Caesarea Philippi and the revelation on the Mount of Transfiguration, we see mostly an invitation to relationship. But in the Gospels that include these events, something else happened between these two episodes.

After Peter's confession, Jesus began to speak about his death.[14] Armed with his newfound Covenant confidence, Peter took Jesus aside privately and assured him of his disciple's support:

"Never, Lord! This shall never happen to you!" (Matthew 16:22)

"Jesus turned and said to Peter, 'Get behind me, Satan! You are a stumbling block to me; you do not have in mind the things of God, but the things of men.'" (Matthew 16:23)

Notes

13: "And it came to pass, when the time was come that he should be received up, he steadfastly set his face to go to Jerusalem." (Luke 9:51 KJV)

14: "He then began to teach them that the Son of Man must suffer many things and be rejected by the elders, chief priests and teachers of the law, and that he must be killed and after three days rise again." (Mark 8:31) See also Matthew 16:21-28 and Luke 9:22-27.

Peter is challenged to his core!

A moment before, Peter had spoken out of revelation given to him direct from God the Father, and now he was speaking on behalf of the devil?

Jesus quickly pressed home his point:

"If anyone would come after me, he must deny himself and take up his cross and follow me. For whoever wants to save his life will lose it, but whoever loses his life for me will find it." (Matthew 16:24-25)

The level of challenge that Jesus brought to Peter appeared to be almost brutal. But the challenge given was commensurate with the level of invitation Peter had received. Jesus had invited Peter to relate on a very deep level, and thus, the challenge was equally deep.

When we observe the patterns of behavior Jesus took toward his followers, we see him constantly calibrating invitation and challenge to draw them on in their discipleship. Invitation and challenge were the two constants. If it was the crowd who knew little of him, then Jesus offered both invitation and challenge at a lower level to that which he shared with his closest followers.

We can expect the Lord will do the same with us. By his Spirit, he continues to disciple his followers in the same way that he always has. He invites us to share deeply in a relationship of love with him. But at the same time, he challenges us to represent him in ever-widening spheres of influence.

Jesus still uses "invitation and challenge" today.

"Therefore go and make disciples of all nations, baptizing them in the name of the Father and of the Son and of the Holy Spirit. And teaching them to obey everything I have commanded you. And surely I am with you always, to the very end of the age."[1]

The Great Commission is simply being a disciple who makes other disciples. The last wish of Jesus before he ascended to his throne in heaven was that we multiply ourselves. We are to do this by immersing (baptizing) the world in the truth of the Trinitarian God, and we multiply disciples of Jesus by teaching them everything he taught. Jesus was constantly inviting his disciples into a deeper relationship and continuously challenging them to represent him as the King. Invitation and challenge build on the understanding that a disciple is basically one who imitates the life of the discipler. Paul said:

"Therefore I urge you to imitate me."[2]

He then gave an example of the imitation he was calling for:

"For this reason, I am sending to you Timothy, my son whom I love, who is faithful in the Lord. He will remind you of my way of life in Christ Jesus, which agrees with what I teach everywhere in every church."[3]

Timothy had been discipled by Paul and now reflected not only Paul's pattern of life but also the character of Christ.[4]

---

1 Matthew 28:19-20
2 1 Corinthians 4:16
3 1 Corinthians 4:17
4 "Join with others in following my example, brothers, and take note of those who live according to the pattern we gave you." (Philippians 3:17) See also Philippians 4:9; 1 Thessalonians 1:6; 2 Thessalonians 3:7a, 9; and Hebrews 13:7-8.

Different people will be more adept at one or the other, but we must learn to calibrate invitation and challenge to make our own disciples.[5] For us, the process of discipleship is the same as that of Jesus. In many ways, as Paul suggests, discipleship is adopting another person into our family. We introduce people to our Father and invite them into a relationship with him. We invite them into a Covenant relationship of friendship with us and challenge them to do the works of the Kingdom. They discover that the God who has become their Father is also the King of the universe, and that their challenge, like ours, is to represent him. At the point when the process is as complete as we can make it, our disciples then function as our family, and our attitude becomes one of support and challenge rather than invitation.

Becoming a disciple is really about learning how to function as a child of heaven. As we mature, we learn to strengthen each other by supporting our Covenant bond in ever-deepening relationships and together taking on the call and commission of God who is our King. We will worship, pray, study and work together to build the Covenant community and extend God's kingly rule.

---

5 You might like to read Building a Discipling Culture by Mike Breen and Steve Cockram © 2009 3dm Publishing, www.weare3dm.com

Chapter 13

Journey to Jerusalem and the Cross

$\mathcal{T}$here is a growing sense of tension in the text as Jesus draws within touching distance of the Holy City. Jesus had made several visits to his dear friends in Bethany—Mary, Martha and Lazarus. On one occasion, Jesus even raised Lazarus from the dead! But even this caused opposition toward him to increase[1] As he looked upon David's ancient city, Jesus paused and lamented:

"O Jerusalem, Jerusalem, you who kill the prophets and stone those sent to you, how often have I longed to gather your children together, as a hen gathers her chicks under her wings, but you were not willing! Look, your house is left to you desolate. I tell you, you will not see me again until you say, 'Blessed is he who comes in the name of the Lord.'" (Luke 13:34-35)

A little while later, Jesus entered Jerusalem to the adulation of the masses—riding on a donkey's colt as prophesied of the coming King.[2]

If Jesus had wanted an earthly kingdom, it would have been there that the battle would have been fought. With his personal charisma and the adulation of the crowd, he could have shaken Israel even from the grasp of Rome. But Jesus had another Kingdom in mind, and his final battle would be more different than anyone could have imagined.

As the "hosannas!" subsided, Jesus went into the temple and drove out the money changers. The spiritual life of Israel had been compromised by commercialization of their religion. Jesus did not allow that to pass without comment. Of course, the demonically inspired antagonism of Israel's leaders toward him only deepened.

Jesus withdrew to prepare.

183

Notes

1: See John 11:45-53

Jesus walks into the shadow of the Cross.

2: "Rejoice greatly, O Daughter of Zion! Shout, Daughter of Jerusalem! See, your king comes to you, righteous and having salvation, gentle and riding on a donkey, on a colt, the foal of a donkey." (Zechariah 9:9)

Circumstances don't define me.

3: "I no longer call you servants,
because a servant does not
know his master's business.
Instead, I have called you friends,
for everything that I learned from
my Father I have made known to
you." (John 15:15)

4: As I have previously noted, the
word "remembrance" used here
is an interesting Greek word—
"anamnesis." It appears to mean
"don't forget who you are."
Jesus seems to be saying that
as we eat bread and drink wine
we honor his death for us—but
we also remember that our
identity is bound up in him. We
"remember who we are."

PASSOVER – JESUS IS THE NEW COVENANT

First, he celebrated Passover with his disciples whom he now called his closest friends.[3] During the supper, Jesus took the unleavened bread and the cup of blessing and used them in a special way:

"And he took bread, gave thanks and broke it, and gave it to them, saying, 'This is my body given for you; do this in remembrance of me.' In the same way, after the supper he took the cup, saying, 'This cup is the new covenant in my blood, which is poured out for you.'" (Luke 22:19-20)

The most important celebration of Israel's Covenant with God was gathered up by Jesus into the New Covenant in him. It was a Covenant that would be established in his death and sealed with his blood.[4] The blood of Passover daubed on the doors of the Israelites meant that they could go into freedom, having been rescued from death. The blood of Jesus means that we are released from the prospect of spiritual death because he died in our place. And now we walk free because of his sacrifice.

THE BATTLE IN THE GARDEN

After the Passover meal, Jesus left the city and went to the Garden of Gethsemane. This was near the camp on the Mount of Olives that he frequented on his visits to Jerusalem.[5] In the garden, he knelt in prayer and in great anguish. Before he could face his final battle, he had to settle the struggle within.

"He withdrew . . . knelt down and prayed, 'Father, if you are willing, take this cup from me; yet not my will that yours be done.'" (Luke 22:41-44)

Jesus deliberately chose to accept in himself the full consequences of human rebellion. In the Garden of Eden, the parents of the human race had forsaken their relationship with the Lord and rebelled against him. Because of this, they lost their relationship and their right to represent him. With their rebellion came exclusion from his presence and estrangement from the source of life. Of course, what was true for them was also true for their universal family.

Spiritual and physical death ensued, and our nemesis and God's enemy installed himself on the throne of the earth. Jesus had come to reverse all this. He would force the devil from the throne and be enthroned by the Father in the devil's place. Jesus would pay the penalty for human estrangement and surrender his life, and the Father would give it back.[6]

As the inner battle was won in darkness, so the soldiers were led in by the traitor Judas. There in that garden, Jesus, as he healed Malchus's severed ear, told Peter to put his sword away.[7] This battle would not be won using earthly methods.

With Jesus' decision to go to the Cross, he was able to tell another to put away his sword—the angel with a fiery flashing sword protecting the way back to God. In the Garden of Gethsemane, Jesus was pressing in to another Garden. In the Garden of Eden, humanity had lost its first battle against temptation. In the Garden of Gethsemane, the first battle of the new humanity in Jesus was won.

185

6: This dynamic picture lies behind Paul's writing in Philippians 2:8-11: "Christ Jesus . . . made himself nothing . . . and became obedient to death—even death on a cross! . . . that at the name of Jesus every knee should bow." Given that many scholars believe that Paul was quoting these words from a New Testament-era hymn, we can assume that this was generally accepted theology in the New Testament church.

7: See Luke 22:50-51 and John 18:10-11.

COVENANT SACRIFICE – THE LAMB ON THE CROSS

8: "He was oppressed and afflicted, yet he did not open his mouth; he was led like a lamb to the slaughter, and as a sheep before her shearers is silent, so he did not open his mouth." (Isaiah 53:7)

The Covenant perspective of the Cross.

9: You may have heard this taught from the point of view of "penal substitution" that pictures us in a law court with God as judge. Our accuser the devil argues that we deserve death, but our advocate Jesus says that he will die in our place. Paul used this picture especially when writing to Jews who understood the legal implications of wrongdoing. According to Covenant theology, we know that for us to have the new life that God offers, we must die in our old life. Jesus did this on our behalf, and now we live as if our old life has ended and our new life has begun. This is what Jesus meant by "taking up our cross" (Matthew 16:24) and what Paul meant when he said, "count yourself dead to sin." (Romans 6:11)

10: "My God, my God, why have you forsaken me? Why are you so far from saving me, so far from the words of my groaning?" (Psalms 22:1)

Jesus died during the celebration of Passover. As the lambs were being led away to slaughter, so Jesus, without a word, was led away to die.[8] Throughout the Scriptures, Jesus is clearly presented as the sacrificial substitute for our death. For us to receive the new life of a relationship of "oneness" with God, there had to be "at-one-ment." Jesus was the atoning sacrifice.

Jesus took our place and walked the pathway of blood on our behalf. He had once traveled a pathway of blood at his own birth, passing from one side of the Covenant exchange to the other. In his death, he traveled the pathway back to reconnect us with God. He was born as one of us and died on behalf of us all.[9]

He accepted all our sin in himself, suffering the alienation and dereliction that only sin can cause. That is why he cried out:

"My God, my God, why have you forsaken me?" (Matthew 27:46)

No doubt Jesus truly felt the full meaning of these words. But he was also quoting Psalm 22 and pointing to the clearest prophecy of Messiah's crucifixion in the Old Testament.[10]

He took the alienation caused by sin to the grave, and he left it there.

And because of his sacrifice, and our Covenant relationship with our Father, we can have Covenant relationships with each other. Jesus illustrated this in one of the tenderest moments of the crucifixion narrative. John recorded in his account that Jesus looked down from the Cross and saw his mother and John.

Jesus connected them as mother and son. When Mary was bereft of her eldest son and protector, John would replace him:

"When Jesus saw his mother there, and the disciple whom he loved standing nearby, he said to his mother, 'Dear woman, here is your son,' and to the disciple, 'Here is your mother.' From that time on, this disciple took her into his home. (John 19:26-27)

KINGDOM BREAKTHROUGH – THE KING ON THE CROSS

In Matthew, Mark and Luke, the Crucifixion is presented as a visitation of the last battle that will be fought and won against the enemy of God, culminating in the Day of Judgment. Darkness, earthquakes and the opening of tombs are elements seen in the prophecies of the last judgment.

The last day of history visited the earth in the crucifixion of Jesus.

In the same way that the blessings of the Kingdom were poured through Jesus in his life, so the "Last Battle" and the Day of Judgment were revealed in his death.

The Day of Judgment will certainly come to the enemies of God, but we who are in his family will be exempt. God's children will always be accountable to him for their actions, but this will never mean that we are judged along with his enemies. The Scriptures tell us that this day will certainly come. It will herald the beginning of a new creation where our King's love and power will flow to all his creatures through us. According to the terms of the New Covenant, we need never fear the Day of

At the Cross, we find ourselves invited by Jesus to surrender and give up our self-will. When we do this, God is able to fashion and restore any Covenant relationship.

The Kingdom perspective of the Cross.

Notes

11: "And so we know and rely on the love God has for us. God is love. Whoever lives in love lives in God, and God in him. In this way, love is made complete among us so that we will have confidence on the day of judgment, because in this world we are like him. There is no fear in love. But perfect love drives out fear, because fear has to do with punishment. The one who fears is not made perfect in love." (1 John 4:16-18)

12: See Matthew 27:45-54 and Luke 23:44-45.

13: "When you were dead in your sins and in the uncircumcision of your sinful nature, God made you alive with Christ. He forgave us all our sins, having cancelled the written code, with its regulations, that was against us and that stood opposed to us; he took it away, nailing it to the cross. And having disarmed the powers and authorities, he made a public spectacle of them, triumphing over them by the cross." (Colossians 2:13-15)

14: "To him who loves us and has freed us from our sins by his blood." (Revelation 1:5b)

Judgment. Our destination is already settled; our sins have been paid for and judged in Jesus. We go free, and can live in the confident expectation of an eternal life with God our Father.[11]

The images of the Last Day are everywhere in the accounts— the earth was shaken, the sky was darkened and the graves of the dead were opened.[12] Jesus echoed the cry of dereliction of all those alienated from God. The commanding officer at the crucifixion, seeing creation in tumult, recognized that something terrible had been perpetrated and echoed the words of the Father at Jesus' baptism:

"Surely he was the Son of God!" (Matthew 27:54b)

Watching Jesus condemned and led away to die, no doubt the devil believed that he had won. He presumed that he would now have unrestricted control over humanity. Surely, he believed that his main instrument of control—his most powerful weapon (sin)—would only increase.

But he was wrong! As Jesus walked toward Calvary, the greatest battle would be fought on ground hidden from every eye, in his body.[13]

Satan had rebelled against God and had enslaved humanity in chains forged of sin, separating us from our Creator. The "sinless one"—our champion—stepped into the fray and accepted the penalty for wrongs he had never committed. The power of sin was overcome in his body. His undeserving death meant that we—rebels held captive by sin and destined for death—could go free![14]

With victory assured and his human life coming to an end, Jesus cried out:

"It is finished." (John 19:28-30)

He had won the battle. He had surrendered only to the Father:

"Father, into your hands I commit my spirit." (Luke 23:46)

At this, the curtain in the temple (separating us from the physical representation of God's presence) was torn from top to bottom. It was as though God took the curtain in his own hands and removed the barrier forever.

At the beginning of Jesus' ministry, the sky had been torn above the River Jordan, and the Kingdom had come flooding through Jesus. At the end of his ministry, the curtain was torn, and the gates of glory were thrown open. The invitation to "enter in" was made by God himself.

And who would be the first to cross the threshold now that the invitation had been made? Could it be the thief who died beside Jesus? No doubt the angels bent to wonder at the sight. But it was true—the first to benefit from the invitation to Paradise was an undeserving sinner, given access simply because he had an invitation from the King.[15]

An eerie peace settled over the hilltop battlefield. The bloodstained Cross was empty. Mary and her friends washed the body of Jesus and wrapped him in strips of cloth, as she had done when he was born. They laid him in a tomb and sealed the entrance. But his victory over Satan and sin meant the death could not hold him.

Paul teaches that, on the Cross, Jesus disarmed the evil powers that hold us captive.

15: See Luke 23:39-43

Jesus rose the Victor and burst from the grave.

"'Death has been swallowed up in victory.
Where, O death, is your victory?
Where, O death, is your sting?' . . . Thanks be to God!
He gives us the victory through our Lord Jesus Christ."
(1 Corinthians 15:54b-57)

The Lord's Prayer

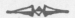

When Jesus says, "Ask in my name," it is a call to pray in terms of the Covenant.[1] He is not handing us a magic formula to success in prayer. He does not want us to tack his name on to the end of a prayer as some superstitious tradition, hoping for a hearing because of the use of his name. The reason that Jesus says "in my name" is this: he and we have the same identity given to us by the same Father. Because we are one, we have access to everything that each of us owns. As in marriage, we and Jesus say, "all that I have is yours, and all that you have is mine." He is our Covenant partner, and he invites us to use his name to gain access to all he owns.

We should have access to all that is ours.

The Covenant gives us great confidence as we ask, but the Kingdom is not yet fully revealed. Sometimes our Father tells us that we have to wait, but the wait is not forever. When we ask in the name of Jesus, we ask for things that are consistent with his identity and therefore that are consistent with his purposes.[2] If we ask with this attitude, then eventually we will receive them, either in this world or the next.

Jesus gave the clearest pattern for our prayer that addresses God both as Father and King:

"Our Father in heaven, hallowed be your name, your Kingdom (Kingship) come,"

The King is our Father, and so we ask him to enter a world of need and express his loving Kingship in every situation:

"Your will be done on earth as it is in heaven."

As a Father, he calls us to rely upon his provision:

"Give us today our daily bread."

---

1 "And I will do whatever you ask in my name, so that the Son may bring glory to the Father." (John 14:13) "If you remain in me and my words remain in you, ask whatever you wish, and it will be given you." (John 15:7)
2 Matthew 7:7-11

He settles family disputes:

"Forgive us our debts, as we also have forgiven our debtors."

As King, he wants us to surrender to his will and seek his protection as we move against his enemy—the leader of the rebellious force in the world—the devil.

"And lead us not into temptation (trials), but deliver us from the evil one."[3]

We pray as confident children of our Father with a tender heart toward a world that needs him.

3 Matthew 6:9-13

Chapter 14

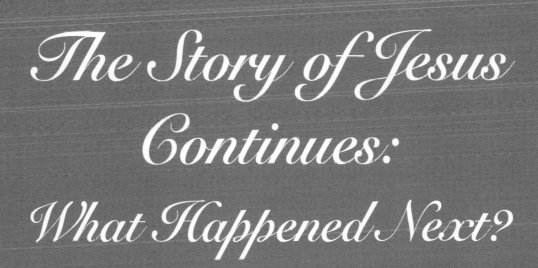

The Story of Jesus Continues:

What Happened Next?

*J*esus came onto the pages of Scripture and onto the stage of history to bring the full revelation of the Covenant and the Kingdom.

On the Cross, which bore the title of the one who hung there,
our enemy was driven back and defeated.
Jesus revealed the victory of the Kingdom.

On the cross, a sacrificial lamb was given up in our place.
Jesus ratified the New Covenant in his blood.

But, of course, the Cross was not the end of the story.

The door to the borrowed tomb stood open. Jesus was out. The open grave was no longer a fear-filled sign of death. It was now an invitation to a new life. As the portal to the coming Kingdom, even his dead body could not hold back the future blessings that God had stored up. Though his body was dead, life came to his body and raised him up.

THE LORD'S SCARS

After the Resurrection, for the better part of six weeks, Jesus met with his disciples. The women were first, then the "Twelve" (now eleven) and then the many others within the inner circle of faithful followers. They met at fellowship meals designed to reinforce their Covenant understanding.[1]

On one such occasion, Jesus wove an important thread into their minds and memories. He revealed his Covenant scars—

The Empty Grave

The Resurrection is the completion of the story of the Cross.

1: For example: "When he was at the table with them, he took bread, gave thanks, broke it and began to give it to them." (Luke 24:30)

"And while they still did not believe it because of joy and amazement, he asked them, 'Do you have anything here to eat?'" (Luke 24:41)

"Jesus said to them, 'Come and have breakfast.' None of the disciples dared ask him, 'Who are you?' They knew it was the Lord." (John 21:12) his hands and feet and side that were still marked. He had a perfect resurrected body able to act supernaturally (he could appear and disappear), yet his body still bore the marks of the Crucifixion.

At least one of the disciples had not been present and still wrestled with doubt. Again, <u>Jesus appeared and revealed his hands and feet</u>—<u>Thomas saw the scars and believed.</u>[2]

But it was not for the purposes of Thomas' unbelief that Jesus bore scars in his body. It was a sign of the permanence of his Covenant commitment. In the prophecies of Isaiah, God encouraged his people to look at his hands and see that their identity was permanently engraved there. God has signs of his Covenant commitment on his hands for all to see:

"See, I have engraved you on the palms of my hands." (Isaiah 49:16)

Of course, we also bear a Covenant sign—a hidden, spiritual scar. The circumcision of the heart that Moses spoke about in Deuteronomy 30:6 is now a reality:

Our scar <u>"Circumcision is of the heart, by the Spirit."</u> (Romans 2:29)

<u>All who have received Jesus, and therefore his Holy Spirit, are marked by the presence of the Spirit.</u> <u>When we receive Jesus, the Holy Spirit becomes a permanent presence in our life—as though our hearts were scarred.</u>

Jesus took his place on the throne his Father had prepared for his Son. <u>Jesus wears the Crown of Kingship</u> and he bears the <u>marks of Covenant.</u> Incredibly, humanity has been admitted into the Godhead, and in Jesus, we sat down in heaven.

2: "A week later his disciples were in the house again, and Thomas was with them. Though the doors were locked, Jesus came and stood among them and said, 'Peace be with you!' Then he said to Thomas, 'Put your finger here; see my hands. Reach out your hand and put it into my side. Stop doubting and believe.' Thomas said to him, 'My Lord and my God!'" (John 20:26-28)

THE ASCENSION

Before he was "taken up into heaven," Jesus instructed his disciples to wait for the infilling of the Spirit that would energize their mission and launch them into their ambassadorial roles:

"Stay in the city until you have been clothed with power from on high." (Luke 24:49)

As they were left staring into heaven, two angels came to encourage the disciples to do as Jesus as asked.[3] They returned to the city and waited as instructed. In a large pilgrim's room built on top of a Jerusalem home, they were tightly packed in and praying. It had been ten days since a cloud had covered Jesus and he had left them. As he had blessed them, he had said:

"But you will receive power when the Holy Spirit comes on you; and you will be my witnesses in Jerusalem, and in all Judea and Samaria, and to the ends of the earth." (Acts 1:8)

Soon, the fire would fall, and the wind would blow. And the flames of global mission would be ignited.

Notes

The transition from the ministry of Jesus to the ministry of the early church begins.

"When he had led them out to the vicinity of Bethany, he lifted up his hands and blessed them. While he was blessing them, he left them and was taken up into heaven. Then they worshiped him and returned to Jerusalem with great joy. And they stayed continually at the temple, praising God." (Luke 24:51-53)

3: ""They were looking intently up into the sky as he was going, when suddenly two men dressed in white stood beside them. 'Men of Galilee,' they said, 'why do you stand here looking into the sky? This same Jesus, who has been taken from you into heaven, will come back in the same way you have seen him go into heaven.'" (Acts 1:10-11)

THE DAY OF PENTECOST

Suddenly the room was filled with the sound and sensation of rushing wind.[4] This was the beginning of the new creation, and the breath of God was filling all the disciples and giving them life. This was a new and deeper revelation of God, and "the fire"—the symbol of God's presence from the beginning—settled on each one. Jesus had said that the Father would send them what he had promised, and John had also prophesied that Jesus would baptize them with fire.[5]

The Creator had breathed his life into Jesus' disciples. Through the death of Jesus, a Covenant had been made that gave the opportunity for humanity to be restored to its original place. God's intention had always been to win human beings back to himself and fill them with his presence so that the void in their life, created when they pulled away from him, could be filled again. As the Holy Spirit filled the disciples, his presence and power remade the connection, and he began the process of personal transformation. As we come to Christ, all of us receive the Holy Spirit who does the same for us. He connects us to our Creator and begins remaking us in his image.

At that time in Jerusalem, many nationalities had gathered for the Jewish feast of Pentecost.[6] Most had stayed on after Passover to take in the second festival. As the disciples were propelled out among the people and Peter preached, many hearts were opened to the good news that the disciples proclaimed. Thousands came to know the risen Savior through the message of these new disciples.

They spoke in "tongues" so that all other nationalities could understand their message. The curse of Babel had been reversed.[7] At Babel, God had confused the language of humankind so that the ensuing divisions would ultimately drive them toward him.

With the new Covenant, these disciples were truly his family. Now he could entrust them to live and share the unity and power that would represent him to the world.

7: See Genesis 11:1-9

Chapter 15

The Story of Jesus Continues:
The Message Spreads

$\mathcal{W}$e have walked through the landscape of the life of Jesus and have paused at its most holy places. We have been to the head waters from where the New Covenant flows. Now we are on the final leg of our journey to the end of the New Testament.

This part of the story, after Jesus ascended and the Holy Spirit came, tells us how a small, once-discouraged group of disciples set in motion a movement that reached the world. We see the Covenant community of disciples functioning with the same Kingdom authority and power seen in Jesus' life.

Following Pentecost, the Covenant community of Jesus began to emerge and organize. The household and the Temple appear to be the principal contexts in which the Jerusalem Church gathered.[1]

The undisputed leader of the early church was Peter. Perhaps more than anyone, he modeled the courage and boldness that would be necessary for the community of Jesus to break through the bonds of religious control. On one occasion, Peter and John healed a cripple who was begging outside the Temple. When they were brought before the religious establishment to explain themselves, Peter boldly declared:

"Rulers and elders of the people! If we are being called to account today for an act of kindness shown to a cripple and are asked how he was healed, then know this, you and all the people of Israel: it is by the name of Jesus Christ of Nazareth, whom you crucified but whom God raised from the dead, that this man stands before you healed. He is 'the stone you builders rejected, which has become the capstone.' Salvation is

The church is born.

Feeling discouraged doesn't stop progress.

1: "Every day they continued to meet together in the temple courts. They broke bread in their homes and ate together with glad and sincere hearts." (Acts 2:46)

2: "When they saw the courage of Peter and John and realized that they were unschooled, ordinary men, they were astonished and they took note that these men had been with Jesus." (Acts 4:13)

Do I?

3: "On that day a great persecution broke out against the church at Jerusalem, and all except the apostles were scattered throughout Judea and Samaria. Godly men buried Stephen and mourned deeply for him. But Saul began to destroy the church. Going from house to house, he dragged off men and women and put them in prison. Those who had been scattered preached the word wherever they went." (Acts 8:1-4)

found in no one else, for there is no other name under heaven given to men by which we must be saved." (Acts 4:8-12)

The Sanhedrin were amazed at Peter and John's courage: how could such men as these speak and act with such authority?[2] The answer was simple. They had been discipled by Jesus. They understood that their identity was bound up with that of their Lord. They were men who had a living Covenant relationship with God. They knew who they were, and knew that they were authorized to act on his behalf. They knew deep within that they carried the authority and power of the King.

Their success put pressure on the Jerusalem establishment, which sought to suppress them with brutal persecution. A young Jewish zealot in good standing with the higher echelons of Jewish society led the charge. Saul was present at the stoning of Stephen and was behind many of the arrests and beatings meted out to the new believers.

HOUSEHOLD CHURCHES – COVENANT COMMUNITIES

Interestingly, this persecution of the Church was used by God to further his purpose for the world.[3] The believers were forced out of Israel's capital, but they gossiped the gospel everywhere as they were scattered across Judea and beyond.

But there was something else. Saul's persecution also removed the opportunity for "public" gatherings. Meeting at the Temple was no longer possible.

From this point on, the early church principally gathered around the preexisting social unit of the household (or "oikos"). These extended families were the cornerstone of first-century social life and were adopted by Christians as their way of "doing life" together. Small enough to care, but large enough to dare, these "house churches" lived out the (Covenant) love of God and demonstrated his (Kingdom) power.

The New Testament church was an unstoppable force! Meeting in these households, the church functioned beyond the coercive control of the social institutions of the day. Rooted in the local community, the church was capable of touching the lives of every person in a neighborhood.[4]

The importance of the household as the social context of the church was seen in the almost casual way in which the church is referred to In the greetings at the end of Paul's letters.[5] The New Testament household church was a Covenant community with a Kingdom mission.

A HERO EMERGES

Saul's zeal knew no bounds. Eventually, he asked for permission to pursue the followers of Jesus to other parts of the region. Saul was on his way to Damascus when he was knocked to the ground by one more powerful than he:

"As he neared Damascus on his journey, suddenly a light from heaven flashed around him. He fell to the ground and heard a voice say to him, 'Saul, Saul, why do you persecute me?' 'Who

4: The model of the early church is established. It was a lightweight, low-maintenance instrument in the hands of God.

5: For example: "Greet also the church that meets at their house." (Romans 16:5) See many more examples, such as Romans 16:10-11, 1 Corinthians 16:19, Philippians 4:22 and Colossians 4:15.

Saul the persecutor meets Jesus.

are you, Lord?' Saul asked. 'I am Jesus, whom you are persecuting,' he replied. "Now get up and go into the city, and you will be told what you must do." (Acts 9:3-6)

Saul, who later took the name Paul, was totally transformed. As he lay groveling on the ground, Jesus revealed his Covenant calling and Kingdom purpose. Paul could not escape Jesus' sovereign decision to confront his follower. Jesus wanted a Covenant relationship that would lead to Kingdom breakthrough.

Jesus asked Saul, "Why do you persecute me?" The Lord was so connected to his followers through the New Covenant that when they were hurt by persecutors such as Saul felt it. This revelation later became the basis of Paul's theology of the church—he went on to describe it as "the body of Christ." "Just as each of us has one body with many members, and these members do not all have the same function, so in Christ we who are many form one body, and each member belongs to all the others." (Romans 12:4-5)[6]

But Jesus also revealed that he was the King. He wanted Paul to represent him. For the rest of Paul's life, he would be a witness to the rule of Christ, even before earthly kings.[7] In a few days, Paul would meet a disciple of Jesus called Ananias and be baptized. The temporary blindness inflicted on the road to Damascus would leave Paul, and from that moment, he would become one of the great examples of a life in the hands of God.

The record of his conversion, reported three times in the Acts of the Apostles, is the central event of early church history. By his life and teaching, Paul framed New Testament theology, and his team was responsible for writing a large part of the New Testament. The church he founded in Ephesus was not only the

6: See also 1 Corinthians 12:12-27 and Ephesians 4:16.

The familiar phrase "in Christ" also describes this Covenant relationship. We have a relationship of "oneness," which means we share all that belongs to Jesus—for example: "But now in Christ Jesus you who once were far away have been brought near through the blood of Christ." (Ephesians 2:13) "Now if we are children, then we are heirs – heirs of God and co-heirs with Christ, if indeed we share in his sufferings in order that we may also share in his glory." (Romans 8:17)

7: This is particularly clear in the other accounts of Paul's conversion that he gave as testimony to others: See Acts 22:3-16 and 26:9-18. It is also made clear by Jesus when he speaks to Ananias of Paul's significance in Acts 9:15-16.

He feels our pain.

epicenter of the Christian faith for several hundred years but also where the last books of the New Testament—those of John—were written.

After an initial foray into his future preaching ministry, Paul disappeared from the pages of the New Testament for more than a decade. When we check the chronology of the New Testament church against his testimony of hardship, we realize that during this time Paul suffered greatly—beaten, stoned, shipwrecked.[8] Jesus had predicted that Paul would know great suffering, and it seems that his "hidden years" were part of the fulfillment.[9]

After all that he had gone through, it must have seemed like an eternity before Barnabas came and found Paul with great news. What Jesus had told Paul about the Gentiles had begun to happen. In Antioch, one of the great cities of the Roman Empire, many were becoming believers. Paul entered the work with great gusto. In time, he was sent with Barnabas and the young John Mark as the first missionaries from this vibrant church.

THE WORD BEGAN TO SPREAD

Their missionary journey began in Barnabas's homeland—the island of Cyprus. Paul quickly emerged as the new leader of the team clearly endorsed by the remarkable favor of God upon his life. From there, they returned to the mainland and traveled into the mountainous region of Galatia.

Afraid of what might happen when they entered this area well-known for its barbarism, Mark returned home. Perhaps it was

8: "This man is my chosen instrument to carry my name before the Gentiles and their kings and before the people of Israel. I will show him how much he must suffer for my name." (Acts 9:15b-16)

9: "Five times I received from the Jews the 40 lashes minus one. Three times I was beaten with rods, once I was stoned, three times I was shipwrecked, I spent a night and a day in the open sea, I have been constantly on the move." (2 Corinthians 11:16-33 extracts) Most of these events could not have occurred in Paul's missionary journeys by the time 2 Corinthians was written. Therefore, we must conclude that these events occurred before the missionary journeys recorded in Acts of the Apostles.

10: Was the "young man" in Mark 14:51-52 Mark himself? Perhaps after returning defeated from his first missionary journey, he was reminded that he had run away once before (from Gethsemane).

11: See Acts 8:1

12: "When Peter came to Antioch, I opposed him to his face, because he was clearly in the wrong. Before certain men came from James, he used to eat with the Gentiles. But when they arrived, he began to draw back and separate himself from the Gentiles because he was afraid of those who belonged to the circumcision group. The other Jews joined him in his hypocrisy, so that by their hypocrisy even Barnabas was led astray. When I saw that they were not acting in line with the truth of the gospel, I said to Peter in front of them all, 'You are a Jew, yet you live like a Gentile and not like a Jew. How is it, then, that you force Gentiles to follow Jewish customs?'" (Galatians 2:11-14)

13: "No, a man is a Jew if he is one inwardly; and circumcision is circumcision of the heart, by the Spirit, not by the written code. Such a man's praise is not from men, but from God." (Romans 2:29)

during this time that Mark first began to write down Peter's sermons; he had recently arrived in Antioch from Jerusalem. His gospel—fast paced and full of emotional "cut and thrust"—reads like no other.[10]

Matthew, probably still based with the other apostles in Jerusalem and Judea,[11] perhaps was beginning his own gospel at this time. Mark's gospel is clearly written for the kind of Gentile public found in the Antioch church. Matthew's gospel, though following the same chronology, is quite different. His gospel appears to be written for Jewish believers. Scholars tell us that even in the Greek Mark's gospel contains the flavors of the Aramaic in which perhaps his gospel was first written.

COVENANT CONTROVERSY

When Paul returned with Barnabas from his first missionary trip, Paul reported to the church all that had happened. But they encountered a new and disturbing reality in the church. Some believers from Jerusalem had begun to teach that the Gentile Christians were not Jewish enough. These believers taught that circumcision was necessary for the followers of Jesus to be fully connected with him in the Covenant. For a while, even Peter appeared to be influenced by their teaching.[12] Paul corrected Peter and argued that the mark of the Covenant was now internal. Paul later wrote that circumcision was no longer an external "fleshly" reality but a matter of the heart.[13]

This unhelpful teaching had already spread rapidly, perhaps encouraged by the new leader of the church in Jerusalem,

Jesus' own brother James. Before long, the teaching reached the churches that Paul had planted in Galatia. Furious about the potential consequences of such harmful teaching, Paul wrote his first letter—Galatians. In it, he argued that the Old Testament Covenant had now been gathered up, reinterpreted and fulfilled in the New Covenant relationship with Christ.

Paul contended that the Holy Spirit within the churches was the permanent mark of a new Covenant relationship with God. Paul encouraged people to be "filled with the Spirit," to "walk with the Spirit," to demonstrate the "fruit of the Spirit" in their lives and to live by his "power" daily.[14] Eventually the dispute was settled in Jerusalem. Paul and Barnabas were sent by the church in Antioch to settle the matter with James and Peter. Paul and Barnabas came back from Jerusalem with a letter that exonerated Paul and his teaching and released the Gentiles from the regulations of the Old Covenant.[15]

Paul was eager to read this letter to the churches he had planted in Galatia that had been so troubled by the controversy. He also wanted to continue the mission that he had been given by Jesus. So Paul began his second missionary journey. "He went through Syria and Cilicia, strengthening the churches." (Acts 15:41) Paul and Silas appear to have read the letter from the meeting of the Apostles in Jerusalem to all the churches the two encountered.[16]

14: See, for example, Galatians 5:16, 22, 25 and Ephesians 1:13-14, 3:16, 20 and 5:18.

15: "Brothers, you know that some time ago God made a choice among you that the Gentiles might hear from my lips the message of the gospel and believe. God, who knows the heart, showed that he accepted them by giving the Holy Spirit to them, just as he did to us. He made no distinction between us and them, for he purified their hearts by faith . . . We believe it is through the grace of our Lord Jesus that we are saved, just as they are." (Acts 15:1-29 extracts)

16: "As they traveled from town to town, they delivered the decisions reached by the apostles and elders in Jerusalem for the people to obey." (Acts 16:4)

PAUL'S TRAVELS WITH SILAS, TIMOTHY AND LUKE

This time, Barnabas did not go with Paul. They disagreed on whether to bring John Mark along as their assistant. Barnabas was keen to give John Mark a second chance, but Paul knew that they were going into hostile territory again and was concerned that John Mark might not have the strength to see the mission through to the end. Both Paul and Barnabas knew the heartache of a Covenant partnership that was broken. But neither wanted to continue alone, and so both sought to build new Covenant relationships that would sustain the men in their mission for the King. Therefore, Barnabas and Mark retraced the early stages of their first journey and went to Cyprus. Paul took Silas—a leader from Jerusalem—and traveled through Galatia, continuing east into Asia Minor.

During this journey, a young man called Timothy joined the team.[17] Later, Paul described Timothy as a spiritual son, and he was the model disciple who imitated Paul's life and teaching in every way. "Therefore I urge you to imitate me. For this reason I am sending to you Timothy, my son whom I love, who is faithful in the Lord. He will remind you of my way of life in Christ Jesus, which agrees with what I teach everywhere in every church." (1 Corinthians 4:16-17)

Paul was a great mission strategist. It appears as though Paul was trying to make for the principal city of Asia Minor—Ephesus. But either by external circumstance or internal prompting, Paul felt that God was directing them elsewhere.[18] Eventually, they came to the end of the westward road and found themselves at Troas. There, Paul had a vision of a man

Paul builds a missionary team.

Interesting. This messy life has broken covenant relationships. Still on mission for the King + in covenant with Him.

17: "He came to Derbe and then to Lystra, where a disciple named Timothy lived, whose mother was a Jewess and a believer, but whose father was a Greek. The brothers at Lystra and Iconium spoke well of him. Paul wanted to take him along on the journey." (Acts 16:1-3a)

18: See Acts 16:6-8

from Macedonia asking him and his team to come and help them. At this point in the story of Acts of the Apostles, Luke appears to have joined the team. The next episode—the first foray into Europe—is an eyewitness account.[19]

By now, Paul and his team were a community of mission. They had many remarkable adventures from the first city the team visited (the Latinate city of Philippi) to the last (the teeming and populous city of Corinth). It was there that Paul suffered the now familiar persecutions that accompanied him on his journeys. But this time, he came to the end of himself. Paul's Covenant partner—Jesus—had provided for and protected Paul and his team along the way. Jesus, the ruler of Paul's life, appeared to Paul in the night to calm his fears and encourage him:

"Do not be afraid; keep on speaking, do not be silent. For I am with you, and no one is going to attack and harm you, because I have many people in this city." (Acts 18:9-10)

19: Luke uses "we" from Acts 16:10-15.

Chapter 16

*The Story Nears
Its Fulfillment*

*T*he fresh ground of the missionary movement had been broken. Although the early church leaders would suffer much for their faith, the movement they had begun now had an unstoppable momentum.

PAUL'S LETTERS TO THE EARLY CHURCH

Paul stayed on in Corinth for another eighteen months and there penned the letters to the Thessalonian churches and a letter of introduction to the church in Rome that he hoped to visit on his way to Spain.[1]

In all Paul's missionary adventures, Covenant and Kingdom were deeply entwined in his message and methods.

The ministry of Jesus was flowing through Paul. Paul testified to this when he later reminded the Corinthians that, although lacking eloquence, his message was authenticated by demonstrations of the Holy Spirit's power:

"My message and my preaching were not with wise and persuasive words, but with a demonstration of the Spirit's power." (1 Corinthians 2:4)

But with all of this demonstration of power, his objective was always to call people to faith in Christ and gather them into the Covenant community of God. Paul's letters are riven through with references to our Covenant relationship with God.[2]

Even though the power of God expressed in the life of Paul was already functioning at a remarkable level, he would discover

215

Paul's "race" is almost run.

1: 1 Thessalonians 3 seems to indicate that Paul was in Corinth during this correspondence. Romans 16:23-24 speaks of Gaius and Erastus, known from external sources to be residents of Corinth at the time.

2: For example: "Remember that at that time you were separate from Christ, excluded from citizenship in Israel and foreigners to the covenants of the promise, without hope and without God in the world. But now in Christ Jesus you who once were far away have been brought near through the blood of Christ." (Ephesians 2:12-13) Also: "By abolishing in his flesh the law with its commandments and regulations. His purpose was to create in himself one new man out of the two, thus making peace." (Ephesians 2:15) how surrender would give him access to even more. The many difficulties and persecutions that he suffered at the hands of those whom he probably described as his "thorns in the flesh" were the way in which God brought Paul to a fresh level of submission and an extraordinary experience of God's power.

Piecing together the story in Acts of the Apostles and Paul's letters, it appears to have happened in this way: in Corinth, Paul seems to have reached the end of his tether. The many threats of violence brought him to the place where the Lord needed to intervene so that Paul would continue with his mission in that city. Jesus appeared to Paul and told him not to fear the many assaults that he might suffer:

"Do not be afraid; keep on speaking, do not be silent. For I am with you, and no one is going to attack and harm you, because I have many people in this city." (Acts 18:9)

Though Paul continued with his mission in Corinth, as he prepared to leave, he made a "Nazerite vow".[3] He cut all the hair from his body and collected it in a bag to place on the altar in Jerusalem as a token of himself. He was determined to ask God to remove the people from his life who were causing him and his churches so much trouble. These opponents had wearied and worn Paul down to the point that he wanted God to take them away forever. Paul asked the Lord three times to remove "the thorn in his flesh."

Paul took a boat and left for Jerusalem. Calling in at Ephesus, he left Priscilla and Aquila—trusted team members from the Corinthian mission—to start the work of planting a church in that great city.

3: "Paul stayed on in Corinth for some time. Then he left the brothers and sailed for Syria, accompanied by Priscilla and Aquila. Before he sailed, he had his hair cut off at Cenchrea because of a vow he had taken." (Acts 18:18)

Interesting

Fulfilling his Nazerite vow in Jerusalem was a conscious act of submission. As he placed his own hair on the altar, he was offering himself as a living sacrifice.[4]

REST AND RECREATION

Having fulfilled his vow in Jerusalem, he returned to Antioch for a well-earned rest. Within a short time, Paul was on the road again, visiting the churches he had planted and making his way to Ephesus. There he planted his most important church—birthed with remarkable Kingdom power.[5] It seems as though Paul's submission to God allowed the Lord to use him to release even greater levels of Kingdom power.

It was in Ephesus that Paul wrote the first part of his Corinthian correspondence.[6] The remarkable success in planting the church in Ephesus caused a huge spiritual backlash, and Paul barely escaped with his life. He left to visit the churches that he and his team had planted in Europe, completing his Corinthian correspondence while on the road.

His plan was to go to Jerusalem again—this time with a financial gift from the Gentile churches for those in need. Though he was warned by prophets along the way that he would be imprisoned, he determined to continue, believing that this was part of his destiny.[7]

Paul's life of faith had begun when he met Jesus on the road to Damascus. There, Jesus had given Paul a gracious invitation to live in a Covenant relationship with the Son of God. Even though Paul had brutally persecuted Jesus' followers, Jesus loved Paul.

217

Notes

4: Interestingly, it was in Corinth that Paul wrote to the Romans (Romans 12:1) and instructed them to offer themselves as "living sacrifices." Perhaps Paul was thinking of this metaphor in relation to himself at the time.

5: See Acts 19:11-20

6: See 1 Corinthians 16:8

7: "When we heard this, we and the people there pleaded with Paul not to go up to Jerusalem. Then Paul answered, 'Why are you weeping and breaking my heart? I am ready not only to be bound, but also to die in Jerusalem for the name of the Lord Jesus.' When he would not be dissuaded, we gave up and said, 'The Lord's will be done.'" (Acts 21:12-14)

Persecutions as opportunities?
Submitted & surrendered

Such grace had overwhelmed Paul. Grace became the central message of his life. With the Lord's grace-filled invitation had also come a call to responsibility. Paul was determined to go to Jerusalem to carry the name of Jesus to "the Gentiles and their kings."[8] He would be arrested, and this would be the means by which he could complete his call. Jesus the King of Kings would send a message through his Covenant brother Paul to the rulers of the world.

PAUL'S ARREST AND TRIALS

In Jerusalem, Paul was arrested and carried under armed guard to prison in Caesarea, the Roman administrative capital. There he had the opportunity to preach to the Roman governor of Judea and the vassal King Agrippa. Paul had already claimed the rights of a Roman citizen, and thus, his case would be heard only by Caesar himself.

When the preparations had been made, Paul undertook the perilous journey, still under armed guard, to Rome. Barely escaping with his life, and somehow surviving a shipwreck, Paul arrived at his destination.

During this period of imprisonment, Paul wrote the letters of Ephesians, Philemon and Colossians. Though the personal letter to Philemon and the epistle to the Colossian church speak of Covenant and Kingdom themes, Ephesians is perhaps the most complete rendering of the two themes found in the New Testament letters. In this general letter, probably read in the church at Ephesus and the other churches of the region,

Paul used Covenant and Kingdom as the framework of his teaching. The first part of the letter[9] is given over to an exposition of our relationship with Christ. For example: "And God raised us up with Christ and seated us with him in the heavenly realms in Christ Jesus, in order that in the coming ages he might show the incomparable riches of his grace, expressed in his kindness to us in Christ Jesus. For it is by grace you have been saved, through faith—and this not from yourselves, it is the gift of God." (Ephesians 2:6-8a) "Remember that at that time you were separate from Christ, excluded from citizenship in Israel and foreigners to the covenants of the promise, without hope and without God in the world. But now in Christ Jesus you who once were far away have been brought near through the blood of Christ." (Ephesians 6:12-13)

The middle part[10] applies this Covenant theology to the whole church, for example: "Be imitators of God, therefore, as dearly loved children and live a life of love, just as Christ loved us and gave himself up for us as a fragrant offering and sacrifice to God." (Ephesians 5:1-2)

The last part of the letter[11] handles the spiritual warfare that we can expect as Kingdom representatives. For example: "Finally, be strong in the Lord and in his mighty power. Put on the full armor of God so that you can take your stand against the devil's schemes. For our struggle is not against flesh and blood, but against the rulers, against the authorities, against the powers of this dark world and against the spiritual forces of evil in the heavenly realms." (Ephesians 6:10-12)

Paul was taken to Rome, and the Acts of the Apostles closes with him awaiting trial in a rented house preaching without

Notes

9: Chapters 1-3.

10: Chapters 4-5.

11: Chapter 6.

hindrance to any who would come to hear him.[12] After this, Paul was released, probably without charge, to continue his mission to the Gentiles. After visiting various places where he had planted churches (for example, Crete), he wrote to Titus, and it seems that he then went on to Spain. He returned to Rome sometime around AD 66.

Peter may already have been in Rome and perhaps wrote his own two letters there.[13] He was crucified upside down by the mad Emperor Nero. The early leader of God's mission and the charismatic head of the first church in Jerusalem was honored by Jesus as he gave Peter the opportunity to witness to the Son of God by the same death that he suffered. Many scholars believe that Mark's gospel is the record of Peter's preaching and teaching about Jesus. Whether Peter knew this or not, the witness of his life was complete.

By now, Paul was languishing in a Roman dungeon and knew his time had come. It was in this period that he probably wrote his letters to Timothy, who was the leader in Ephesus[14] and was being severely tested by heresy in the church. Clearly, Paul's admonitions and Timothy's leadership were successful. The Ephesian church continued to thrive and assumed a preeminent place in the early church. No one knows for certain who wrote the letter of Hebrews, but if it was Paul, as the early church fathers believed, it would probably have been around this time that he wrote the letter.

THE DEATH OF A GREAT APOSTLE

Even though Paul's life was drawing to a close, he knew that he had fulfilled the calling that he had been given by Jesus on the road to Damascus:

"For I am already being poured out like a drink offering, and the time has come for my departure. I have fought the good fight, I have finished the race, I have kept the faith. Now there is in store for me the crown of righteousness, which the Lord, the righteous Judge, will award to me on that day—and not only to me, but also to all who have longed for his appearing." (2 Timothy 4:6-8)

Paul was executed under Emperor Nero. Because Paul was a Roman citizen, he was beheaded.

Soon after, Timothy left Ephesus. Tradition tells us that, around the same time, the aging apostle John arrived in Ephesus with Jesus' mother, Mary. He buried the saintly lady there and assumed the leadership of the churches in the city and the surrounding region. John's letters and the last book of the New Testament—Revelation—were written for these Christians.

REMARKABLE SUCCESS OF THE EARLY CHURCH

The astonishing success of the early church can be attributed to three things: the message that the church proclaimed, the practices that the believers lived by and the power of God at work among them. They proclaimed a grace-filled invitation of love. Their household churches were lightweight enough to be

Paul's race is run.

able to be planted in almost any context, and the power of their Kingdom ministry was such that the early church had a reputation for healing and deliverance. Even though the early churches were mercilessly persecuted, the compelling life of their community and the power at work among them drew many into a relationship with God.

The New Testament was completed by AD 100. Within seventy years of the death, resurrection and ascension of Jesus, the Bible we read today was complete, and most had been written much earlier than this before the destruction of Jerusalem in AD 72.

THE BOOK OF REVELATION

Similar to so many of Jesus' apostles, John was persecuted. He was sent to a prison camp on the island of Patmos. The highly symbolic "apocalyptic" language of Revelation often repels Western readers. But its message is clear—whatever circumstances the people of God may be facing, the Lord is working out his purposes to bring about ultimate victory. The book of Revelation is a window on the future; in chapter 5, we see that Jesus is portrayed as a lamb that has been slain. He is seated on a throne—our Covenant substitute is also our sovereign. By the time we reach the conclusion of John's apocalypse, we see that Jesus is also a mighty warrior, riding a white charger. He has come to make war on all the enemies of God and bring release to the prisoners held in darkness so that a new world can begin with a new humanity. The Covenant people of God will see the Kingdom win through and the rule of darkness will be vanquished. Between now and then, we are encouraged to see things from God's perspective and realize that his plans will come to their fulfillment with the triumphant return of Christ.

The New Testament closes on a triumphant note with the promise of a returning King. When all the battles are fought and won, our King Jesus will return and gather his Covenant community to himself. Then heaven and earth will be remade, and the New Creation revealed:

> "'Behold, I am coming soon! Yes, I am coming soon.' Amen.
> Come, Lord Jesus."
> (Revelation 22:12, 20)

Our study is almost complete. By now, I trust you are becoming familiar with the themes of Covenant and Kingdom and how they interrelate within the text of Scripture. Before we look at the practicalities of identifying these themes in any passage of the Bible (see the following chapter, "Tools for Interpretation"), perhaps we should look back through the New Testament and summarize what we have learned so far.

SUMMARY OF COVENANT IN THE NEW TESTAMENT

As Jesus reveals his relationship with his heavenly Father, Jesus invites us into a new depth of understanding of the Covenant. He offers to us the relationship that he enjoys with the Father.

FATHER

John's gospel—the gospel of the Covenant—defines the relationship that exists between God the Father and the Son. The Son is revealed as Jesus throughout the gospel.

Jesus says that he does only what he sees the Father doing (John 5:19). In shared identity, common purpose is forged. As his disciples mature in their relationship with him, Jesus reveals that they will share in a common relationship with the one that he calls Father and that together they will fashion the cords that will hold the Covenant together:

"If anyone loves me, he will obey my teaching. My Father will love him, and we will come to him and make our home with him." (John 14:23)

Jesus came as one who was and is in radical, deep and intimate Covenant with the God of heaven. Today, he draws people to himself and builds a community of people who follow him, who want to become more like him and enter more into the realities of the Covenant that Jesus shares with his Father.

IDENTITY

Identity flows from the one who gives us life. We are children of God, born again into a new family, given a new name and a new identity by which we can gain access to all of the resources of our Covenant partner.

The New Testament teaches that when we are baptized we embrace our new identity. Jesus connects us to God and defines who we are. We bear his Name, and everything he has is ours. Our identity is so caught up with God's that the New Testament is able to say that we are heirs of heaven and co-heirs with Christ. God's commitment to us is written indelibly in the blood of Jesus. As we share in the Covenant meal that Jesus gave, the bread and wine help us to remember who he is and who we are.

OBEDIENCE

The New Covenant means that God's code of behavior for his people—"the Law"—is now written in our hearts. This happens when the Holy Spirit fills us and gives us new life when we are born again as God's children. Now we are free to obey God because this is truly a reflection of who we are. We choose to obey because this is the most consistent way of expressing our identity. What we do tells the world who we are:

"If you love me, you will obey what I command." (John 14:15)

Obedience is always an act of love. Because of our shared Covenant identity with Jesus, we do the things he did:

226

"I tell you the truth, anyone who has faith in me will do what I have been doing. He will do even greater things than these, because I am going to the Father." (John 14:12)

Exercising this life of Covenant oneness means living a life of security and confidence:

Don't have these with that oneness w/ the Lord.

"And I will do whatever you ask in my name, so that the Son may bring glory to the Father. You may ask me for anything in my name, and I will do it." (John 14:13-14)

It may be helpful to sum this up visually in the same way that we did in the Old Testament Summary:

The Covenant begins with the Father, who gives us our identity. Now we are able to obey because as children of God we are empowered to do so. At times, we may find ourselves seeking to approach God through obedience rather than in simple recognition of our identity. When we do this, we fall into the trap of the Pharisees whom Jesus encountered. As we are God's children, he is already pleased with us, and this knowledge liberates us from the legalistic observance that so often leads to frustration and guilt.

SUMMARY OF KINGDOM IN THE NEW TESTAMENT

It is not with a show of majestic judgment that Jesus revealed the Kingship of God. Rather, it was with servant-hearted tenderness toward us, his wayward subjects. His sacrificial love brought the ultimate victory of the Kingdom over our enemies of sin, death and hell.

Until the birth of Jesus, the prophets foresaw only the coming of the King. But now the King has come among us. The King of heaven has taken on flesh and has chosen to walk among his wayward subjects, to reveal the future he has prepared for us, a future that we can taste now if only we will surrender to his Kingship.

In almost every expression of earthly kingdom, the monarch benefits most from its existence. With the Kingdom of heaven, however, the Kingdom is for the subjects. The King is a servant King who wants his people to be the greatest recipients of its benefits. In response to receiving all the blessings, the people of the King offer him their love and loyalty, glory and honor.

Again the Kingdom (or Kingship) of God is expressed in three key words: King, authority and power.

KING

As the servant King, Jesus constantly offered himself as the doorway to the future Kingdom. He looked for those who needed forgiveness; he searched for those who needed restoration or healing. Jesus the King was single-minded in his determination to reveal his Kingship. He sought the lost, fed the hungry, mended the broken and healed the sick. He told stories, painting pictures of a life worth living and a future worth dying for.

Usually the King's glory was veiled, but occasionally he was seen in all his splendor: at his baptism when heaven stood open, on the Mount of Transfiguration with the enveloping cloud of glory and in the Ascension when he made the return journey to the heavenly Kingdom.

AUTHORITY

The Kingdom is all about the King and his Kingship. But this King is completely committed to his subjects, desiring that they might fully reflect him as they represent him, doing all that he did and living as he lived.

Authority simply means the qualification to act. In the gospels, we read of Jesus' amazing authority as he represented God's Kingship. In turn, having followed him and learnt to imitate his life, his disciples chose to receive his authorization to act on his behalf. In the same way, we are commissioned to act on his behalf. Disciples choose to give as they have received—giving forgiveness, healing, deliverance and blessing.

POWER

In the United States and some other countries, police officers acting on behalf of their commissioning government are given two vital symbols of office—a badge to identify who they are and a gun that enables them to carry out their job. We need to carry the badge and the gun. If authority is our badge of office, then power is our gun with which we are equipped to take on the task.

Similar to Jesus, our power comes from the presence of the Holy Spirit. The Spirit of God himself connects us to the Kingdom for which we long. It is by him that we "taste the powers of the coming age" (Hebrews 6:4-5).

As with the Old Testament Summary, it may be helpful to portray graphically the connection of these three vital elements. The Kingdom begins with the King, who exercises authority through us his representatives, and with that authority, he sends power for us to be able to do all that he wants us to do:

Chapter 17

Tools for Interpretation

*T*his book has been about Covenant and Kingdom—two lenses that help us understand more clearly the meaning of Scripture. These two lenses give us a "binocular vision" of the Bible, helping us to see breadth and depth.

Even familiar passages come alive in a new way when viewed from the binocular vision of Covenant and Kingdom. Being able to identify the main themes of any passage, no matter how obscure, will be an essential skill as you seek to apply the Bible's truth to your life. No human mediator between you and God is needed. The Bible is God's gift to you—be confident as you read it, asking him for personal application.

QUESTIONS TO ASK AS YOU ARE GETTING STARTED

When you come to a passage of Scripture, you might ask yourself some simple questions, such as the following:

- Is the passage mainly about Covenant, or is the passage about Kingdom? (Often, the passage contains elements of both.) If you are not sure:
- Is it about "being one with God" or "doing something for God"? ("being" always refers to Covenant; "doing" often refers to Kingdom)
- If Covenant is being revealed, then the relationship with our Father God is the primary theme, and the passage will reveal insights into that relationship, which flows into all other relationships. We will become more aware of who God is, how he gives us a true sense of our identity and what obedience to him really means.
- If the text appears to be about the Kingdom, you might ask yourself, how does it reveal God as King and his call to represent him?
- Does the verse or passage in question reveal God's desire to extend his rule of mercy and love through us? Such a verse will reveal something of

our authority, our calling, to "do" something in his Kingdom. It will reveal God's power given to us. <u>He gives us the capacity to do what he asks because we are empowered by his Spirit.</u>

- If you are not sure, don't worry—taking a broader view of the passage or even the book as a whole often helps to clarify things.

THE COVENANT PERSPECTIVE

Approaching the Bible by asking these kinds of questions helps us recognize when a passage is speaking about Covenant or Kingdom. To put it simply, anything referring to relationships is about our Covenant with God or his people. Such passages reveal something about God as our <u>**Father**</u>, our <u>**identity**</u> as his children or our call to <u>**obey**</u> him.

Let's look at a few verses where I have highlighted some of the essential words that reveal the theme of Covenant:

 FATHER – family – protection – provision ("bread") – promise

As a father has compassion on **his children,**
so the Lord has compassion on those who fear him;
for he knows how we are formed,
he remembers that we are dust.

Psalms 103:13-14 (the whole Psalm is helpful on Covenant)

So do not worry, saying, "What shall we eat?" or "What shall we drink?" or "What shall we wear?" For the pagans run after all these things, and **your heavenly Father knows that you need them.**
Matthew 6:32 (see also 6:25-33)

Give us today our daily **bread**.
Matthew 6:11

This mystery is that through the gospel the Gentiles are **heirs** together with Israel, **members** together of one body, and **sharers** together in the **promise** in Christ Jesus.
Ephesians 3:6

Now let's look at some verses that reveal our Covenant **identity** through our relationship with God:

IDENTITY – being one in Christ – being known – calling – anointing – belonging – nation – tribe – inheritance – shepherd – flock

Now if you obey me fully and keep my **covenant**, then out of all **nations** you will be **my treasured possession**. Although the whole earth is **mine, you will be for me** a kingdom of priests and a **holy nation**. These are the words you are to speak to the Israelites.
Exodus 19:5-6

What shall we say, then? Shall we go on sinning so that grace may increase? By no means! We died to sin; how can we live in it any longer? Or don't you know that all of us who were **baptized into Christ Jesus** were **baptized into his death**? We were therefore buried with him through baptism into death in order that, just as Christ was raised from the dead through the glory of the Father, we too may live a new life.

If we have been **united with him** like this in his death, we will certainly also be **united with him** in his resurrection. For we know that our old self was **crucified with him** so that the body of sin might be done away with that we should no longer be slaves to sin—because anyone who has died has been freed from sin.

Now if we **died with Christ**, we believe that we will also **live with him**. For we know that since Christ was raised from the dead, he cannot die again; death no longer has mastery over him. The death he died, he died to sin once for all; but the life he lives, he lives to God.
Romans 6:1-10

For you did not receive a spirit that makes you a slave again to fear, but you received the Spirit of **sonship**. And by him we cry, "**Abba, Father.**" The Spirit himself testifies with our spirit that we are **God's children**. Now if we are children, then we are **heirs—heirs** of God and **co-heirs** with Christ, if indeed we **share** in his sufferings in order that we may also **share** in his glory.
Romans 8:15-17

And you also were included in Christ when you heard the word of truth, the gospel of your salvation. Having believed, you were **marked in him with a seal, the promised Holy Spirit**, who is a **deposit guaranteeing our inheritance** until the redemption of those who are God's possession—to the praise of his glory.
Ephesians 1:13-14

The third big theme within the Covenant is **obedience**, often described in the Bible as "walking" or "life"—anything that calls us to act in a way that reflects our relationship with God. In the Old Testament, this is called "Law," and in the New Testament is a description of behavior that is consistent with being children, such as pursuing holiness. Let's look at a selection of verses that reveal this understanding. Here are a few key words to look out for:

 OBEDIENCE – command – oath – vow – obey – holiness – loving one another – walk – path – hear/listen – law – code

Be careful to **follow every command** I am giving you today, so that you may **live and increase** and may enter and possess the land that the Lord **promised on oath** to your forefathers.
Deuteronomy 8:1

You, dear **children**, are **from God** and have overcome them, because the one who is in you is greater than the one who is in the world. They are from the world and therefore speak from the viewpoint of the world, and the world listens to them. We are **from God**, and whoever knows God **listens** to us; but whoever is not from God does not listen to us. This is how we recognize the Spirit of truth and the spirit of falsehood. Dear friends, **let us love one another**, for love comes from God. **Everyone who loves has been born of God and knows God.**
1 John 4:4-7

This is my **command: Love** each other.
John 15:17

Aside from the three key concepts of Father, identity and obedience, other words and ideas cluster around the theme of Covenant. Often, they deal with how God has initiated the relationship and how the connection is maintained. Let's look at words that refer to God's initiative and his commitment to maintaining a relationship with us:

GOD'S INITIATIVE: choose – predestined – blood – sacrifice – atonement – lamb – grace – favor – gift – loving kindness (the Covenant word for love is "hesed," translated as loving kindness, goodness and mercy)

You did not choose me, but **I chose you and appointed you** to go and bear fruit—fruit that will last. Then the Father will give you whatever you ask in my name.
John 15:16

For those God **foreknew** he also **predestined** to be conformed to the likeness of his Son, that he might be the firstborn among many brothers. And those he **predestined**, he also **called**; those he called, he also justified; those he justified, he also glorified.
Romans 8:29-30

Then they are to take some of the **blood** and put it on the sides and tops of the doorframes of the houses where they eat the **lambs** . . . The **blood** will be a sign for you on the houses where you are; and **when I see the blood**, I will pass over you. No destructive plague will touch you when I strike Egypt.
Exodus 12:7 and 13

Slaughter it in the Lord's presence at the entrance to the Tent of Meeting. Take some of the bull's **blood** and put it on the horns of the altar with your finger, and pour out the rest of it at the base of the altar.
Exodus 29:11-12

In the same way, after supper he took the cup, saying, "This cup is the new covenant in my **blood**; do this, whenever you drink it, in remembrance of me."
1 Corinthians 11:25

God presented him as a **sacrifice** of atonement, through faith in his **blood**. He did this to demonstrate his justice, because in his forbearance he had left the sins committed beforehand unpunished—
Romans 3:25

The Lord appeared to us in the past, saying:
"I have loved you with an **everlasting love**;
I have **drawn you** with **loving-kindness**.
Jeremiah 31:3

Surely **goodness and love** will follow me
all the days of my life,
and I will dwell in the house of the Lord
forever.
Psalms 23:6

Moses said to the Lord, "You have been telling me, 'Lead these people,' but you have not let me know whom you will send with me. You have said, 'I know you by name and you have found **favor** with me.' If you are pleased with me, teach me your ways so I may know you and continue to find favor with you. Remember that **this nation is your people**."
Exodus 33:12-13

Through whom we have gained access by faith into this **grace** in which we now stand. And we rejoice in the hope of the glory of God.
Romans 5:2

For it is by **grace** you have been saved, through faith—and this not from yourselves, it is **the gift of God**.
Ephesians 2:8

Next we should look at words that refer to our response to God's initiative. This is directed in love toward him, toward other Covenant partners with God (his people) and toward others who do not yet know him. Some key words referring to our response to God are the following:

 LOVE FOR GOD – love for other Christians – love for the world – thanksgiving – worship – confidence in prayer

He answered: "**Love the Lord your God** with all your heart and with all your soul **and with all your strength and with all your mind**"; and, "**Love your neighbor as yourself.**"
Luke 10:27

Dear friends, let us **love one another**, for love comes from God. Everyone who loves has been born of God and knows God. Whoever does not love does not know God, because God is love. This is how God showed his love among us: He sent his one and only Son into the world that we might live through him. This is love: not that we loved God, but that he loved us and sent his Son as an

239

atoning sacrifice for our sins. Dear friends, since God so loved us, we also ought to **love one another**. No one has ever seen God; but if we **love one another**, God lives in us and his love is made complete in us.
1 John 4:7-12 (and onwards)

He answered: 'Love the Lord your God with all your heart and with all your soul and with all your strength and with all your mind'; and, **'Love your neighbor as yourself.'**
Luke 10:27

So then, just as you received Christ Jesus as Lord, continue to live in him, rooted and built up in him, strengthened in the faith as you were taught, and overflowing with **thankfulness**.
Colossians 2:6-7

Yet a time is coming and has now come when the **true worshipers** will **worship the Father in spirit and truth**, for they are the kind of worshipers the Father seeks. God is spirit, and his worshipers must worship in spirit and in truth."
John 4:23-24

I tell you the truth, anyone who has faith in me will do what I have been doing. He will do **even greater things than these**, because I am going to the Father. And **I will do whatever you ask in my name**, so that the Son may bring glory to the Father. **You may ask me for anything in my name, and I will do it.**
John 14:12-14

Therefore, brothers, since we have **confidence to enter the Most Holy Place** by the blood of Jesus, by a new and living way opened for us through the curtain, that is, his body, and since we have a great priest over the house of God, **let us draw near to God with a sincere heart in full assurance** of faith, having our hearts sprinkled to cleanse us from a guilty conscience and having our bodies washed with pure water.
Hebrews 10:19-22

This is my command: **Love each other.**
John 15:17

THE KINGDOM PERSPECTIVE

As we come to the Bible equipped with the insights of God's Kingdom, we are able to recognize when a passage is speaking of God's Kingship and our responsibility to represent him as King. Throughout this book, we have seen that the themes of king, authority and power are the principal ways to understand this foundational concept. Let's look at some passages that reveal Kingdom and the key words that cluster around it:

 KING – reigning – ruling – splendor – majesty – throne – other regal references

Lift up your heads, O you gates;
be lifted up, you ancient doors,
that the **King of glory** may come in.
Psalms 24:7 (the whole Psalm)

which God will bring about in his own time—God, the blessed and only **Ruler, the King of kings and Lord of lords**, who alone is immortal and who lives in unapproachable light, whom no one has seen or can see. To him be honor and might forever. Amen.
1 Timothy 6:15-16

The Lord **reigns**, he is **robed in majesty**;
the Lord is **robed in majesty**
and is armed with strength.
The world is firmly established;
it cannot be moved.

241

Your **throne** was established long ago;
you are **from all eternity**.
Psalms 93:1-2

Now let's look at some key words and passages that reveal the Kingdom authority given to Jesus and to us, by which we act on God's behalf:

AUTHORITY – go (commission) – send (mission) – task

Then Jesus came to them and said, "**All authority** in heaven and on earth has been given to me.
Matthew 28:18

I have given you **authority** to trample on snakes and scorpions and to overcome all the power of the enemy; nothing will harm you.
Luke 10:19

He said to them, "**Go** into all the world and preach the good news to all creation.
Mark 16:15

Again Jesus said, "Peace be with you! As the Father has sent me, **I am sending you**."
John 20:21

The third big theme within the Kingdom is power, whether seen in astonishing signs and miracles or in less obvious supernatural ways, such as the power to forgive. Let's look at just a small selection of verses that reveal power in the Bible. Here are a few key words to look out for:

I am going to send you what my Father has promised; but stay in the city until you have been **clothed with power from on high**."
Luke 24:49

God did **extraordinary miracles** through Paul, so that even handkerchiefs and aprons that had touched him were taken to the sick, and their illnesses were cured and the evil spirits left them.
Acts 19:11-12

At that time **the sign** of the Son of Man will appear in the sky, and all the nations of the earth will mourn. They will see the Son of Man coming on the clouds of the sky, **with power** and great glory.
Matthew 24:30

Whoever believes and is baptized will be saved, but whoever does not believe will be condemned. And these **signs** will accompany those who believe: In my name they will drive out demons; they will speak in new tongues; they will pick up snakes with their hands; and when they drink deadly poison, it will not hurt them at all; they will place their hands on sick people, and they will get well."
Mark 16:16-18

If you forgive anyone his sins, **they are forgiven; if you do not forgive** them, **they are not forgiven**."
John 20:23

As well as the three key concepts of king, authority and power, other words and ideas expand our understanding of Kingdom activity, either by confirming God's capacity to rule from the heavenly realms, expressing the certainty that Jesus will return or emphasizing our responsibility to act on his behalf. Let's look first at some words that refer to God's heavenly place:

The Lord is in his holy temple;
> the Lord is on **his heavenly** throne.
> He observes the sons of men;
> his eyes examine them.

Psalms 11:4

The Lord looks down from **heaven**
> on the sons of men
> to see if there are any who understand,
> any who seek God.

Psalms 14:2

From **heaven** you pronounced judgment,
> and the land feared and was quiet-

Psalms 76:8

Next we should look at words that refer to the Kingdom that is yet to come in all its fullness. We are assured that Jesus will return as our King and that his people are to eagerly await that day. Some key words referring to the coming Kingdom are the following:

Coming Kingdom – glory – Jesus returning – judgment

I saw the Holy City, the new Jerusalem, **coming down out of heaven** from God, prepared as a bride beautifully dressed for her husband.
Revelation 21:2

At that time men will see **the Son of Man coming in clouds with great power and glory**. And he will send his angels and gather his elect from the four winds, from the ends of the earth to the ends of the heavens.
Mark 13:26-27

Then I saw a great white throne and him who was seated on it. Earth and sky fled from his presence, and there was no place for them . . . The dead were judged according to what they had done as recorded in the books.
Revelation 20:11-13

Behold, **I am coming soon!** My reward is with me, and I will give to everyone according to what he has done. I am the Alpha and the Omega, the First and the Last, the Beginning and the End.
Revelation 22:12-13

The Bible speaks of many kinds of battles. A key Kingdom perspective is that Christians are called to arm themselves to fight for the extension of God's Kingdom. Persecution will occur, but Jesus' ultimate victory is assured. Let's look at some passages where we might see some of those ideas:

**Warfare – battle – struggle – victory – weapons – armor
– taking frontiers – suffering – persecution**

All those gathered here will know that it is not by sword or spear that the Lord saves; for **the battle is the Lord's**, and he will give all of you into our hands.
1 Samuel 17:47

"Where, O death, is your victory?
    Where, O death, is your sting?" The sting of death is sin, and the power of sin is the law. But thanks be to God! **He gives us the victory** through our Lord Jesus Christ
1 Corinthians 15:55-57

Finally, **be strong** in the Lord and in his mighty power. Put on the **full armor of God** so that you can **take your stand** against the devil's schemes. For our **struggle** is not against flesh and blood, but against the rulers, against the authorities, against the powers of this dark world and against the **spiritual forces** of evil in the heavenly realms. Therefore put on the **full armor of God**, so that when the day of evil comes, you may be able to **stand your ground**, and after you have done everything, to **stand**. Ephesians 6:10-13 (read on to verse 18)

From the days of John the Baptist until now, the kingdom of heaven has been **forcefully advancing**, and **forceful men lay hold** of it.
Matthew 11:12

Who shall separate us from the love of Christ? Shall **trouble or hardship or persecution or famine or nakedness or danger or sword**? As it is written:

"For your sake **we face death** all day long;
we are considered as sheep to be slaughtered." No, in all these things we are **more than conquerors** through him who loved us. For I am convinced that neither death nor life, neither angels nor demons, neither the present nor the future, nor any powers, neither height nor depth, nor anything else in all creation, will be able to separate us from the love of God that is in Christ Jesus our Lord.
Romans 8:35-39

SOME FINAL THOUGHTS ON INTERPRETING THE BIBLE

Now that you can identify the themes of Covenant and Kingdom in any Bible passage or story, you can ask God the Holy Spirit to reveal his Word more fully to you. For instance; if a verse or passage is primarily about Covenant, then you might consider how this Scripture reveals the ways in which your Father in Heaven loves you. You will be able to reflect on your identity as a child of God and your response to knowing this. If it seems to be a Kingdom passage, you will no doubt be learning what it means for your Father God to also be the King of the Universe. You will be able to reflect on how his authority is supposed to work through you as you face your common enemies and what expression of his power is needed to do this. You are now ready to read the Bible from a fresh perspective. You will need to trust in the Holy Spirit - the author of the Word - and other believers with whom you can seek to understand the Scriptures. But be confident! You do not need a 'mediator' or an 'expert' - the Holy Spirit working through the people of God is enough.

In defining the main themes of the Bible as Covenant and Kingdom, I am not suggesting for one moment that you should not still study the Word from the point of view of author, place, date and purpose along with other scholarly insights. It is still important to ask ourselves who wrote the text and what was its original purpose. It is also important to remember that, as you study, the Bible stands over you and not you over it. It is God's Word.

Of course, those used by God to write down the Scriptures left their personal mark, but the illumination is from God alone. Each of the books of the Bible is like a different stained-glass window; the author may provide hue and structure, but the light coming through the window is the Lord himself. The Bible is the revealed Word of God.

"And we have the word of the prophets made more certain, and you will do well to pay attention to it, as to a light shining in a dark place, until the day dawns and the morning star rises in your hearts. Above all, you must understand that no prophecy of Scripture came about by the prophet's own interpretation." (2 Peter 1:19-21)

"All Scripture is God-breathed and is useful for teaching, rebuking, correcting and training in righteousness, so that the man of God may be thoroughly equipped for every good work." (2 Timothy 3:16-17)

The Bible has changed individuals and whole nations. Having access to the meaning of Scripture is a life-transforming adventure. As you search the Scriptures, seeing the themes of Covenant and Kingdom, I trust that you will find the extraordinary riches that God has stored for you.

Conclusion

*A*t the outset of our journey, we recognized that, although Scripture can be approached from the details or the overview of the text, the fundamental meaning of the Bible is found somewhere between the two.

The Bible is about human beings relating to God and to one another.

Detailed analysis may help us on occasion, and the biggest picture will help us maintain perspective. However, the Bible is essentially about God, our loving Father, inviting us to know him in the most intimate of relationships. It is about discovering that this God whom we call "Daddy" is also the King of the universe, who calls us to represent him in the world.

We will always wrestle with a sense of inadequacy when faced with this task, but this, surrendered into the hands of a loving Father, becomes the context through which his life and power flow. It is in weakness that God's power is made perfect.

The Bible is the most important book you will ever read. As you seek to plumb its depths, like many before, you will discover unfathomable riches of love and inexpressible joy. My prayer for you as we conclude this journey is that this study has emboldened you to traverse this landscape many more times. I trust that as you become more familiar with its highs and lows, breadth and depth, you will find yourself drawing nearer to the one who caused it to be written, the one whom we know as Father and King.

To read additional books by Mike Breen and the 3DM team, here are two more books we highly recommend. You can find them at www.weare3DM.com

Building a Discipling Culture

We do not have a leadership problem in the church, nor do we have a church growth problem. We have a discipleship problem. If we make disciples like Jesus did, we will have more leaders than we know what to do with and a missional movement the likes of which we have never seen. The isue is that we don't know how to make disciples, which was the last and most important thing Jesus asked us to do. *Building a Discipling Culture* is a practical guide showing you a way to do this.

Launching Missional Communities: A Field Guide

This is a book about where Missional Communities came from, how they developed and how your community can begin launching Missional Communities, using them to see people who don't know Jesus begin the journey of discipleship. It is a practical, insiders look, giving you the tools to make MCs come alive in your church. If you want to know *how* to launch, sustain, disciple people and multiply Missional Communities, this book is for you.

Now available on Kindle and iPad.

THE GOURMET
VEGETARIAN
SLOW COOKER

THE GOURMET
VEGETARIAN
SLOW COOKER

Simple *and* Sophisticated Meals *from* around *the* World

Lynn Alley

PHOTOGRAPHY BY

Leo Gong

TEN SPEED PRESS
Berkeley

Published in the United States by Ten Speed Press, an imprint of the
Crown Publishing Group, a division of Random House, Inc., New York.
www.crownpublishing.com
www.tenspeed.com

Ten Speed Press and the Ten Speed Press colophon are registered
trademarks of Random House, Inc.

Library of Congress Cataloging-in-Publication Data
Alley, Lynn.
  The gourmet vegetarian slow cooker : simple and sophisticated meals
from around the world / Lynn Alley ; photography by Leo Gong. — 1st ed.
      p. cm.
  Includes index.
  Summary: "A vegetarian approach to the slow-cooker phenomenon,
from the author of the best-selling Gourmet Slow Cooker series,
featuring innovative and time-saving meatless recipes from Indian,
Mexican and Southwestern, Asian, Italian, French, Greek, and Middle
Eastern cuisine"—Provided by publisher.
  1. Electric cookery, Slow. 2. Vegetarian cookery. I. Title.
  TX827.A436 2010
  641.5'636—dc22
                            2009034719

ISBN 978-1-58008-074-3

Printed in China

Cover design by Chloe Rawlins based on an original design
by Catherine Jacobes
Text design by Catherine Jacobes
Production by Chloe Rawlins
Food styling by Karen Shinto
Prop styling by Christine Wolheim

10 9 8 7 6 5 4 3 2 1

First Edition

To M., as always, with love and gratitude.

CONTENTS

Acknowledgments

Many streams of thought, many recipes, many meals, and many people converge within the pages of a book.

So acknowledging everyone is a daunting thought. Let me start where I can and wend my way along until I've covered those who seem to have played a most important role in the book.

To begin with, let me send warm thank yous out to Aunt Sarah and Aunt Mae, my mother's aunts, who showed me how wonderful vegetables straight from the garden could be. To France, spiritual home to good cooks everywhere, where at one time visitors would be hard-pressed to find a bad meal, and weekly markets were a joy to behold.

To some of the chefs and authors who have inspired me: India-born chefs Neela Paniz and Suvir Saran for their dedication to the cooking of their homeland. To Laurel Robertson for lighting the way and inspiring so many of my generation to kick the meat habit back in the '70s. To Alice Waters for skillfully drawing my attention to the excitement of vegetables. To Deborah Madison for her pioneering role in elevating vegetarian cooking to an art form. To Julia Child for being the light that she was in the world, both personally and professionally.

To my editors at Ten Speed, Melissa Moore and Dawn Yanagihara, for their guidance and hard work. To Phil Wood, now "publisher emeritus" at Ten Speed, for always supporting my manuscripts and encouraging my work. To the very kind Aaron Wehner, who has taken over the helm at Ten Speed, one of the few publishers willing to work well and directly with their authors. To Kristin Casemore, Ten Speed's hardworking cookbook publicist. To Chloe Rawlins, Leo Gong, and Karen Shinto for creating such a lovely book.

On the very practical side, I'd like to thank Valerie Gleason of the EdgeCraft Corporation for making the most wonderful knife sharpener available to the home cook. To Melissa Palmer at the All-Clad Corporation.

To Chibi, Jai, and the many animal friends who have provided unconditional love, warmth, support, friendship, and grounding. They all deserve better than being eaten.

To my dear friend Kathy Fleming, of Accomplishment Coaching, the world's clearest and most astute friend and coach.

To Beth Hensperger, an inspired cook and a hardworking author, who has taught me some invaluable lessons.

To my mom, Margaret Zink, for being a good friend and helper.

Introduction

As I wrote in the introduction to *The Gourmet Slow Cooker*, my first experiments with a slow cooker involved beans.

I was living in a mobile home on a farm in Davis, California, for several months, and the only equipment in the old kitchen was a vintage 1970s slow cooker and a very clunky, battle-scarred frying pan. The drive in to town was more than just the hop down the road I was used to at home, so I tried to buy up at the beginning of the week and keep it really simple.

The solution to the problem seemed to be beans. I went to the Davis Co-op and bought as many different kinds of beans as they had. Each day, I'd put a different kind of bean on to cook in the slow cooker. When the beans were tender, I'd add some good salt and choose an herb or two from the small herb garden outside the double-wide. A dash of olive oil gave my beans a bit of staying power.

And that was how I learned to appreciate the fact that not all beans taste the same. And not all beans have the same color or texture, for that matter.

This was a terrific experiment for me. It enabled me to experience something that country folk throughout the world have long known: how to take what you've got in the back forty and turn it into something that will keep you happy and well nourished.

In Italy, such cooking has been dubbed *la cucina povera*, roughly translated as "the cooking of the poor," or, more graciously, "country cooking." It doesn't entail using exotic and expensive ingredients from around the world. It involves the artful combining and preparing of what is at hand.

Examples abound throughout this book. Think of the simple Cracked Wheat Berries with Honey and Ricotta breakfast, or the Risotto with Lentils from the Italian chapter. Or the French Alpine Cheese, Tomato, and Onion Soup which utilizes summer tomatoes, onions, bread, and cheese from France's alpine regions. Or the Scalloped Potatoes Auvergnats, which calls for potatoes and blue cheese made in the central French region of Auvergne. Or the Baby Limas with Spinach of the Greek chapter. Or the Armenian Apricot Soup, which juxtaposes apricots from the region of their birth with the humble lentil.

Although I am a food and wine writer, and have partaken of many very elegant meals prepared by professional kitchen artists and craftspeople, I admit that some of my favorite meals have been the simplest. Fried okra, just picked from a friend's garden and piping hot on a paper towel. Warm, fresh-picked tomatoes that have never seen the inside of the refrigerator, dusted with a pinch of salt. Bread fresh from a Spanish oven with a cooling gazpacho of tomatoes, cucumbers, and onions.

Those wonderful slow-cooked beans, too, remain in my heart and in my pantry. (Nowadays, I often slow-cook a pot full of beans, salt them, then freeze them in individual portions so that I have something on hand either to eat unembellished or to use as a base for a soup, stew, or salad when the need arises.)

It is my hope that the recipes in this book will honor the traditions of those people who have used what they had in their kitchens, pantries, and gardens in countries around the world.

Some of the dishes (such as the Italian and French recipes) come from cultures where "bare bones basic" works. Some (like the Indian and Mexican recipes) come from cultures that have traditionally drawn upon a more complex mélange of ingredients and cooking techniques.

All the dishes, however, are vegetable-based and reflective of the cultures from which they are drawn, and hence timely for the modern American kitchen, in terms of both health interests and economic considerations, in a world where many of us are realizing that we can live well and happily on a lot less than what we've been conditioned to believe.

Most important, recipes without meat make a statement of compassion for the animals cruelly confined to factory farms throughout the world. Whether or not we consumers choose to see and acknowledge their suffering, it exists and we can choose to be a party to it or not through our food choices.

Cooking Times

You will find this book contains a mélange of dishes inspired by cultures around the world and a variety of cooking times. Some of the dishes require relatively short periods of cooking (2 to 3 hours or so). These dishes have generally been chosen because they highlight something the slow cooker does particularly well, such as taking the tedious stirring out of making risotto or polenta, or baking a successful custard over a longer period of time than is required in the oven. Bread puddings turn out particularly well in a slow cooker. And melting chocolate, like making a fondue, can be done especially well with the gentle, controlled heat provided by a slow cooker.

Other dishes call for a moderate period of cooking, anywhere from 4 to 6 hours. These are dishes that are either based on legumes, like lentils, that do not require extensive cooking, or sturdier vegetables (such as carrots, potatoes, and winter squashes) that can actually stand up to and be improved by moderate cooking times.

And lastly, there are recipes, generally based on grains or beans, that are at their best when subjected to a nice, long, juicy slow cook.

Unless otherwise stated, all the recipes in this book were tested in a 5-quart slow cooker. (I keep a 3-quart slow cooker for making risotto, polenta, and small amounts of anything, and for melting chocolate, but I do nearly everything else in a 5-quart slow cooker. I also keep two 7-quart slow cookers for entertaining, and a couple of very small ones for when I want to cook for just myself.)

This means that the recipes in the book are calculated to "work" at the specified times in a 5- or 6-quart slow cooker. So the first time you try a recipe from this book, you may want to watch it carefully and adjust your cooking times accordingly, especially if you are using a slow cooker of some other size. The cooking time for a 7-quart slow cooker, for instance, may be significantly shorter than for a 5-quart cooker.

Cooking times may also vary according to manufacturer and price. I am a firm believer in using the relatively cheap slow cookers that I buy at Walmart or Home Depot. They are generally very effective. The only real drawback I have found is that often the heating coils in a cheaper slow cooker may heat less evenly than those in the more expensive models.

This uneven heat source may mean that one side will brown more rapidly than the other. And the only time this makes a real difference is if you are baking a cake, which few people except me do in a slow cooker, or making a custard or bread pudding. (My makeshift solution to the problem has been to use very thick oven mitts to lift and turn the slow cooker insert halfway through the cooking period for a more even cooking. This must be done very carefully, if at all, because the insert is likely to be quite hot.)

The more expensive models also often have digital control panels rather than manual. To me, this means one more thing that could go wrong if the digital panel goes on the fritz. I prefer the manual controls found on most of the cheaper models.

The more expensive models may have more bells and whistles, such as a classy-looking gourmet "finish," or the ability to program the cooker to turn off after a certain number of hours. If this kind of stuff is important to you, then by all means, invest in the bells and whistles.

All-Clad has a lovely, relatively expensive cooker that offers a cast-aluminum insert, rather than the conventional porcelain, that can go straight from the stove top into the slow cooker. This innovation saves on cleanup when you are browning ingredients before slow-cooking them.

And lastly, cooking times may vary in accordance with different types of ingredients. Not all potatoes, for instance, cook at the same rate. New potatoes tend to be waxy and have a firm texture that holds up under longer cooking periods, while tiny white rose potatoes or russets cut into cubes can be cooked in a matter of a couple of hours. "Old" beans take longer to cook than relatively recently harvested beans.

Ingredients and Resources

BEANS

Each type of bean has a unique texture and flavor, many of which I discovered during my first forays with a slow cooker years ago. It's no wonder that some form of bean dish is found in nearly every culture on earth. Beans have provided protein and energy for human health, life, and growth—especially when combined with grains—for thousands of years. And beans were among the first offerings to the gods and goddesses after the harvest.

The liquid left from cooking beans, when not served with them, is a bonus that can enliven soups and other dishes. Large white beans, for instance, leave lots of starch in their cooking broth, making the thick, gelatinous liquid almost perfect for thickening vegetable soups and stews.

Slow-cooked beans taste great, and the long, slow cook often yields an almost creamy product that absorbs the flavors of herbs, spices, fats, and aromatic vegetables added to the pot.

Dried beans should ideally be cooked and eaten within a year of harvest, but most of the time we as consumers have no idea about the condition of our beans. So here are a couple tips for buying beans.

- Look for a store or source that has a rapid turnover of beans. They are more likely to be selling recently harvested beans than stores where the beans have been sitting on the shelf for eons.

- The appearance of the beans can give you some clues as to how long they've been stored. Beans that are split, cracked, or chipped have probably been around for longer than we would like.

Remember that the condition and length of storage of the beans may affect cooking times. Occasionally, I will hear a cook complain about cooking beans for as long as 14 hours, only to find skins that still remain tough and inedible. "Fresh" dried beans will always cook within a reasonable amount of time.

OLIVE OIL

Some olive oil is suitable for cooking, while some is more suitable for what chefs call "finishing" a dish. The less expensive olive oils, usually found in large quantities at a grocery store, are often suitable for cooking purposes. You can use them to brown onions or sauté vegetables. But the more expensive extra virgin olive oils are best when not subjected to the high heat of cooking, and are instead drizzled over a dish or stirred in at the last minute.

SALT

Most of us grew up thinking that salt is salt, but there can be great variations in flavor, texture, and even color depending on where the salt came from, how it was formed, and what's in it.

I rarely use conventional "table salt" in my cooking anymore (with the exception that I still use salt from a box for basic, large-scale cooking needs, such as soups and stews). This is because I have found that the "good" salt called for in my recipes has so much more to offer in terms of flavor and often texture than does good old Morton's. A sprinkling of my favorite gray sea salt, for instance, is often all it takes to elevate a poached egg on toast to something very special.

For this reason, you will find my recipes call for "salt to taste" rather than specific amounts of salt. If you are using conventional table salt, for instance, you should know that it is considered to be twice as potent by volume as kosher or large-grained specialty salt. So let your taste be your guide when it comes to salting your creations.

Most specialty salts are large-grained and require some crushing before you can sprinkle them on your food. To this end, many stores sell special salt mills, which are like pepper mills, only designed for salt. Trouble is, many specialty salts are somewhat moist, and this moisture can gum up the works of a salt mill, even those made for specialty salts. So I have taken to grinding salt crystals by hand in a small Japanese *suribachi* (a sort of Japanese mortar with a ridged inner surface and wooden pestle) purchased at Sur La Table (www.surlatable.com). I have one for grinding salt and one for grinding other spices.

Sea Star Sea Salt is my delicious all-purpose standby. Sea Star (www.seastarseasalt.com) is owned by chef Holly Peterson, who teaches food and wine dynamics at the Culinary Institute of America in Napa Valley. Holly sources her salt from Brittany, where it is farmed in the traditional manner. I have a handmade ceramic seashell that sits on a shelf above my kitchen stove and holds my salt stash. Next to it stands the little *suribachi* for grinding. It takes just a few minutes to smoosh up a batch of salt, but it makes all the difference in the world.

Another "trick" I like to use is adding smoked salt for a smoky flavor to a vegetable dish that might ordinarily get its flavor from a smoked meat such as sausage, ham, or bacon. (See the Smoky Potage Saint-Germain recipe on page 79.)

Playing around with and learning about this basic ingredient is a lot of fun, and although salts are not inexpensive by grocery store standards, a little bit can do a great deal to make an inexpensive meal taste like "the Ritz."

Here are a few sources where you can learn a bit and order salt:

www.napastyle.com

www.saltworks.us

www.salttraders.com

www.seastarseasalt.com

www.atthemeadow.com

SPICES

Although most of the herbs I use come fresh from my garden, spices (usually the seeds or bark of a plant rather than the leaves) are not so easily grown at home. My favorite source for most spices is Penzeys Spices (www.penzeys.com). I order from them online regularly. They source high-quality spices and have a large and rapid turnover offered at reasonable prices. Sit back, thumb through the online catalog, and go shopping right from your armchair!

I should also note that I generally buy spices whole so that I can grind them fresh just before using. Just as freshly ground pepper is more pungent and aromatic than preground pepper that has been sitting on the shelf for who-knows-how-long, spices, too, have more to offer if they are ground just before using. In addition, grinding your own spices means that you have more control over the texture of the finished product. Sometimes I like my spices ground to a fine powder, much like how they would come out of a jar. Other times, I like them to retain some texture, especially in dishes where I want to convey a very "rustic" feel. For this reason, I have both an electric coffee grinder that is used only for spices and a couple of small Japanese *suribachi* that I use for crushing spices. (See further discussion and sources, page 10.)

USEFUL EQUIPMENT

Electric Coffee Mill

An electric coffee mill that is dedicated to grinding spices is a very useful item to have on hand. Instead of buying your spices ground, you will find fresher and more interesting flavors if you buy whole spices and grind them yourself just before using. It takes only a few minutes more, but makes a great deal of difference in your cooking.

Immersion Blender

A handheld immersion blender looks like a long stick with a handle at one end and a tiny metal detector at the other end. It makes life with a slow cooker a breeze. Gone are the days when you have to transfer large batches of stuff by hand from the crock to a blender, blend them, then return them to the pot, leaving soup slopped all over the countertop and your clothes. You just plunge the head of the immersion blender into your beans (or what-ever), turn on the blender, and purée your ingredients within minutes. It is important to keep the head of the blender *under* the surface of your food. If the head rises above the surface, stuff will fly everywhere—all over you and your kitchen.

Mortar and Pestle

I have many different sizes of mortars and pestles and have collected them for years. (The most beautiful one I have ever used was in France. It was an antique and belonged to the proprietor of a French farmhouse where I had gone to teach cooking classes. It must have weighed at least 40 pounds and was large enough to make a quart of mayonnaise in. If I thought I could have carried it home on the plane, I would have tried to buy it!) I find them most useful for grinding spices by hand, liberating flavors and aromas while retaining some interesting textures. I strongly recommend that if you really love to cook, you look around for some interesting examples and try them.

India

Spiced Basmati Rice Breakfast Cereal 15

Curried Chickpeas with Fresh Ginger and Cilantro 17

Creamy Dal 18

Dal with Ground Cinnamon, Cloves, Cardamom, and Cumin 19

Stuffed Peppers with Yogurt Sauce 20

Waari Muth 21

Potatoes and Carrots in Coconut Curry 22

Mogul Eggplant 23

Minted Potato and Chickpea Curry 25

Spicy Indian Lentil and Tomato Soup 26

Tomato, Rice, and Coriander Soup 27

What could be more perfect for a book on vegetarian slow cooking than a chapter on India, a country where the majority of people are vegetarian?

In northern India, you may find meat eaters, Muslims and sometimes Sikhs, whose roots and traditions come from the meat-eating cultures to the west of India. This is the home of lamb, beef, and chicken curries. It is interesting to note that in the United States, just as Greek restaurants offer a somewhat limited picture of true Greek cuisine, most "Indian" restaurants are run by immigrants from northern India, often Sikhs, and their culinary traditions include plenty of meat dishes. For the most part, however, the vast majority of Indians are Hindus and do not consume flesh. As a result, the Indian subcontinent is a vegetarian's dream come true in terms of variety, color, and flavor.

Perhaps the most distinguishing hallmark of Indian cuisine is the use of a wide array of spices. Traditionally, each cook mixes her own spices. And traditionally, there is no such thing as "curry powder" among Indian cooks. There are just custom spice blends. (Curry powder is considered to be an invention of the British, who wanted an easy way to approximate the complex flavors found in Indian dishes.)

True, there are characteristic spices that appear over and over again in Indian dishes, but the proportions and specific blends are very much an individual or regional thing. For this reason, most of the dishes in this chapter call for spices to be blended by the cook either in a mortar and pestle or in an electric coffee mill. If you plan to grind spices in a coffee mill, I suggest keeping one mill for your coffee and one just for spices so that the flavors don't mix with one another. You can buy mortars and pestles from any number of different sources, but India-born chef Suvir Saran has designed one specifically to grind Indian spices by hand easily (http://americanmasala.com/collection/main.html).

WINES WITH INDIAN FOOD

India does not have a long-standing tradition of winemaking and wine drinking, probably due to the pervasive Muslim influence in the country. Typically, affluent Indians would offer cocktails before dinner (à la British raj), then drink water or beer with the meal itself. Things are now changing as affluent Indians adopt Western ways, including the taste for wine. There is even a small but growing government-supported wine industry in India.

The complexity of flavors and spices found in Indian cuisine makes it perhaps the most difficult of Asian cuisines for matching with wines. In general, I like aromatic whites such as Gewürztraminer, Riesling, Pinot Blanc and Gris, Müller-Thurgau, Albariño, and Chenin Blanc. Off-dry whites may also work well. Prosecco and other sparkling wines are often great partners for Indian food.

Rosé wines can also work with Indian dishes. Appropriate reds are a bit more difficult to find, and you will want to avoid anything with a lot of tannins, because tannins tend to intensify heat. You'd probably be better off sticking with the lighter, fruitier, younger reds such as French or Oregon Pinot Noir, Grenache, and Beaujolais.

SPICED BASMATI RICE BREAKFAST CEREAL

Most Americans would consider eating oatmeal for breakfast, but for the vast majority of Asians, rice is the breakfast food of choice. Here is a distinctively Indian variation on the Asian breakfast theme that can be cooked while you sleep and be ready for breakfast when you wake up.

Place the rice and water in the slow cooker insert, cover, and cook on low overnight, about 8 hours.

In the morning, grind the cinnamon, cardamom pods, and nutmeg to a powder in an electric coffee mill or a mortar and pestle.

Add the currants and spices to the rice and stir in 15 minutes before serving.

Divide the rice among 4 cereal bowls and pour ½ cup milk on top of each serving.

Sprinkle each bowl with the toasted coconut and nuts. Drizzle with honey.

SUGGESTED BEVERAGE: A cup of hot spiced chai would be a perfect complement.

1½ cups organic brown basmati rice, rinsed well

3½ cups water or soymilk

1½ sticks cinnamon

2 green cardamom pods

½ teaspoon nutmeg, freshly grated if possible

½ cup currants or raisins

2 cups milk, heavy cream, rice milk, or soymilk

3 tablespoons coconut, flaked and toasted

½ cup walnuts or almonds, coarsely chopped and toasted

Honey, for drizzling (optional)

CURRIED CHICKPEAS WITH FRESH GINGER AND CILANTRO

~ Serves 6 to 8 ~

As anyone familiar with Indian food knows, chickpeas are one of the most common types of legumes found on Indian tables. In this popular recipe, the spices and fresh ingredients are added at the very end of the cooking time to preserve optimum flavor and freshness. Regulate the heat by the amount of cayenne you use.

Thoroughly rinse the chickpeas and place them in the slow cooker insert along with the water. Cover and cook on low for 6 to 8 hours, until the chickpeas are tender.

In a large sauté pan, brown the onion in the sesame oil until dark brown in color, about 15 minutes.

Combine the cumin seeds, peppercorns, cloves, cardamom, chile powder, ginger, turmeric, garam masala, and cayenne in an electric coffee mill or a mortar and pestle and grind to a coarse powder.

Add the coarsely ground spices to the onion and continue to cook for another 5 minutes, then add the onion and spices to the cooked chickpeas. Recover and continue cooking for another 30 to 60 minutes.

Using a handheld immersion blender, purée some of the chickpeas in the insert to thicken the mixture.

Add salt to taste, then stir in the lemon juice. Ladle into bowls, add a dollop of yogurt, and garnish with the chile slices and cilantro leaves.

SUGGESTED BEVERAGE: I would enjoy a light- to medium-bodied white wine, such as a Pinot Gris, Pinot Blanc, or Spanish Rueda or Albariño.

2 cups dried chickpeas

6 cups water

1 red onion, finely chopped

$^1/_4$ cup sesame or vegetable oil

1 tablespoon cumin seeds

$^1/_4$ teaspoon black peppercorns

4 whole cloves

4 green cardamom pods

$1^1/_2$ teaspoons pure chile powder

$1^1/_2$-inch piece fresh ginger, peeled and minced

$^1/_2$ teaspoon ground turmeric

1 teaspoon garam masala

$^1/_2$ teaspoon cayenne (optional)

Salt to taste

Juice of 1 lemon

Yogurt, for serving (optional)

3 fresh serrano chiles, seeded, deveined, and cut into julienne, for garnish

A few fresh cilantro leaves, for garnish

CREAMY DAL

⮞ Serves 4 ⮜

In southern India, dal is traditionally served thin like a soup, then ladled over rice. But in northern India, where dal is traditionally scooped up with roti or served on rice, it is usually made thicker, almost the consistency of a porridge. I've suggested 4 to 5 cups of water so that you can make it thin like the southern Indians or thicker like a northern "stew." In addition, you can vary the heat intensity in the finished dish by the number of serrano chiles you add. Keep in mind that one serrano will add heat to the whole dish.

Thoroughly rinse the lentils, being sure to remove any small stones or dirt, then place them in the slow cooker insert and add the water (the amount will depend on the consistency you desire).

Cover and cook on low for 4 to 6 hours, until the lentils are tender. While the lentils are cooking, prepare the remaining ingredients.

In a sauté pan, melt the butter and add the chopped onion. Sauté until the onion is medium brown, about 10 minutes. Add the cumin seeds, mustard seeds, ginger, and chiles and continue cooking for another 5 minutes over medium heat. Add the tomato and continue to cook for another 5 minutes.

When the lentils are ready, add the sautéed onion mixture to the pot and stir together gently. Continue cooking just until all ingredients are heated through, 10 to 15 minutes.

Add a pinch of curry powder and salt to taste, then stir in the half-and-half.

Serve hot, garnished with sprigs of cilantro.

SUGGESTED BEVERAGE: Because of the richness of the cream in this dish, I could go with a light- to medium-bodied white wine, a good blanc de blanc (sparkling wine), or even a rosé.

1 cup dried lentils

4 to 5 cups water

1 tablespoon unsalted butter

$1/2$ yellow onion, chopped

$1/4$ teaspoon cumin seeds

$1/4$ teaspoon mustard seeds

$1/2$-inch piece fresh ginger, peeled and grated

1 or 2 serrano chiles, seeded, deveined, and cut into julienne

1 large tomato, chopped

Pinch of curry powder

Salt to taste

$1/2$ cup half-and-half or heavy cream

Several sprigs fresh cilantro, for garnish

DAL WITH GROUND CINNAMON, CLOVES, CARDAMOM, AND CUMIN

⮞ Serves 4 ⮜

Dal can be a soup or stew (depending on how much liquid you use) of dried lentils, vegetables, and seasonings. Traditionally served over rice in much of India, it is a staple of the Indian diet. Millions of variations exist from region to region and cook to cook. Here is just one of many variations. This recipe makes use of the Indian technique of adding some last-minute ingredients for freshness rather than subjecting them to the full cooking time.

Thoroughly rinse the lentils, being sure to remove any small stones or dirt, then place them in the slow cooker insert.

In an electric coffee mill or a mortar and pestle, grind the cinnamon, cloves, cardamom pods, cumin seeds, and turmeric to a fine powder.

Add the spices and water (the amount will depend upon the consistency you desire) to the slow cooker insert, cover, then cook on low for 4 to 6 hours or on high for 2 hours. Add salt to taste.

To make the tempering oil, heat the oil in a sauté pan and sauté the onion until beginning to brown, then add the garlic, ginger, and chile and cook just long enough to soften the chile, about 15 seconds.

Stir half of the tempering oil into the dal along with half of the cilantro and all of the lemon juice.

Ladle the dal into bowls and spoon what remains of the tempering oil over the top of each bowl. Sprinkle with the remaining cilantro and serve.

SUGGESTED BEVERAGE: Again, I would opt for one of those light- to medium-bodied, very chilled white wines, such as a light, French-style Chardonnay, a crisp Albariño, or perhaps a Pinot Blanc.

1 cup dried lentils

1-inch piece cinnamon

3 whole cloves

4 green cardamom pods

1 teaspoon cumin seeds

1/2 teaspoon ground turmeric

4 to 5 cups cold water

Salt to taste

Tempering Oil

2 tablespoons oil or ghee

1 onion, finely chopped

3 cloves garlic, finely chopped

1 tablespoon peeled, minced fresh ginger

1 fresh hot green chile, minced

1/4 cup fresh cilantro leaves

Juice of 1/2 lemon or lime

STUFFED PEPPERS WITH YOGURT SAUCE

Serves 4

Practically every country in the world has a recipe for stuffing peppers: Spain, Greece, Italy, Hungary, and Mexico, to name a few. India is no exception. The following recipe offers a variety of colors, textures, and flavors, with the stuffing being relatively mild and the raita-like sauce offering much of the dish's flavor and texture. For a really stunning presentation, garnish with a sprinkling of fresh pomegranate seeds, Mogul style.

Prepare the peppers by slicing off their tops and removing any seeds and veins from the inside.

To make the stuffing, grind the cumin and coriander seeds coarsely in an electric coffee mill or a mortar and pestle. In a sauté pan, melt the butter and sauté the onion and almonds just until lightly browned, 5 to 7 minutes. Add the ground spices and sauté for another minute. Thoroughly mix in the rice, spinach, and raisins and add salt to taste. The spinach should wilt and cook from the heat of the other ingredients.

Stuff the bell peppers with the rice mixture and place the peppers in the slow cooker insert. Pour in the water and cook on low for 4 hours, or until the peppers are tender when pierced with a fork. While the peppers are cooking, prepare the sauce.

To make the sauce, place the yogurt in a bowl. Grind the cumin and coriander seeds to a coarse powder in an electric coffee mill or a mortar and pestle. Mix them into the yogurt. Using a garlic press, press the garlic into the yogurt and mix in thoroughly.

Half an hour before serving, mix the cucumber, fresh mint, chiles and onion into the yogurt sauce and add salt to taste.

4 red, green, yellow, or purple bell peppers

Stuffing

1 teaspoon cumin seeds

1 teaspoon coriander seeds

1 tablespoon butter

1/2 cup chopped yellow onion

1/2 cup sliced almonds

2 cups cooked basmati rice

6 ounces fresh spinach leaves

1 cup raisins

Salt to taste

1 cup water

Sauce

2 cups plain yogurt

1 teaspoon cumin seeds

1 teaspoon coriander seeds

2 cloves garlic

1/2 cucumber, peeled and chopped

1 teaspoon chopped fresh mint

When the peppers are done, remove each one from the slow cooker insert and place in a pasta bowl (best for catching any juices), then slit it open and pour a generous stream of sauce over the top.

Sprinkle with the chopped cilantro and pomegranate seeds and serve.

SUGGESTED BEVERAGE: How about a glass of Prosecco?

- 1 or 2 fresh serrano chiles, seeded, deveined, and finely chopped
- 1/2 small red onion, finely chopped
- Salt to taste
- 1/4 cup chopped fresh cilantro leaves, for garnish
- 1/4 cup pomegranate seeds (optional)

WAARI MUTH

⤳ Serves 4 to 6 ⤶

When most of us think of Indian food, we think of lentils or chickpeas as the legumes of choice. However, because most Indians are vegetarians, beans form an important protein source in the Indian diet. The array of beans that actually appears on the table in India is far vaster than we imagine. Waari muth is a Kashmiri recipe calling for black beans, similar to the kind of beans found in Mexican, Cuban, and Southwestern dishes. It's a simple dish, yet with the typical seasonings of the Indian subcontinent, and very nourishing. Serve either in a bowl by itself garnished with cilantro, or over rice.

Wash the beans thoroughly, then place them in the slow cooker insert with the water.

Using a mortar and pestle or an electric coffee mill, coarsely grind the fennel seeds, then add to the beans. Stir in the turmeric, ginger, and garam masala. Cover and cook on high for about 8 hours, or until the beans are tender.

Add the pepper flakes and salt to taste, then spoon individual portions into a bowl and top with a sprinkle of cilantro.

SUGGESTED BEVERAGE: I think I'd go for the "fire and ice" principle on this one: a crisp, chilled, medium-bodied aromatic white wine, such as a Gewürztraminer or an Albariño.

- 2 cups dried black beans
- 6 cups water
- 2 teaspoons fennel seeds
- 2 teaspoons turmeric powder
- 1 teaspoon ground ginger
- 1 teaspoon garam masala or curry powder
- 1/2 teaspoon red pepper flakes
- Salt to taste
- 1/4 cup coarsely chopped fresh cilantro leaves, for garnish

POTATOES AND CARROTS IN COCONUT CURRY

~ Serves 4 to 6 ~

This is one of my all-time favorites in my repertoire of Indian dishes. The addition of coconut milk identifies it as a typical southern Indian dish, where coconut milk is a common ingredient. (Coconut milk is rarely found in the cooking of the colder, mountainous climate of northern India, where coconuts don't grow.) It can be made in about 5 hours and served hot, warm, or at room temperature, like a traditional potato salad. Cooking times will vary according to the type and size of potatoes you use.

Wash the potatoes thoroughly, then place them in the slow cooker insert and add the water. Cover and cook on low for 4 to 5 hours, or until the potatoes are fairly tender. (Cooking time will depend on the size and the type of potato you use. Tiny red potatoes, for instance, will probably cook in less than 4 hours, so use a fork to determine doneness. If your potatoes are fairly large, you may wish to cut them carefully into quarters before proceeding with the rest of the recipe.)

In a sauté pan, heat the oil and sauté the onion over medium-high heat until golden brown, about 10 minutes. Add the garlic, cumin seeds, and fennel seeds and continue cooking for another 2 to 3 minutes.

Add the onion, carrots, and curry powder to the potatoes, and carefully stir in the coconut cream. Recover and continue cooking for 1 hour.

Add salt to taste, then spoon the curry into a bowl or onto plates and garnish with the chile slices and cilantro.

Note: Coconut cream is a thicker version of coconut milk. It will say coconut "cream" right on the can. The mouthfeel of the cream is much richer than that of the milk, and as you might imagine, it is also higher in calories. You can substitute coconut milk for the cream in this recipe, but it is soooo good with the cream.

SUGGESTED BEVERAGE: I picture something chilled and white: Gewürztraminer or Pinot Gris, perhaps? Maybe even a citrusy New Zealand Sauvignon Blanc?

3 pounds red potatoes

1 cup water

2 tablespoons vegetable oil

1 onion, finely chopped

2 cloves garlic, coarsely chopped

2 tablespoons cumin seeds

2 teaspoons fennel seeds

1 pound carrots, sliced into rounds

2 tablespoons curry powder

1 can (about 14 ounces) coconut cream (see Note below)

Salt to taste

4 serrano chiles, seeded, deveined, and cut into julienne, for garnish

1/4 cup chopped fresh cilantro leaves, for garnish

MOGUL EGGPLANT

~ Serves 4 ~

Muslims from Persia and Central Asia invaded India from the north and ruled much of the country during the sixteenth to eighteenth centuries. As a culture, they are called "Mogul." They brought with them a period of relative peace and affluence, unifying the native cultures and cuisines of India with those of the Persian Empire. Adding yogurt to a dish is a Mogul touch, as is sealing food with dough in a clay pot and cooking it directly over the coals of a fire. The following recipe is a typical Mogul-style dish, cooked in your slow cooker instead of over a fire. Add the yogurt at the last minute to avoid curdling. (Note: If you cut the eggplant into cubes, the dish makes an excellent sauce for pasta.) Serve with basmati rice.

In an electric coffee mill or a mortar and pestle, grind the cumin seeds and cloves to a fine powder. Add the ginger and garlic and continue to grind until a powdery paste forms.

Place the eggplant slices in the slow cooker insert.

In a bowl, combine the ground spice—ginger mixture, garam masala, turmeric, paprika, cayenne, and crushed tomatoes, mix thoroughly, and then pour the spiced sauce over the eggplant slices, spreading it evenly over them.

Cover and cook on low for about 4 hours, or until the eggplant is tender and cuts easily. When the eggplant is done, turn off the heat, remove the lid, and allow the dish to sit for 10 minutes. Carefully mix in the yogurt and add salt to taste

Serve hot, sprinkling the fresh cilantro and chiles over the top of the eggplant.

SUGGESTED BEVERAGE: Once again I revert to my chilled, light- to medium-bodied white wine on this one. A rosé, I think, would also work nicely. Even a fruity, young red wine might go well.

1 teaspoon cumin seeds

6 whole cloves

1 tablespoon peeled, minced fresh ginger

2 teaspoons minced garlic

2 small eggplants, peeled and sliced into quarters vertically

2 teaspoons garam masala

1 teaspoon ground turmeric

1 tablespoon paprika

1/4 teaspoon cayenne (optional)

1 (28-ounce) can crushed tomatoes

2 cups plain yogurt

Salt to taste

1/4 cup chopped fresh cilantro leaves, for garnish

2 fresh serrano chiles, seeded, deveined, and cut into julienne, for garnish

MINTED POTATO AND CHICKPEA CURRY

~ Serves 4 ~

This potato and chickpea curry, with its coconut milk and sugar, is more characteristic of southern Indian cooking than northern. The chickpeas themselves take a nice, long cook, while the remaining ingredients are added about an hour before serving.

Thoroughly rinse the chickpeas and place them in the slow cooker insert along with the water. Cover and cook on low for 6 to 8 hours, or until the chickpeas are just tender.

Remove the cover and gently stir in the chile powder, turmeric, potato, tomatoes, coconut milk, and sugar. Add salt to taste, replace the cover, and continue cooking for about 1 hour longer, or until the potatoes are tender.

Spoon into bowls and top each serving with 1 tablespoon each of chopped mint and cilantro, and a pinch of chopped jalapeño.

SUGGESTED BEVERAGE: Surprise! Why not try a sparkling Shiraz with this dish?

2 cups dried chickpeas

6 cups water

2 teaspoons pure chile powder

1 teaspoon turmeric

1 russet potato, peeled and diced

2 tomatoes, coarsely chopped

$^1/_2$ cup unsweetened coconut milk or coconut cream

1 to 2 teaspoons palm sugar or brown sugar

Salt to taste

$^1/_4$ cup chopped fresh mint leaves

$^1/_4$ cup chopped fresh cilantro leaves

1 jalapeño chile, seeds and veins removed, finely chopped

Spicy Indian Lentil and Tomato Soup

❧ Serves 4 ❧

One of the beautiful things about traditional Indian cooking is that each cook grinds her own spices, and each dish therefore bears the unique thumbprint of its creator. Freshly ground spices give this simple soup a gourmet touch.

Wash the lentils thoroughly, being sure to remove any small stones or dirt. Place them, along with the water, in the slow cooker insert.

In an electric coffee mill or a mortar and pestle, grind the cumin seeds, coriander seeds, and peppercorns to a coarse powder.

In a bowl, combine the ground spices, turmeric, tamarind concentrate, tomatoes, and garlic; add to the lentils.

Cook, covered, on low for 5 to 6 hours, or until the lentils are quite tender and the flavors have melded.

Add the corn and salt to taste just before serving so that the corn retains its fresh flavor and texture.

To make the tempering oil, heat the ghee in a frying pan, then add the mustard seeds and broken chile and sauté until the seeds begin to pop. Quickly remove from the heat and drizzle a tiny bit over each bowl of soup.

Sprinkle with the fresh cilantro and serve.

SUGGESTED BEVERAGE: Any chilled, aromatic white wine will do nicely here.

1 cup dried lentils

6 cups water

1 teaspoon cumin seeds

1 tablespoon coriander seeds

8 black peppercorns

1 teaspoon ground turmeric

1 teaspoon tamarind concentrate (see Note on pages 51–52)

3 large tomatoes, coarsely chopped

3 cloves garlic, finely minced

Kernels cut from 2 ears fresh corn, or 1 cup frozen corn

Salt to taste

Tempering Oil

2 teaspoons ghee

2 teaspoons black mustard seeds

1 dried red chile, broken into bits

1/4 cup chopped fresh cilantro leaves

TOMATO, RICE, AND CORIANDER SOUP

~ Serves 4 ~

Another delicious Indian soup, similar to the Spicy Indian Lentil and Tomato Soup (page 26), but with rice and a very different blend of spices.

Using the side of a chef's knife, smash together the ginger and garlic, being careful not to cut your fingers.

In an electric coffee mill or a mortar and pestle, grind the cinnamon, cloves, cardamom, peppercorns, and cumin seeds to a coarse powder.

In a skillet, heat the ghee and sauté the onion over medium high heat until brown, about 10 minutes, and then add the garlic, ginger, and spices to the onion. Continue to cook for 2 to 3 minutes more.

Place the onion mixture, carrots, tomatoes, water, and rice in the slow cooker insert. Cover and cook on low for 4 to 6 hours, or until the rice and carrots are thoroughly tender. Stir in the lemon juice and add salt to taste.

Ladle into bowls and garnish with the chopped cilantro and chiles. Add a dollop of yogurt and serve immediately.

SUGGESTED BEVERAGE: A bright, light fruity Pinot Gris would do nicely with this soup.

1-inch piece fresh ginger, peeled and finely minced

3 cloves garlic, finely minced

1 cinnamon stick

4 cloves

6 green cardamom pods

8 black peppercorns

2 teaspoons cumin seeds

1 tablespoon ghee or vegetable oil

1 onion, finely chopped

2/3 cup peeled, sliced carrots

3 tomatoes, coarsely chopped

6 cups water

2 tablespoons brown basmati rice

3 tablespoons fresh lemon juice

Salt to taste

1/4 cup chopped fresh cilantro leaves, for garnish

2 serrano chiles, seeded, deveined, and thinly sliced, for garnish

Yogurt, for serving (optional)

Mexico and the Southwest

What most of us think of as "Mexican" food today includes some fairly simple ingredients: chicken, beef, lots of cheese, tomato sauces, and peppers, cooked in a limited number of ways.

But real Mexican cooking is a skillful blending of ingredients from the Old and New Worlds. The flavors are those used by the indigenous peoples of the Americas—unsweetened chocolate, peppers, potatoes, beans, tomatoes, and native herbs and seasonings—with a rich overlay of ingredients brought originally by Spanish explorers and missionaries: beef, chicken, lamb, goat, dairy products, wine, and wheat, to name a few.

The combination of these ingredients in the hands of Mexican cooks has produced some of the most exciting and complex dishes on the face of the planet.

According to legend, for instance, *mole poblano*, Mexico's national festive dish, was created in the sixteenth century by nuns at the Convent of Santa Rosa in Puebla de los Angeles. The story goes that the archbishop was planning a visit and the nuns had nothing suitably grand to serve him, so guided by divine inspiration, they began chopping and mixing pantry ingredients they had on hand: chiles, chocolate, nuts, day-old bread, and a host of other ingredients.

Whether the legend is true or not, its theme of loving hands combining the ingredients of two very different cultures and peoples into one magnificent creation is accurate.

Many dishes in Mexico—both ancient and modern—were baked in an oven in earthenware *cazuelas* for long periods of time, making dishes of both Mexico and the Southwestern United States (so influenced by Mexico) perfect candidates for adaptation to slow cookers.

WINES WITH MEXICAN FOOD

Matching wines with often complex Mexican flavors can be just about as intimidating as matching wines to complex, often fiery Indian cuisine. Not surprisingly, many of the types of wines that work well with Indian food also work well with Mexican foods.

Dry or off-dry aromatic whites such as Gewürztraminer, Riesling, Pinot Blanc and Gris, Müller-Thurgau, Albariño, and Chenin Blanc can cool the heat of dishes with lots of chiles and spices. As with Indian food, Prosecco, cava, champagne, and other sparkling wines can make refreshing pairings.

In general, I would avoid pairing tannic wines with foods rich in chiles and spices, but you never know. The sweetness of a *mole poblano*, for instance, might render it a good pairing with the right Cab, Nebbiolo, or Garnacha.

Wines from Spain and California might be especially good choices for your Mexican and Southwestern dishes, but you can also draw upon some of the increasingly wonderful wines being made in the Southwestern United States. One of my favorite sparkling wines, for instance, is made by the Gruet family (of Champagne fame) in southwestern New Mexico. It is very good and very reasonably priced. There are also growing fine wine industries in both Arizona (centered around Sonoita) and New Mexico.

Although winemaking in Mexico was suppressed for all but the clergy for two or three hundred years, a modern-day boutique wine industry has blossomed in the Valle de Guadalupe, just an hour and a half south of San Diego in Baja California. If you have an opportunity to taste some of the wines of this region, by all means, take it. A growing number are very good. You can occasionally find Mexican wines in American specialty wine shops, too, especially if you live in the Southwest—or you might just want to take a road trip through Mexican wine country.

MY FAVORITE CHILI

Serves 6 to 8

Chili, a quintessential slow cooker meal, is not a traditional Mexican dish. Rather, it seems to be Southwestern in its inception. It is sort of a combination of the dried beans and chiles so readily available in the Southwest with the wonderful spices brought by Europeans to Mexico. This particular version is generously seasoned with spices and chili powder and has been pieced together by me over the course of a few years. The following recipe makes a big mess o' chili and is best done in a 6- or 7-quart slow cooker.

Thoroughly wash the beans and place them, along with the water, in the slow cooker insert. Grind the allspice, cinnamon, oregano, cumin, aniseed, and coriander seeds in an electric coffee mill or a mortar and pestle and add to the beans. Cover and cook on low for 6 hours, or until the beans are tender.

Add the diced onion, garlic, tomatoes, cocoa powder, and chili powder to the beans and continue cooking for 2 hours.

About half an hour before serving, add the red and green bell pepper and corn kernels to the beans so they retain their crisp, fresh taste and texture.

Ladle into bowls and top each bowl with a dollop of sour cream and a sprinkling of green onion and cilantro.

SUGGESTED BEVERAGE: Although you could also choose fruity red wine to drink with this dish, I would prefer a good Mexican beer.

2 cups dried kidney, pinto, pinquito, or pink beans

6 cups water

6 allspice berries

1 stick cinnamon

$^1/_2$ teaspoon dried Mexican oregano

$^1/_2$ teaspoon cumin seeds

$^1/_4$ teaspoon aniseed

$^1/_2$ teaspoon coriander seeds

$^1/_2$ onion, diced

3 cloves garlic, finely minced

1 (28-ounce) can crushed tomatoes

$^1/_4$ cup unsweetened cocoa powder

1 to 2 tablespoons chili powder

$^1/_4$ cup diced red bell pepper

$^1/_4$ cup diced green bell pepper

$^1/_2$ cup fresh or frozen corn kernels

$^1/_2$ cup sour cream or nonfat yogurt

$^1/_4$ cup thinly sliced green onions, green part only, for garnish

$^1/_2$ cup chopped fresh cilantro leaves, for garnish

Vegetable Amarillo

⌐ Serves 4 ⌐

Amarillo means "yellow" in Spanish, and it is also the name of one of the seven classic moles, or sauces, from Oaxaca, known as "The Land of Seven Moles." Though far from yellow (it's more of a brick red), it can be used as a base for a delicious and very spicy vegetable stew that can stand alone or be served over rice to cut its heat.

To make the sauce, wash the dried chiles well (they are often dusty). Toast them in a frying pan briefly and lightly on each side. Do not allow them to burn or they will become bitter. When they cool, remove their stems, slit them open, and remove the seeds and veins. Tear them into pieces and place them in the slow cooker insert. Cover with the water.

In an electric coffee mill or a mortar and pestle, grind the allspice, cloves, and cumin seeds to a powder, then add to the chiles.

Add the garlic, oregano, oil, raisins, onion, tortilla, and tomatillos. Cover and cook on high for about 1 hour.

Using an immersion blender, blend the mixture as smooth as possible right in the slow cooker insert. Be sure to keep the head of the blender below the surface of the sauce or you will splatter sauce all over the place. (Wear an apron just in case!) The sauce can be made 1 day ahead of time.

Sauce

12 dried guajillo chiles

3 cups water

4 whole allspice berries

4 whole cloves

$1/4$ teaspoon cumin seeds

9 cloves garlic, peeled

1 tablespoon dried Mexican oregano

2 tablespoons oil (sesame has good flavor)

$1/4$ cup raisins

$1/2$ onion, cut in half and lightly charred under the broiler

1 corn tortilla, torn into pieces

3 tomatillos, washed, husked, and quartered

To make the vegetables, add the chayote, potatoes, and butternut squash to the sauce in the slow cooker insert. Recover and cook on low for 3 to 4 hours, or until the potatoes are tender but still hold their shape.

Add the sliced mushrooms, orange juice and zest, and green beans and continue cooking for 30 to 40 minutes, just until the beans are al dente.

Serve topped with crumbled feta and chopped cilantro.

SUGGESTED BEVERAGE: Try a young, fruity red wine with some body, such as a Zinfandel or a Grenache, or even a rosé.

Vegetables

1 large chayote, peeled and cut into 1-inch chunks

1 pound red potatoes, unpeeled and cut into 1-inch chunks

1/2 pound butternut squash, peeled and cut into 1-inch chunks

3 portobello mushrooms, thickly sliced

Juice and zest of 1 orange

6 ounces green beans, trimmed and halved

Garnishes

1/2 pound Mexican queso fresco or feta cheese, crumbled

1/4 cup chopped fresh cilantro leaves

Slow-Cooked Grits with Chile and Cheese

Serves 2 to 4

Grits, a traditional Southern breakfast dish, are often served topped with butter and cheese. They fill hungry bellies and stick to the ribs for many hours. Technically, grits are coarsely ground hominy, and they are white in color, while polenta is ground, dried yellow corn. But in the United States (outside the Deep South), the two are often used interchangeably. It's best if you can find the stone-ground real thing, but if not, you can use the instant grits that are available in nearly every grocery store or mail-order them from a source that specializes in grains, such as Bob's Red Mill in Oregon. I recommend using a 2- to 3-quart slow cooker so that your grits don't dry out overnight.

Place the grits, salt, and water in the slow cooker insert. Cover and cook on low overnight, about 8 hours.

In the morning, simply stir in the chiles, adjust the salt to taste, and stir in half the cheese. Spoon up a bowlful for each person, then top with the remaining cheese.

SUGGESTED BEVERAGE: No wine here, but a good, hearty cup of coffee at breakfast time or a Mexican beer at lunch or dinner.

1 cup grits

$1/2$ teaspoon salt

4 cups water

1 (7-ounce) can diced green chiles

1 cup grated sharp cheddar or smoked gouda (or a combination)

SPAGHETTI SQUASH WITH MEXICAN SPICES

～ Serves 4 ～

The spaghetti squash gets its name from the fact that its insides, when cooked, separate into spaghetti-like strands that can be used in exactly the same way you would use spaghetti. You can either top the strands with Tomato-Mushroom Sauce (page 63) or toss it with your favorite Mexican spices. Choose a squash that will fit in the slow cooker insert. If need be, the squash can be halved to fit, but the cooking time will be shorter.

Wash the spaghetti squash, then place it in the slow cooker insert and add the water. Cover and cook on low for 5 to 6 hours, or until the squash is tender when pierced with a fork. Remove the squash from the slow cooker and allow it to cool slightly while you prepare the spices and butter.

Using an electric coffee mill or a mortar and pestle, crush the cumin seeds, coriander seeds, cloves, cinnamon, and red pepper flakes together. Leave some texture to them rather than powdering them.

Melt the butter in the microwave or on the stove top. Using a garlic press, press the garlic into the butter. Stir in the spices and remove from the heat.

Carefully halve the squash lengthwise (it will give off steam) and remove and discard the seeds. Working over a bowl, scrape out the flesh with a fork, loosening and separating the strands as you remove them from the skin. Toss with the butter and spices and add salt to taste.

To serve, garnish each portion with cilantro and sprinkle with cheese.

SUGGESTED BEVERAGE: I'd like something nice and light with this dish, with a hint of spice to complement the seasonings. A chilled Gewürztraminer or even a Mexican Chenin Blanc would be perfect.

1 spaghetti squash

1 cup water

1 teaspoon cumin seeds

1 teaspoon coriander seeds

4 whole cloves

1 teaspoon ground cinnamon

$1/8$ teaspoon red pepper flakes

4 tablespoons unsalted butter or olive oil

3 cloves garlic, minced

Salt to taste

$1/4$ cup chopped fresh cilantro leaves, for garnish

$1/2$ cup Mexican queso fresco or feta cheese

MEXICAN BLACK BEAN SOUP

❧ Serves 4 to 6 ❧

I think of black beans in Mexican cuisine as an almost upscale replacement for pinto beans, but in actual fact, they have been part of the meso-American culinary repertoire for thousands of years. This is a simple, flavorful, nutritious one-pot meal.

Thoroughly wash the beans and place them, along with the water and onion, in the slow cooker insert. Cover and cook on low for about 8 hours, or until the beans are tender.

Using a handheld immersion blender, purée some of the beans to thicken the soup. (How much you purée depends on how much texture you'd like remaining in the soup.)

Add salt to taste, then ladle into bowls. Top each serving with some crumbled cheese, a sprinkle of cilantro, and some tortilla strips.

SUGGESTED BEVERAGE: This is a relatively mild dish, so I'd choose a chilled, medium-bodied white wine, perhaps with a little spice. A Gewürztraminer or even an off-dry Muscat Canelli would work well. A beer would do nicely, too.

2 cups dried black beans

8 cups water

1 white onion, finely diced

Salt to taste (smoked, if possible)

1/2 cup crumbled Mexican queso fresco or feta cheese

1/4 cup chopped fresh cilantro leaves, for garnish

4 corn tortillas, sliced into 1/8-inch-wide strips and fried until crisp, or 1/3 cup corn chips, crumbled into large pieces, for garnish

Rustic Potato and Poblano Gratin

~ Serves 4 ~

Potatoes and chiles are "New World" stuff, and yet, as it turns out, they have nourished millions of people around the world since they were brought to the "Old World" by European explorers just a few hundred years ago. Here is a simple dish combining the Old World and New World ingredients, stewed together in the pot—in this case, the slow cooker. Unlike conventional scalloped potatoes baked in a gratin pan, where "design" matters, I recommend gently stirring these potatoes once or twice during their cooking time to evenly distribute the good stuff and ensure even cooking.

To roast the chiles, place them on a baking sheet lined with aluminum foil about 8 inches from the broiler. Broil them until the skin blisters and turns black on both sides. (Do not burn the chiles themselves.) Remove the baking sheet from the oven and quickly cover the chiles with a clean dish towel. Let them sit, covered, until they are cool. Using a paring knife or your fingers, carefully peel off the skins, then slit one side and remove the seeds and veins. Cut the chiles into thin strips.

Melt the butter in the bottom of the slow cooker insert.

Place a layer of the sliced potatoes in the bottom of the slow cooker insert. (I use a bit more than one potato per layer.) Sprinkle lightly with freshly ground smoked or regular salt. Place a thin layer of cheese (about one third of the cheese) on top of the potatoes. Place about half of the chile strips on top of the cheese. Repeat with another layer of potatoes, salt, cheese, and chiles. Finish with a layer of potatoes.

Pour the water over the potatoes. Cover and cook on low for about 1½ hours, or until the potatoes are beginning to get tender.

Using a garlic press, press the garlic into the cream; pour the cream mixture over the potatoes, then add a last layer of cheese sprinkled with a bit of salt. Recover and cook for another 3 hours, or until the sauce has thickened and the potatoes are quite tender.

SUGGESTED BEVERAGE: A dry white wine of light to medium body would work for me with this dish. A French or Mexican Chardonnay or even a cava (Spanish sparkling wine) would also be nice.

4 poblano chiles

1 tablespoon unsalted butter or olive oil

4 large russet potatoes, peeled and thinly sliced

Salt to taste (smoked, if possible)

¼ pound flavorful jack or sharp cheddar cheese, grated or sliced

½ cup water

3 cloves garlic, peeled

1 cup heavy cream or half-and-half

STACKED CAULIFLOWER ENCHILADA WITH GREEN CHILE SAUCE

~ Serves 4 to 6 ~

Most of us are familiar with "rolled" enchiladas: some kind of savory filling rolled up in a tortilla, then baked. But a stacked enchilada is even easier to make, and the results, especially when done in a slow cooker, are a lot like a casserole. A layer of corn or flour tortillas, a layer of fresh vegetables, another layer of tortillas, another layer of filling, and so on until the slow cooker insert is a bit over half full. Then a nice long, slow cook that allows all the juicy vegetable flavors to meld and blend. You can certainly vary the type of vegetables according to the season and what's in your garden or farmers' market at any given time. This is great freshly cooked and is even better as leftovers.

Trim and core the cauliflower, then wash and slice the head vertically. (You will be placing it in layers in the casserole, so you want the pieces fairly thin.) Pull the onion layers apart.

In a large bowl, combine the cauliflower, onion, olives, tomatoes, and beans using your hands.

Oil the inside of the slow cooker insert. Place 2 or 3 overlapping tortillas in the bottom of the insert. Add a layer of half the mixed vegetables and top it with a generous sprinkling of cheese (about one-third of the cheese). Pour $^1/_2$ cup of the enchilada sauce over the layer.

Add another layer of tortillas, then half of the remaining vegetables and another one-third of the cheese. Pour on another $^1/_2$ cup of sauce. Finish with an additional layer of tortillas and the remaining $2^1/_2$ cups sauce. (Even though you may appear to have an excess of sauce, much of it is absorbed into the tortillas and vegetables as they cook.)

1 head cauliflower

1 white onion, cut vertically into 8 pieces

1 cup sliced pitted California olives, drained

2 tomatoes, coarsely chopped

1 (15-ounce) can black beans, drained

6 to 9 corn tortillas

$^1/_2$ pound smoked or regular cheddar or Monterey Jack cheese, grated

1 (28-ounce) can green enchilada sauce

$^1/_4$ cup chopped fresh cilantro leaves, for garnish

$^1/_2$ cup sour cream, for garnish

Cover and cook on low for 5 to 6 hours, or until the cauliflower is tender. Top the casserole with the remaining cheese, cover, and cook for an additional 30 minutes, or until the cheese is melted.

Turn off the heat and allow the contents of the insert to sit for 10 to 15 minutes to set, then carefully scoop up generous individual servings of the enchilada into bowls. Top each serving with a sprinkle of cilantro and a dollop of sour cream.

SUGGESTED BEVERAGE: A nice, light, summery rosé would be great with this dish.

Sopa de Ajo

❧ Serves 4 ❧

There is a Mexican restaurant in my town that specializes in caldos, *or Mexican broth-based soups like this* sopa de ajo. *Everyone goes there to get take-out* caldo *when they feel a cold or flu coming on, but most of the time, everyone goes there just because they like* caldo!

Place the water and garlic in the slow cooker insert, cover, and cook on low for 6 to 8 hours, or until the garlic is quite tender.

Add the bread to the broth and allow to soften for about 10 minutes, then purée the garlic and bread using a handheld immersion blender. Add the olive oil and salt to taste.

To serve, place some of the avocado, oregano, cheese, tomato, and green onions in the bottom of each bowl, then ladle in the broth over the ingredients. Top each bowl with a sprinkle of cilantro.

SUGGESTED BEVERAGE: I would enjoy a light-bodied white wine or possibly a light, fruity, young red wine with this soup.

6 cups water

2 large heads garlic, cloves separated and peeled

4 slices French or country bread

$1/4$ cup fruity olive oil

Salt to taste

1 ripe avocado, cut into $1/2$-inch dice

1 teaspoon dried Mexican oregano

3 ounces Mexican queso fresco or feta cheese, crumbled

1 ripe tomato, diced

4 green onions, thinly sliced, green part only

$1/4$ cup chopped fresh cilantro leaves, for garnish

MEXICAN CHOCOLATE PUDDING CAKE

Making puddings is one of the tasks the slow cooker does especially well. This scrumptious blend of flavors often found in Mexican chocolate and desserts is a wonderful ending to a meal, or an afternoon or evening snack all by itself. I like to eat it hot, warm, or at room temperature, topped with a generous dollop of whipped cream and dusted with cocoa powder or grated chocolate.

To make the pudding, in a food processor, finely grind the chocolate. Add the butter, brown sugar, flour, buttermilk, eggs, vanilla and maple extracts, apple pie spice, coffee, baking powder, and a pinch of salt and process until the mixture is relatively smooth. (There will still be tiny flecks of chocolate in the mixture.)

Pour the mixture into the slow cooker insert, cover, and cook on low for about 2 hours, or until the edges are set. The center of the pudding will still appear to be somewhat uncooked, and this is fine.

Once the pudding is done, with a hand mixer or an immersion blender, whip the cream until frothy, then add a tablespoon or two of confectioner's sugar (to taste). Continue whipping until peaks form.

To serve, spoon a serving of the pudding cake into a bowl, then top with a dollop of softly whipped cream and garnish with grated chocolate.

SUGGESTED BEVERAGE: Cold milk, hot coffee, or a glass of tawny port would be perfect with this pudding cake.

Pudding

8 ounces bittersweet chocolate, cut into chunks

$1/2$ cup (1 stick) unsalted butter, cut into pieces

$1/2$ cup packed dark brown sugar

$1/4$ cup all purpose flour

$1^1/2$ cups buttermilk

4 large eggs

1 teaspoon pure vanilla extract

$1/2$ teaspoon pure maple extract

1 tablespoon apple pie spice

1 tablespoon finely ground coffee

$1/2$ teaspoon baking powder

Pinch of salt

1 cup heavy cream

1 to 2 tablespoons confectioner's sugar

Grated chocolate or unsweetened cocoa powder, for garnish

Asia

One of the problems with creating Asian-inspired dishes for the slow cooker is that traditionally in Asian cultures, most dishes are cooked quickly on the stove top or over a fire.

Everyone, for instance, is familiar with the Chinese wok and its relatives that appear throughout Asia. Asian culinary traditions in general contain far fewer long, slow-cooked one-pot meals than do those of the Western world.

The Korean Style Black Beans, Soy-Braised Potatoes, and Potatoes and Peas in Red Curry Sauce could all be considered exceptions to this quick-cooking, stove top tradition. And the Japanese-Style Braised Tofu is so darn good that I just couldn't leave it out, even if it takes only a couple of hours to cook. It offers the perfect opportunity to put something easy on to cook when you come home from work, so you can put your feet up, savor a glass of wine, and have dinner on the table without much ado an hour or two later. The Butternut Squash in Green Curry Sauce is visually exciting, and the Green Vegetable Curry, though clearly of stove top origins, works well.

In this chapter, I have drawn from a number of very different culinary traditions, from the soy-based sauces often found in Japanese and Korean dishes to the unique seasonings found in Malaysian food and the more Indian-like flavors of Thai cooking.

Thai curries are in some ways similar to those of their Indian neighbors, but with the addition of certain characteristic Thai ingredients, such as lemon grass, galangal (a type of ginger), and coconut milk—ingredients that are not easily found in the United States (unless, of course, you live near a good Asian market). So do what Asian cooks often do: use curry pastes that have been prepared by someone else, someone who specializes in making spice pastes. In Thailand, you can often buy prepared pastes at the local shop or in the market. Here, you can often find different Thai curry pastes on the shelves of Whole Foods or other cosmopolitan supermarket chains.

WINES WITH ASIAN FOOD

Although it may be difficult to try to lump the foods of a region as vast as Asia into one big category for pairing with wines, you can probably make a few assumptions that apply to the interesting flavors many of them share in common.

Many of the flavors we like best in Asian foods, including soy sauce, chiles, ginger, lemon grass, and galangal, can make a serious dent in the flavor profile of a good wine. In general, some of the same principles that apply to pairing wines with Mexican and Indian cuisines apply to pairing them with Asian flavors. Wines to avoid would be heavy, oaky Chardonnays and wines such as Cabernets and Merlots with lots of tannins. And wines that might work well with Asian flavors would be your crisp, clean, acidic wines, such as New Zealand Sauvignon Blancs, Pinot Grigios from Italy, crisp whites from British Columbia, and some northern Italian whites. The same goes for aromatic white wines: Gewürztraminer, Riesling, and Viognier. Fruity red wines (as opposed to the more tannic varietals) like Syrah and Zinfandel might make good matches. And, just as with Indian and Mexican foods, anything with bubbles in it ought to go well.

Soy-Braised Potatoes

~ Serves 4 ~

Wherever they are grown around the world, potatoes fill the belly and warm the heart. Although potato dishes are less common in Asian countries than in Western and Eastern European countries, they can still fill the belly and warm the heart, Asian style. A crisp green salad would make a fine accompaniment to the dish.

Place the potatoes and water in the slow cooker insert. (The smaller the pieces, the faster they will cook. Also, the greater the surface area of the potato that is exposed, the more the sauce will be soaked up, and the more flavorful your potatoes will be.)

Cover and cook on low for about 3 hours, or until the potatoes are somewhat tender when pierced with a fork, stirring now and again to keep all sides of the potatoes cooking evenly.

In a small bowl, combine the sugar, soy sauce, sesame oil, and garlic and pour over the potatoes, tossing thoroughly to coat all sides. Recover and continue cooking for about 30 minutes longer.

Serve garnished with the toasted sesame seeds, sliced green onion, and red pepper flakes.

SUGGESTED BEVERAGE: I'm thinking perhaps a lighter-style Roussanne or Rhône-style white blend from California.

2 pounds red or white rose potatoes, washed and halved or quartered

1/2 cup water

1 tablespoon sugar

1/4 cup soy sauce

1 tablespoon toasted sesame oil

2 cloves garlic, peeled and crushed

1 tablespoon sesame seeds, toasted, for garnish

1 green onion, thinly sliced, green part only, for garnish

Red pepper flakes, for garnish (optional)

POTATOES AND PEAS IN RED CURRY SAUCE

∼ Serves 4 ∼

Thai curries differ from northern Indian curries in that they add some typically Thai ingredients, such as dried red chiles, onion, garlic, coconut milk, galangal, lemon grass, and kaffir lime, to the warm Indian spice blends. They are categorized as red, yellow, or green based on the kind of chile or ingredients used in them (but not necessarily by the color of the finished product), and they have an element of sweetness to them that is lacking in some Indian curries. They can be made from scratch, but most Thai home cooks today rely on either commercially prepared pastes or pastes prepared by a vendor down the street. Many supermarkets in the United States carry Thai curry pastes. And if you really want to save time, you can purchase a jar or two of Thai Red Curry Simmer Sauce (Whole Foods and Trader Joe's are two good bets) and save yourself the trouble of doing any mixing at all! Most Thai curries, including this one, should be served with steamed rice.

Wash the potatoes thoroughly and place them, along with the onion, in the slow cooker insert.

Mix the coconut cream, red curry paste, sugar, and soy sauce together and pour over the potatoes. Cover and cook on low for about 3 hours, or until the potatoes are somewhat tender when pierced with a fork.

Add the sweet potato, cover, and continue to cook on low for another 2 to 3 hours, or until all the vegetables are tender. Add the peas along with salt to taste and continue to cook, uncovered, for 15 minutes longer.

To serve, sprinkle each portion with 1 to 2 tablespoons cashews and some cilantro.

SUGGESTED BEVERAGE: A Sauvignon Blanc with a hint of citrus ought to complement this dish quite nicely.

2 pounds small red or yellow potatoes, cut into 1¹/₂-inch pieces if necessary

1 yellow onion, sliced vertically into sections

1 can (about 14 ounces) coconut cream (see Note on page 22)

2 to 3 tablespoons red curry paste

2 tablespoons palm sugar or brown sugar

1 teaspoon soy sauce

1 large sweet potato, peeled and cut into 1¹/₂-inch pieces

1 cup fresh or frozen green peas

Salt to taste

¹/₂ cup dry-roasted cashews, for garnish

¹/₄ cup chopped fresh cilantro leaves, for garnish

MARGARET HUGHES'S GREEN VEGETABLE CURRY

~ Serves 4 ~

My dear friend Martha Deaton was raised in Malaysia, where she and her sisters learned to cook traditional Malaysian dishes from their mother. Martha's sister, Margaret Hughes, has built a thriving London catering business based on the dishes of her homeland. The following is one of her most popular recipes. Although this dish, like so many Asian dishes, is traditionally prepared on top of the stove, I think it works well in the slow cooker. See what you think. Serve it hot, on a bed of steamed rice.

Place the eggplant in the slow cooker insert with ½ cup water. Cover and cook on low for about 3 hours, or until the chunks are somewhat tender.

In an electric coffee mill or a mortar and pestle, grind the coriander, fennel, and cumin seeds to a powder.

In a blender, combine the onion, lemon grass, galangal, ground spices, 1 teaspoon salt, coconut cream, tamarind concentrate, the remaining cup of water, soy sauce, bell pepper, nuts, chiles, and oil until you have a nice, fragrant sauce. Set aside.

When the eggplant pieces are nearly tender, add the green beans and cabbage and continue to cook for another 30 minutes, or until the green beans and cabbage are also tender.

About 10 minutes before serving, stir in the sauce and add salt to taste. Serve hot.

Note: Ingredients such as ground galangal (or fresh galangal root, if you're lucky enough to find it), tamarind concentrate, and lemon grass can be found at Asian markets and sometimes at regular supermarkets

1 eggplant, peeled and cut into
    1-inch cubes

1½ cups water

1 tablespoon coriander seeds

1 tablespoon fennel seeds

1 teaspoon cumin seeds

1 onion, peeled and cut into chunks

2-inch piece lemon grass, sliced
    (use the tender bottom 2 inches
    of the stem), or 1 teaspoon
    ground dried lemon grass

1 teaspoon ground galangal
    (sometimes called Thai ginger;
    see Note below)

1 teaspoon salt, plus more to taste

1 (about 14 ounces) can coconut
    cream (see Note on page 22)

1 to 2 tablespoons tamarind
    concentrate (see Note below)

1 tablespoon soy sauce

(continued)

where there is a significant Asian population. For an especially quick and easy version of this dish, purchase generic green curry paste at an Asian market instead of making the sauce from scratch.

SUGGESTED BEVERAGE: Something white, crisp, and refreshing, perhaps a Canadian Gewürztraminer or a New Zealand Sauvignon Blanc.

1 tablespoon soy sauce

1 green bell pepper, seeded, deveined, and cut into chunks

1/4 cup macadamia nuts

3 serrano or jalapeño chiles, stemmed, seeded, deveined, and cut into chunks

1 tablespoon vegetable oil

12 ounces fresh green beans, trimmed and cut into 1 1/2-inch pieces

3 ounces napa cabbage, thinly sliced (about 3 cups)

KOREAN-STYLE BLACK BEANS

~ Serves 6 ~

You might consider this simple recipe the Korean version of New England baked beans: sweet and salty at the same time. The beans are slow-cooked to give the flavors time to meld, and served accompanied by some cooked greens, a salad, or some rice for a complete protein.

Wash the beans thoroughly, then place them in the slow cooker insert along with the water.

Mix together the soy sauce, sugar, and sesame oil and pour over the beans, stirring in thoroughly.

Cover and cook on low for 6 to 8 hours, or until the beans are tender.

SUGGESTED BEVERAGE: Perhaps something with bubbles, such as Prosecco or a sparkling Californian wine. And if all else fails, a good ol' beer would complement this dish nicely (and would be more traditional than wine as an accompaniment).

2 cups dried black beans

6 cups water

1/2 cup soy sauce

1 tablespoon sugar or honey

2 tablespoons toasted sesame oil

Butternut Squash in Green Curry Sauce

Serves 4

My first introduction to Thai curries came while I assisted a friend in preparing a luncheon for Nancy Reagan at the Reagan Presidential Library in Simi Valley, California. What a surprise: the curry sauce was red! Although Thai curries have many ingredients in common with those of neighboring India, they tend to be tinged with a hint of sweetness from the combination of coconut milk and a traditional dash of sugar, and they are often colored red or green by the red or green chiles in them, rather than the more familiar yellow color of Indian curries. As with most Thai curries, serve this over rice.

Place the squash and water in the slow cooker insert. Cover and cook on low for 3 to 4 hours, or until the squash is tender when pierced with a fork.

In a blender, combine the onion, garlic, ginger, chile, 1/2 cup of the cilantro, sugar, and coconut milk. Blend until it forms a smooth green paste, then add salt to taste.

Once the squash is tender, pour in the sauce and continue cooking just until heated through, 20 to 30 minutes.

Serve garnished with the remaining 1/4 cup cilantro leaves and the Thai basil.

SUGGESTED BEVERAGE: A nice crisp, off-dry white wine would be lovely here.

1 butternut squash, peeled, seeded, and cut into 1-inch cubes (about 4 cups)

1/2 cup water

2 tablespoons chopped yellow onion

2 cloves garlic, peeled

1-inch piece fresh ginger, peeled and coarsely chopped

1 serrano chile, stemmed, seeded, and deveined

3/4 cup coarsely chopped cilantro leaves

1 teaspoon sugar

1 can (about 14 ounces) unsweetened coconut milk

Salt to taste

1/4 cup fresh Thai basil leaves, thinly sliced, for garnish (optional)

Japanese-Style Braised Tofu

⤳ Serves 4 ⤳

Even my meat-eating friends, quietly polite when invited to a dinner featuring tofu, rave about this one. It is easy and delicious and contains flavors traditionally considered typical of both Japanese- and Korean-style cooking. Serve over brown rice.

Combine the miso paste, tamari, sesame oil, water, and honey in a soup bowl or shallow dish.

Carefully coat each slice of tofu in the sauce and then lay it in the slow cooker insert, being careful not to break it. Pour the sauce over the top of the tofu.

Cover and cook on low for about 4 hours, or until the tofu is hot all the way through and saturated in sauce.

Just before serving, add the spinach to the slow cooker insert, cover, and cook for about 10 minutes more, or until the spinach is thoroughly wilted.

Carefully remove the spinach and slices of tofu from the slow cooker and place a few slices on each plate. Garnish with the sesame seeds and sliced green onion and serve hot.

SUGGESTED BEVERAGE: Some delicious, light, aromatic white like a Sauvignon Blanc or a Gewürztraminer would be nice. Or something with bubbles. Or the standard beer.

$1/4$ cup white miso paste

$1/4$ cup tamari or low-sodium soy sauce

2 tablespoons sesame oil

2 tablespoons water

1 tablespoon honey

1 pound extra-firm tofu, drained and cut into $1/2$-inch slices

$1/2$ pound fresh spinach leaves

2 tablespoons sesame seeds, toasted, for garnish

1 green onion, thinly sliced, for garnish

Italy

Cracked Wheat Berries with Honey and Ricotta 59

Risotto with Lentils 60

Polenta Lasagna with Tomato-Mushroom Sauce 63

Barley, Mushroom, and Onion Soup 65

Polenta gnocchi in tomato sauce 66

Tuscan White Beans with Sage and Garlic 69

Fonduta Piemontese 70

Red Wine and Cherry Risotto 71

Italy, like France and Greece, has a wonderful repertoire of hours long, oven-baked dishes, many of them based, like all peasant cuisines, on grains, fruits, and vegetables. There are two Italian specialities in particular that lend themselves well to the slow cooker: polenta and risotto. Made the traditional way, both dishes require that the cook stand over the pot and watch, stirring fairly constantly for long periods of time, making sure the dish comes out smooth.

However, thanks to the gentle, even heating provided by the slow cooker, polenta can be put in the pot with an appropriate amount of water and walked away from for 6 to 7 hours. Maybe you'd like to stir it once or twice, but basically, it prepares itself. To my mind, polenta is such a versatile food that it can be eaten for breakfast, lunch, or dinner and sauced with any number of sweet or savory ingredients. Using it as a component in the Polenta Lasagna recipe is only one of many ways it can be served. Try using it as a breakfast cereal topped with milk and honey. Or try mounding it on a plate and topping it with some of the Tomato-Mushroom Sauce and freshly grated Parmesan cheese.

Risotto, too, when made the traditional way, takes careful watching. However, the slow cooker makes the preparation of risotto a snap. Place the rice and water in the slow cooker insert, set on low, and walk away for a couple of hours. Put your feet up. Have a glass of wine. Watch a movie. Come back and enjoy a delicious, nourishing plate of Risotto with Lentils.

Another of the slow cooker's strengths is the gentle melting of cheese and wine for fondue, as in the Fonduta Piemontese. And cleanup is a breeze.

WINE WITH ITALIAN FOOD

My first introduction to Italian wines came from master sommelier Edmund Osterland, the first American to qualify in France as a master sommelier. Ed was teaching a wine appreciation class in San Diego, and he hauled out a couple of northern Italian wines and juxtaposed them with a couple of the more familiar California wines. To my unschooled palate, the difference was amazing. The Italian wines were crisp and acidic and lower in alcohol than their American counterparts. I didn't like them very much. I wanted the heavier mouthfeel and slight sweetness to which I was accustomed. Then Ed explained that the Italian wines are made to go with food, rather than to be sipped or drunk on their own, as American wines are. The idea that wine and food might be made with the intention of consuming them in tandem was novel to me.

Italian wines, like those of any wine-producing region, have grown up alongside the foods of the region. Every little corner of this country produces wine, often from its own unique grape varieties, of which Italy has more than one thousand! (Dizzying thought to those of us brought up in the Cabernet-Chardonnay frame of reference.) To study them is to study the history of the people who have made and planted them.

In general, people seem to be most enthusiastic about the wines of northern Italy, and in particular those of Tuscany, Piedmont, and the northeastern regions of Friuli, Alto Adige, and Veneto. It is the wines from these regions that you are most likely to find in the United States, so you could begin your exploration and experimentation here. But I cannot resist saying that the best way to get a handle on Italian wines and their intimate relationship with Italian foods would be to pack your suitcase.

CRACKED WHEAT BERRIES WITH HONEY AND RICOTTA

�⟩ Serves 3 to 4 ⟨

Although most Americans are familiar with ground wheat hot breakfast cereals such as Wheatena, few of us would consider cracking whole wheat berries at home for breakfast. They are, however, aromatic and delicious, and eaten much like oatmeal (either whole or cracked) in some rural areas of Italy. This recipe works well in the 3-quart slow cooker that I use for risotto and polenta. Just put it on to cook at night before you go to bed and awaken to a delicious breakfast. Be sure to purchase "triple-cleaned" wheat from your health foods store or use a commercially prepared seven-grain cereal if you don't want to go to the trouble of cracking your own wheat.

Pulse the wheat berries briefly in your blender or food processor, just enough to crack them into pieces. Do not powder them.

Place the cracked wheat, water, and salt in the slow cooker insert. Cover and cook on low overnight, about 8 hours.

In the morning, dish up servings of cracked wheat, then top each with a scoop of ricotta cheese. Drizzle generously with honey, and then sprinkle with ground cinnamon and a dusting of cocoa powder.

SUGGESTED BEVERAGE: You could conceivably kick-start your day Italian style with some grappa in your coffee, but I'm thinking a nice espresso or cappuccino after breakfast would do the trick—and make focusing on the drive to work a whole lot safer.

1 cup hard wheat berries

4 cups water

1/2 teaspoon salt

1 1/2 cups fresh ricotta cheese

Honey

Ground cinnamon, for garnish

Cocoa powder or shaved
   semisweet chocolate,
   for garnish

Risotto with Lentils

⤳ Serves 4 ⤳

Over many centuries, every country in the world has developed ways to obtain much-needed protein by combining the simplest of ingredients. In Italy, the combination of lentils and rice has found just as happy a home as it has in India. The trimmings may be a little different, but this simple dish can make a meal in itself when served with a salad, or as an accompaniment to grilled vegetables or stuffed artichokes.

Thoroughly rinse the lentils and rice, being sure to remove any small stones or dirt. Place them in the slow cooker insert along with the water and 1 teaspoon salt.

In a sauté pan, heat the butter and sauté the onion over medium-high heat until the onion is golden brown, about 10 minutes.

Add the onion to the lentils and rice. Cover and cook on high for about 2 hours, or until both the lentils and the rice are tender. Add additional salt, if necessary, and pepper to taste.

Top each serving with a drizzle of the olive oil and a generous sprinkling of the Parmesan cheese and the parsley.

SUGGESTED BEVERAGE: Any good, medium-bodied red wine would be nice with this dish. I might try a Barbera or a young, fruity Zinfandel or one of my favorite easy-drinking Italian varietals, Callaway Vineyards' Dolcetto.

1/2 cup dried lentils

3/4 cup Arborio rice

4 cups water

1 teaspoon salt, plus more to taste

2 tablespoons unsalted butter

1/2 yellow onion, chopped

Freshly ground black pepper to taste

1 tablespoon good, fruity olive oil

1/2 cup freshly grated Parmesan cheese

1/4 cup finely chopped fresh parsley, for garnish

POLENTA LASAGNA WITH TOMATO-MUSHROOM SAUCE

❧ Serves 4 to 6 ❧

For most of us, the mention of lasagna conjures up mouthwatering images of rich tomato sauce layered with rich cheeses and thin noodles. But a type of lasagna can also be made using polenta rather than pasta. In this polenta lasagna, the old familiar formula appears, but the packaging (polenta instead of lasagna noodles) is new. I recommend making the tomato sauce a day ahead of time, and possibly having two slow cookers on hand so that you can pour the polenta quickly from one into the other.

To make the sauce, using a paring knife, cut a cross in the stem end of each tomato, then drop them into a pot of boiling water. When the skins begin to come loose, carefully remove the tomatoes from the water with a skimmer, allow them to cool slightly, and then peel off the skins. Chop the tomatoes very coarsely and place them in the insert of the slow cooker.

Rinse the dried mushrooms, then soak them in a small bowl in about 1 cup of water for 30 minutes. Lift out the softened mushrooms, leaving any grit behind, and squeeze the excess liquid out of them. Add the mushrooms to the tomatoes.

Heat the 2 tablespoons of oil in a skillet and sauté the onion until golden brown, 7 to 10 minutes. Add the garlic and sauté for about 1 minute longer, then add the mixture to the insert. Cover, and cook on low for 6 to 8 hours, or until the sauce has thickened to your liking. Stir in the remaining olive oil and season with salt and freshly ground pepper to taste. The sauce can be made a day ahead and kept refrigerated in a covered container.

To make the polenta, combine the polenta, water, and salt in a clean slow cooker insert. Cover and cook on low for about 6 hours, or until the polenta is creamy and the grains are tender. Stir once or twice during cooking.

(continued)

Tomato-Mushroom Sauce

4 pounds flavorful tomatoes

1 ounce dried porcini or cremini mushrooms

2 tablespoons plus ¼ cup olive oil (preferably a high-quality, fruity olive oil)

½ yellow onion, finely chopped

6 cloves garlic, peeled and finely chopped

Salt and freshly ground black pepper to taste

Basic Polenta

1 cup polenta

5 cups water

1 teaspoon salt

While the polenta is cooking, prepare the lasagna.

To make the lasagna, oil the inside of a slow cooker insert (this is when having two slow cookers comes in handy!) and prepare and set out the other ingredients so assembly will be quick and easy.

In a large bowl, thoroughly combine the Parmesan, mozzarella, parsley, basil, nutmeg, and pepper using your clean hands. In a small bowl and using a garlic press, press the garlic into the ricotta cheese and mix thoroughly.

When the polenta is done cooking, pour half of it into the bottom of the oiled slow cooker insert, carefully smoothing it into a neat layer. Next, carefully pour 1 cup of the sauce over the polenta, trying not to disturb it. Sprinkle half of the Parmesan-mozzarella mixture over the sauce, and then drop balls of ricotta over the cheese, using *all* of the ricotta. Carefully spoon in the remainder of the polenta, trying not to disturb the cheese–tomato sauce layer, then top the layer of polenta with the remaining cheese.

Cover and cook on low for about 2 hours, or until all the cheese is melted and the casserole is hot all the way through.

Allow to set for about 15 minutes after turning off the slow cooker. The portions may not come out set as perfectly as they would from a regular lasagna pan, but the contents will be colorful and delicious. This is another one of those dishes that is just as good the day after!

SUGGESTED BEVERAGE: Anything, just as long as it is red and dry. I can think of all sorts of wines I would enjoy with this dish: California Zin, Barbera, Chianti Classico, or super Tuscan (when I can get it).

Lasagna

2 tablespoons olive oil

1/2 cup Parmesan cheese (freshly grated, if possible)

8 ounces mozzarella cheese, grated

1/4 cup finely chopped fresh parsley

6 large fresh basil leaves, rolled like a cigar, then thinly sliced into strips

1/4 teaspoon ground nutmeg

Freshly ground black pepper to taste

2 to 4 cloves garlic

1 cup ricotta cheese

BARLEY, MUSHROOM, AND ONION SOUP

~ Serves 4 ~

It's delicious. It's typical of the kind of peasant soup you might find in a mountainous region where barley grows plentifully, and mushrooms are to be had in season. And best of all, it's a put-the-stuff-in-the-pot-and-walk-away-from-it no-brainer.

Place the barley and water in the slow cooker insert.

In a sauté pan, heat the oil and sauté the onion until golden brown, about 10 minutes.

Rinse the dried mushrooms and then soak them in a small bowl in about a cup of water for 30 minutes. Lift out the softened mushrooms, leaving any grit behind, and squeeze the excess liquid out of them. Pour the soaking water through a strainer lined with a damp paper towel or a coffee filter. Coarsely chop the mushrooms.

Add the mushrooms and the strained soaking water, the sautéed onion, the tomato sauce, carrot, and celery to the barley. Cover and cook on low for 6 to 8 hours, or until the barley is completely tender. Add the parsley and salt and pepper to taste.

Serve sprinkled with a tablespoon or two of freshly grated Parmesan.

SUGGESTED BEVERAGE: Personally, I'd prefer a beer with this hearty, simple peasant soup.

1 cup pearl barley, rinsed thoroughly

8 cups water

2 tablespoons olive oil

1 onion, thinly sliced

1/2 ounce dried porcini mushrooms

2 tablespoons tomato sauce

1/2 cup diced carrot

1 cup diced celery

2 tablespoons chopped fresh parsley

Salt and freshly ground black pepper to taste

1/2 cup freshly grated Parmesan cheese

Polenta Gnocchi in Tomato Sauce

⮑ Serves 4 to 6 ⮐

You can serve polenta in its most traditional form, but you can also use it to create an easy variation on gnocchi. I first learned this technique from my friend, Milan-born and -raised cooking teacher Nadia Frigieri. Making both the polenta and the sauce in a slow cooker means there's little hands-on effort required to make this stunning dish. Adding a green salad makes this a meal.

Prepare a baking sheet by placing a layer of aluminum foil over the surface, then grease with half of the olive oil.

Spread the just-cooked polenta in a smooth layer on the baking sheet and refrigerate the polenta until cool and firm, 2 to 4 hours. Use a biscuit or ravioli cutter to stamp out rounds of polenta.

Preheat the oven to 400°F. Prepare a baking dish by coating it with the remaining olive oil. Arrange the polenta gnocchi so the pieces are slightly overlapping one another in the bottom of the baking dish. Generously spoon the sauce over the polenta gnocchi and bake until hot, about 30 minutes.

Remove the gnocchi from the oven and sprinkle with the Parmesan and parsley, then grind some fresh pepper over the top. Serve immediately.

SUGGESTED BEVERAGE: A medium- to full-bodied red wine, such as a Sangiovese, super Tuscan, or a Zinfandel, would be a good choice.

$^{1}/_{4}$ cup olive oil

1 recipe Basic Polenta (page 63)

1 recipe Tomato-Mushroom Sauce (page 63)

$^{1}/_{4}$ cup freshly grated Parmesan cheese

$^{1}/_{4}$ cup finely chopped fresh parsley, for garnish

Freshly ground black pepper

Tuscan White Beans with Sage and Garlic

⌐ Serves 4 ⌐

Beans are as much a staple in Tuscany as they are in rural regions anyplace else in the world. Traditionally cooked in an earthenware pot called a fagioliera, *this simple bean dish works beautifully in a slow cooker insert. Embellish it with fresh vegetables such as tomatoes or summer squash if you like, then serve with a crusty loaf of French bread and a green salad. Choosing good-quality salt and olive oil will help elevate the dish to something special.*

Wash the beans thoroughly, then put them, along with the water, bay leaves, and sage sprigs in the slow cooker insert. Leave the head of garlic whole, wrap it in cheesecloth if desired, and add to the beans. Cover and cook on low for 6 to 8 hours, or until the beans are tender.

Remove the garlic and herbs from the beans, then add salt to taste and a pinch of red pepper flakes. Stir in the olive oil.

Ladle individual servings into bowls and garnish each with a fresh sage leaf or two.

SUGGESTED BEVERAGE: I personally would enjoy this simple meal with a hearty red Tuscan (or super Tuscan) wine. I'm not picky. I like most all of them!

2 cups dried cannellini beans

6 cups water

2 bay leaves

2 sprigs sage, plus extra leaves for garnish

1 head garlic

Salt to taste

Pinch of red pepper flakes (optional)

⅓ cup extra-virgin olive oil

FONDUTA PIEMONTESE

~ Serves 4 ~

Fondue has provided nourishment to mountain folk in Switzerland and the Italian and French Alps through many a hard, cold winter. Made from what must have been, at times, the only ingredients at hand, stale bread and hard cheese, the communal rites that developed around the eating of fondue sustained spirits as well as bodies. Although Emmentaler, Gruyère, and fontina are fondue classics, you can actually use any kind of "mountain" cheese, such as Appenzeller, Comté, or Beaufort. The slow, even heat of the slow cooker is just perfect for making a smooth, effortless fondue. I suggest using a 2- or 3-quart slow cooker for the fondue. It fits more easily on the table and is a more suitable size for this amount of fondue.

In a plastic bag, combine the cheese and cornstarch and shake until the cheese is coated with cornstarch.

Place the cheese-cornstarch mixture, the white wine, and the garlic in the slow cooker insert. Cover and heat on low for about 2 hours, stirring occasionally, until the cheese is thoroughly melted and the mixture has thickened. Add a dash of nutmeg.

You can then transfer the fondue mixture to a fondue pot and place it on the table, or you can place the slow cooker on the table and allow people to dip in with the bread cubes speared on skewers.

SUGGESTED BEVERAGE: A dry northern Italian white such as a Pinot Grigio or Cortese would work nicely here. I also think I might enjoy a Nebbiolo or a Barolo.

16 ounces cheese, cubed
  (single variety or a
  combination; see headnote)

1¹/₂ tablespoons cornstarch

1 cup dry white wine

1 clove garlic

Dash of freshly ground nutmeg

1 loaf rustic country bread,
  cut into 1-inch cubes

RED WINE AND CHERRY RISOTTO

⮑ Serves 4 ⮐

Although this unusual risotto could be served with Parmesan cheese shaved over the top as a savory side dish, it's at its best as a dessert. Serve it warm and topped off with a scoop of vanilla ice cream or some sweetened whipped cream. Gobble it all up before the ice cream has a chance to melt.

Rinse the rice thoroughly, then place the rice, butter, wine, water, and cherries in the slow cooker insert.

Cover and cook on high for about 2 hours, or until the rice is tender and the liquid absorbed.

Remove the cover and stir in the cream. Serve warm.

SUGGESTED BEVERAGE: I, personally, wouldn't drink wine with this dish, but would prefer to savor every bite, then follow it with an espresso. However, dessert or ice wine might complement the dish if you'd like to try it.

1 cup Arborio rice

2 tablespoons butter

2 cups dry, fruity red wine

2 cups water

4 ounces dried, pitted tart cherries

1/4 cup heavy cream or half-and-half

France

I remember my first French cooking vessel: an earthenware casserole from Vallauris, purchased at Williams-Sonoma when the only Williams-Sonoma in the world was located in downtown San Francisco. It was recommended by Julia Child as being an excellent vessel for making French stews and casseroles, and I just had to have one. The first meal I made in it came from *Mastering the Art of French Cooking*—*a boeuf bourguignon*, the quintessential French one-pot meal.

Since that time, I have been fascinated by the plethora of French casseroles and dishes that lend themselves so well to the long, slow cook. Many were born of centuries of using similar earthenware vessels baked in a communal oven. (To save fuel and time, many villages had what they called a *four banale*, or common oven, an oven that everyone in the village could use, so that fuel was not wasted in myriad individual homes.)

Many such dishes contained meat, but many, of necessity, as with all cultures around the world, were made of vegetables in season, at times perhaps seasoned with a hint of meat, but more often with aromatic herbs and vegetables that could be gathered in the surrounding hillsides.

I can envision the French Alpine Cheese, Tomato, and Onion Soup, for instance, bubbling away on a stove top for hours, filling the air with the smells of a summer evening in the Alps. Or the Smoky Potage Saint-Germain, with its simple, hearty base of split peas, sending its earthy, smoky fragrance wafting into the air on a cold winter afternoon. And while

I'm not likely to concoct a classic *boeuf bourguignon* these days, I have not given up the wine that so enriches it. On the contrary, I've tossed it into a pot of beans.

WINES WITH FRENCH FOOD

For many of us, French wines served as the door through which we passed into the world of wine. And for many of us, French wines were the yardstick against which we measured wine quality. Winemaking in France has a long and venerable history, going back to the earliest days of the Roman occupation, and probably going back to primitive efforts to ferment wild grapes of the region long before that.

Who doesn't know the names of France's major wine-producing regions and the unique wines that have been made there for centuries—the elegant Pinot Noirs of Burgundy, the crisp whites of the Loire Valley, the rich, inky reds of the southern Rhône, the aromatic whites of Alsace, the imperial reds and whites of the Bordeaux region, and the most spectacular sparkling wines in the world from the Champagne region? Then there are the more rustic but equally interesting wines from more obscure regions: Languedoc-Roussillon, Côtes de Provence, the Jura Mountains, Côtes de Ventoux, and so on.

This is a country in which, like Italy, wines and food have grown up together. The wines are made to accompany food and the foods are made to be consumed with wine. Get a wine map and explore. First from your armchair, then eventually, by exploring France's wine regions and their foods on the ground, because all wines should ultimately be sampled in their natural environs.

FRENCH ALPINE CHEESE, TOMATO, AND ONION SOUP

∾ Serves 4 ∾

One of the great joys of my childhood was having my mother read to me from Heidi. *Heidi drank goat's milk from a bowl for breakfast and had soup for dinner. In the Swiss Alps, Heidi enjoyed a feast that has sustained and nurtured people the world over for many centuries: soups, sometimes featuring the simplest of ingredients (as simple as some oats or flour, a nip of onion, and some broth or milk). Soups like this one have been made and drunk in France's mountainous regions for breakfast, lunch, and dinner. All you need are some really flavorful ingredients, a creative mind, and a loving heart. Note: Don't buy hard, flavorless tomatoes in the dead of winter and expect this simple soup to taste good! Use the best, freshest tomatoes you can find, preferably from your own garden, picked at the peak of ripeness on a late summer's day. This is not a winter soup.*

In a large sauté pan, heat the oil and butter and sauté the onions over medium-high heat until golden brown, about 10 minutes. (I find it easiest to do this in two batches.)

Salt the onions lightly, then sprinkle them with the flour and place them in the slow cooker insert. Add the tomatoes, wine, and water. Cover and cook on low for 6 to 8 hours, or until the onions are quite soft and flavors have had a chance to meld.

When you are ready to serve the soup, adjust the salt to your taste, place a slice or so of bread in the bottom of each soup bowl, then toss in some of the cheese. Ladle some hot soup and vegetables over the top of the bread and cheese and serve.

SUGGESTED BEVERAGE: I would enjoy either a dry, acidic white wine such as an Alsatian Pinot Gris or Riesling, or a good, fruity mountain red.

2 tablespoons vegetable oil

2 tablespoons unsalted butter

2 yellow onions, thinly sliced

Salt to taste (I use both smoked and sea salt)

1/3 cup all-purpose flour

2 pounds tomatoes, coarsely chopped

1/2 cup dry white wine

6 cups water

4 to 6 slices country bread, well toasted

1/2 pound Gruyère or Tomme de Savoie cheese, diced (about 1 cup)

COLD PROVENÇAL WHITE BEAN SALAD

~ Serves 6 to 8 ~

One of the things I enjoyed most on my first visits to France were the cold rice and bean salads. They seemed so simple, and the only rice and beans I had eaten at home were hot and served in soups or casseroles, or under some creamed meat. Here is a typical French-style cold white bean salad.

Thoroughly rinse the beans and place them and the water in the slow cooker insert. Cover and cook on low for 6 to 8 hours, or until the beans are tender. Quickly and gently pour them into a colander and drain them. (You can reserve the cooking water and use it to thicken soups or stews.) Transfer the beans to a serving bowl.

In a small bowl, combine the vinegar, oil, mustard, and garlic. Blend thoroughly with a whisk or an immersion blender.

Pour the dressing over the beans and mix thoroughly. Add the green onions, olives, and salt and pepper to taste, and toss by hand (or if you must, using spoons).

Serve either chilled or at room temperature on lettuce leaves and garnish with the tomato wedges.

SUGGESTED BEVERAGE: A chilled Tavel rosé would be nice.

2 cups dried small white beans

6 cups water

1/4 cup white wine vinegar

1/2 cup olive oil

2 tablespoons Dijon mustard

2 cloves garlic, pressed

4 green onions, green part only, very thinly sliced

1 cup Mediterranean-style olives, pitted and halved

Salt and freshly ground black pepper to taste

6 to 8 large lettuce leaves

2 small tomatoes, cut into wedges, for garnish

SCALLOPED POTATOES AUVERGNATS

❧ Serves 4 to 6 ❧

Few countries do potatoes and cheese as well as France and Switzerland. Raclette, scalloped potatoes, pommes de terre dauphinoises, *whipped, or whatever, a couple hundred years of potatoes and cheese and a knack for cooking have made them experts at the many comforting ways these two inexpensive, favorite ingredients can be combined. The Auvergne is a region in south–central France known, among other things, for its popular blue cheese called Bleu d'Auvergne.*

Arrange a layer of potatoes in the bottom of the slow cooker insert, then sprinkle about 2 teaspoons flour and $1/4$ teaspoon salt evenly over the layer. Place several small dots of butter on the layer. Then sprinkle on a tablespoon or two of cheese.

Repeat, adding layers of potatoes topped with flour, salt, butter, and cheese, until all the potatoes have been used up. (One large potato yields about one layer.) End with a plain layer of potatoes, but save a bit of cheese for a final layer later. Cover and cook on low for about 3 hours.

Remove the lid, pour the milk over all, top with a last layer of cheese, recover, and cook for 1 to 3 hours longer, or until all the potatoes are tender. Do not be afraid to stir the potatoes very gently as they are cooking. When you spoon them out of the insert they will become disarranged—no matter how carefully you have arranged them to start with—and a gentle stir will keep all the good stuff evenly distributed and help disguise any graying of potatoes that are exposed to oxygen.

Let the potatoes rest for 10 minutes, and then scoop large spoonfuls onto plates.

Variations: Some of my favorite variations on the theme of scalloped potatoes and cheese are sharp cheddar and chives, Gruyère and freshly grated nutmeg, and smoked cheddar and fresh parsley.

SUGGESTED BEVERAGE: Perhaps a good, hearty red wine from southwestern France would be nice. A tannic Minervois? A dry rosé? Almost anything that you would pair with a blue cheese would work well here.

3 or 4 russet potatoes, peeled and sliced $1/4$ inch thick

$1/4$ cup all-purpose flour

Salt to taste

2 tablespoons unsalted butter

$1/4$ pound Bleu d'Auvergne, Stilton, Roquefort, or domestic blue cheese, grated, thinly sliced, or crumbled

$1^1/2$ cups milk or half-and-half

SMOKY POTAGE SAINT-GERMAIN

➳ Serves 4 to 6 ➳

Most split pea soup recipes are ridiculously predictable. Some onion, a bit of carrot, maybe some cut-up spuds. A ham hock. Inevitably, split peas are the main attraction, usually cooked to a mushy consistency. But I was looking for texture and additional flavor, so I added some dried chanterelle mushrooms; half an onion, thinly sliced and well browned; some chopped tomatoes; fresh celery leaves; carrots; and spinach. I considered adding liquid smoke because the ham hock was out. But as luck would have it, one of my wooden spoons caught on fire, so I let it burn, then put out the fire and stuck the charred spoon in the soup. If a winemaker can use charred oak to enhance the flavors of her wine, then why can't I use charred wood for that desired essence of smoke in my soup? (P.S. DO NOT try this at home! Using a smoked salt should achieve similar effects without the fire!)

Place the split peas, water, and mushrooms in the slow cooker insert.

In a skillet, heat the oil and sauté the onion over medium-high heat until golden brown, about 10 minutes. Add the onion, celery leaves, tomatoes, and carrots to the split peas. Cover and cook for 6 to 8 hours, or until the split peas are tender.

About 15 minutes before serving, add the spinach leaves and season with smoked salt to taste. Serve piping hot.

SUGGESTED BEVERAGE: A classic beverage for drinking with Smoky Potage Saint-Germain is beer rather than wine.

2 cups dried split peas, washed

8 cups water

$1/2$ ounce dried chanterelles or other mushrooms, rinsed well

1 tablespoon olive or vegetable oil

1 yellow or red onion, thinly sliced

$1/4$ cup chopped celery leaves

$1/2$ cup chopped fresh tomatoes

$1/4$ cup thinly sliced carrots

1 cup fresh spinach leaves

Smoked salt to taste

Egg, Cheese, and Onion Quiche

⌇ Serves 4 to 6 ⌇

A classic quiche Lorraine has long been one of my favorite dishes. You can make a good crustless, meatless version in the slow cooker, drawing upon that gentle heat. I like to use a smoked salt to supply the smoky flavor that bacon would ordinarily give. Serve with a crispy green salad.

In a large sauté pan, heat the oil and sauté the onion until wilted and starting to brown, 5 to 7 minutes. Add the mushrooms and continue to sauté until both the onion and the mushrooms are golden brown, 5 to 7 minutes more. Add the smoked salt and pepper to taste.

Spread the bread crumbs evenly over the bottom of the slow cooker insert. Using a slotted spoon so any excess moisture can drain off, carefully spread the sautéed mushrooms and onion on top of the bread crumbs, being careful not to displace the layer of bread crumbs. Spread the cheese in a single layer on top of the mushrooms and onions.

In a blender or food processor, combine the eggs, a dash of salt, the sour cream, and the nutmeg until thoroughly blended.

Gently pour the egg mixture over the contents of the slow cooker insert. Cover and cook on low for 2 to 3 hours, or until the center still jiggles slightly but is just about set. (Always stop the cooking *before* the quiche is completely set. If you wait until the top is set, the quiche is likely to be dry and overcooked.)

Serve by carefully spooning a generous portion of the quiche out of the slow cooker insert and onto plates or shallow bowls.

Variation: For a nontraditional "americanized" crust, try spreading a cup or two of grated potatoes evenly over the bottom of a well-oiled or buttered slow cooker insert, then proceeding with the recipe above.

SUGGESTED BEVERAGE: An Alsatian Pinot Gris or other nice light, dry white wine would be nice. I think I'd just as well enjoy a sparkling wine, Prosecco, or champagne, too.

2 tablespoons vegetable oil

1 onion, cut in half and thinly sliced

8 ounces fresh mushrooms, sliced

Smoked salt to taste

Freshly ground black pepper to taste

1 cup toasted bread crumbs

1 cup (about 1/4 pound) grated Gruyère or Swiss cheese

6 large eggs

1 cup sour cream

Pinch of freshly grated nutmeg

UNCLE BOB'S GREEN LENTIL SALAD

~ Serves 6 to 8 ~

My uncle Bob, an artist and a designer, has lived in Paris most of his adult life. The last time I visited him, he took me to a small, favorite bistro near his atelier in the 14th arrondissement. We began our meal with a simple, cold green lentil salad, a popular appetizer all over France.

Rinse the lentils thoroughly, being sure to remove any small stones or dirt. Place them in the slow cooker insert along with water to cover by 2 inches. Cover and cook on low for about 2 hours, or until the lentils are tender but still have texture. They should be al dente, so do not overcook them or they will turn to mush. Drain the lentils.

In a small bowl, whisk together the oil and vinegar, and add salt and pepper to taste. Press the garlic into the dressing and mix thoroughly.

Mix the dressing thoroughly into the lentils while they are still warm, then top with the finely chopped onion.

Serve at room temperature.

SUGGESTED BEVERAGE: I think I would enjoy a lively Pinot Noir with this dish (or all by itself, for that matter).

2 cups dried French green lentils

Water

2 tablespoons olive oil

¼ cup red wine vinegar

Salt and freshly ground black pepper to taste

1 clove garlic

½ onion, finely chopped

STEAMED ARTICHOKES

～ Serves 2 to 3 ～

"What's the advantage to cooking artichokes in a slow cooker?" you might ask. The answer is that while the arti-chokes are cooking, you've bought yourself a big chunk of time to do other things while the chokes cook completely unattended. If you are like me, you may get no further than pulling the chokes out of the pot with tongs and sitting down to them with a nice serving of homemade garlic-tarragon mayo. But I've given a few other suggestions in case you get bored.

Trim the stems off the artichokes and strip off any extra leaves. Using a very sharp knife, carefully cut off a generous one-third at the top of each artichoke. This will remove most of the thorns and expose the center of the artichoke.

Rinse the chokes thoroughly, then arrange them in the slow cooker insert (an oval-shaped cooker works best). Pour in the water, cover, and cook on low for about 6 hours, or until a fork easily pierces the stem end of the choke or a leaf can easily be pulled off.

Meanwhile, prepare the stuffing or mayo.

To make the stuffing, break up the bread slices and put them in the bowl of a food processor. Pulse until the bread is in large crumbs. Add the parsley, garlic, tomato, lemon juice, olive oil, and salt to taste and pulse until thoroughly mixed.

To make the mayo, place the vinegar, egg, and mustard in the bowl of a food processor or a blender and mix thoroughly. With the machine running, drop in the garlic cloves, then slowly pour in the vegetable oil. Pouring the oil slowly is important to the process of thickening the mayo. When the mayo has thickened, drop in the tarragon and pulse just until thoroughly mixed in. (If you let the machine continue to run, you will have green mayo, which, in some cases, might be just the ticket.) Add salt and freshly ground pepper to taste.

(continued)

3 medium or 2 large artichokes (or however many will fit in the insert of your slow cooker)

4 cups water

Stuffing (optional)

4 slices country bread, dried out

$1/4$ cup coarsely chopped fresh parsley

2 cloves garlic, finely minced

1 Roma tomato, minced

1 teaspoon fresh lemon juice

2 to 3 tablespoons olive oil

Salt to taste

Garlic-Tarragon Mayo

1 tablespoon white wine, sherry, or apple cider vinegar

1 egg

1 teaspoon Dijon mustard

4 or more cloves garlic, peeled and smashed with a knife

$1^1/2$ cups vegetable oil

1 to 2 tablespoons chopped fresh tarragon leaves

Salt and freshly ground black pepper to taste

Carefully remove the artichokes from the water using tongs and invert them in a colander or strainer so that any excess water can drain out. Using a spoon or your fingers, pull out the fuzzy center choke of each artichoke, leaving a nice hole. (It is important to let the artichokes cool somewhat before attempting to remove the chokes so that you do not burn your fingers.)

If you are using the stuffing, spoon some of the stuffing into each cavity. Spoon the mayo into small bowls for dipping.

Serve warm or at room temperature. (Unstuffed artichokes can be eaten even cold.)

Note: For some fun and entertainment at your next party, give several guests a large mortar and pestle and the ingredients for the mayo and let them make the mayo by hand. Put the vinegar, egg, mustard, and garlic in the mortar and smash it up. Incorporate the vegetable oil a few drops at a time, pounding it in with the pestle, until the mayo is nice and thick. Be sure to keep their wineglasses full!

SUGGESTED BEVERAGE: Artichokes are generally considered a difficult food to pair with wines. I think the fun would be to experiment and find out what, if anything, works. Put out some bottles of rosé, a chilled white or two (Gewürztraminer, Pinot Gris, or Grigio), perhaps a sparkling wine, and maybe even a red.

WALNUT AND APPLE BREAD PUDDING

~ Serves 4 to 6 ~

Apples and walnuts ripen at about the same time, and are often grown in the same region. Pair them with a crusty, rustic loaf of bread, some spices, milk, and eggs, and you've got a perfect dessert for a fall afternoon. Puddings and bread puddings are particularly easy to make in a slow cooker, and the results are nearly always perfect.

Coat the interior of the slow cooker insert with the butter.

In a large mixing bowl, combine the bread, apples, cinnamon, walnuts, and raisins and mix them together as thoroughly as possible. (I use clean hands, the best mixing device I know of.) Place the bread and apple mixture in the slow cooker insert.

In a blender, combine the milk, sugar, and eggs and blend thoroughly. Gently pour the liquid over the bread, using a spoon to press the bread down into the liquid.

Cover and cook on low for about 3 hours, or until the liquid has been absorbed by the bread and a crust is beginning to form.

Turn off the slow cooker and allow the pudding to settle for 15 to 20 minutes, then spoon individual portions into bowls and top each portion with a generous serving of whipped cream and a sprinkling of brown sugar.

SUGGESTED BEVERAGE: Tea or coffee are good choices here. If you can find one, a Canadian apple ice wine would be delightful.

2 tablespoons unsalted butter

6 cups levain or country bread, cut into 1-inch cubes

2 Granny Smith apples, peeled, cored, and cut into 1-inch (or smaller) cubes

2 tablespoons ground cinnamon or apple pie spice

1 cup chopped walnuts

1/2 cup raisins

4 cups whole milk

1/2 cup sugar

4 large eggs

Whipped cream or ice cream, for serving

Brown sugar, for sprinkling

Greece

Like the rustic cooking of all countries, Greek cuisine reflects the many peoples and cultures that have passed through and contributed to making this beautiful country what it is today. And just as rustic dishes may vary greatly from one region of a country to another, so do those of Greece.

For most Americans, Greek food consists of a very limited repertoire of delicious dishes: cured olives, hummus, *melitzanosalata* (mashed eggplant) and feta cheese, moussaka, pastitsio, avgolemono (lemon-flavored chicken soup), and the ubiquitous "Greek salad." But what few of us realize is that what passes for "Greek food" here in the United States is but a very narrow spectrum of the cuisine of the country as a whole.

What most Americans recognize as Greek food has its origins in the islands and the coastal mainland of southern Greece. Travel inland and north and you find a very different culture, architecture, people, and, of course, rustic cuisine.

For instance, Stuffed Peppers Florina makes use of one of Macedonia's (the mountainous region of northern Greece, which the Greeks claim is the true Macedonia of Alexander the Great) most well-known agricultural products: peppers. As Greece-born food writer Diane Kolchilas says, "Peppers are to Macedonia what corn is to Kansas."

WINES WITH GREEK FOOD

You may be scratching your head wondering where to find a Greek wine. And if you do find it, will it be any good? For many of us, our only exposure to Greek wine has been the poor-quality, piney-tasting retsina we may have tried at a Greek restaurant, on a Greek island, or at a Greek Orthodox church festival. Few of us have had any exposure to the wonderful and unique wines coming out of Greece today.

I have a number of terrific Greek wines in my small personal collection, and I would like to encourage you to seek out and try the new generation of wines from boutique winemakers in Greece. Many of Greece's most talented winemakers today have studied winemaking in Bordeaux, California, or Australia. Not only are they growing and making wines from the noble grape varieties with which we are all familiar, but they are also applying cutting-edge European and New World winemaking techniques to their unique repertoire of indigenous Greek grape varieties. Most of these varieties have names that will be difficult for you to pronounce, but believe me when I say that a whole new world of flavors and aromas awaits you in well-made Greek wines. Because of the growing popularity of Greek wines, they are becoming easier to find in American wine shops and markets. I can highly recommend the wines of Kir-Yianni Estate, Gaia Estate, Alpha Estate, Boutari-Matsa Estate, and Château Geravassiliou, to name just a few.

GREEK-STYLE FAVA BEANS AND TOMATOES

～ Serves 6 to 8 ～

Countries all around the world make use of dried beans, and cook them, of necessity, in an oven or on a stove top for a long time, often dressing them in the simplest of ways. The Greeks, who serve them both as a meze *(appetizer) and as a main dish, are no exception. For this dish, I've recommended fava beans, commonly used in Mediterranean countries, but Greeks often use a large, white bean called* gigandas *that can sometimes be found in Middle Eastern markets. Note: If you are using favas, be sure to buy blanched, skinless beans, as favas come encased in a tough, brownish shell and are sometimes sold that way. This dish makes a nice meal with a green salad and a crusty country loaf.*

Rinse the beans thoroughly, removing any dirt or stones, then place them in the slow cooker insert along with the water. Cover and cook on low for 6 to 8 hours, or until the beans are nice and tender.

While the beans are cooking, heat 2 tablespoons of the oil in a sauté pan and sauté the onion until lightly browned, about 7 minutes. Add the tomatoes, bay leaves, and thyme to the pan and cook briefly.

Drain the beans and toss them with the tomato-onion mixture. Using a garlic press, press the garlic into the beans, and add the remaining 4 tablespoons olive oil and the lemon juice. Add salt and pepper to taste.

Serve hot or warm.

SUGGESTED BEVERAGE: I'd probably enjoy a retsina with this dish, or a Greek rosé.

2 cups dried fava beans or other large, white beans

7 cups water

6 tablespoons olive oil

1 onion, coarsely chopped

2 large tomatoes, coarsely chopped

2 bay leaves

2 sprigs fresh thyme

6 cloves garlic, peeled

2 tablespoons fresh lemon juice

Salt and freshly ground black pepper to taste

STUFFED GREEK ONIONS

⁓ Serves 4 ⁓

Stuffed eggplant, tomatoes, zucchini, and, in this case, onions typically make their appearance on the table for special occasions in traditional Greek homes. Vidalia onions, if you can find them, are a bit flatter and sweeter than yellow onions, and they are perfect for stuffing. Just slice a bit off the top and a tad off the bottom, and you've got the perfect "cup" for holding something delicious. Serve these with a plate of tomatoes or a green salad.

Using a sharp knife, slice about one-third off the top of each onion, leaving a flat crown. Then remove a small slice from the bottom so it will remain upright in the slow cooker. Using a grapefruit knife or melon baller, carefully scrape out as much of the onion's core as you can without ruining the onion. Place the onions in the slow cooker insert, pour in the water, cover, and cook on low for about 3 hours, or until the onions are somewhat tender when pierced with a paring knife.

While the onions are cooking, combine the cheeses, olive oil, currants, chopped mint, and pine nuts in a bowl, mix together with a fork, and add a pinch of freshly ground pepper. Remove the cover of the slow cooker and fill each onion with 2 to 3 tablespoons of the mixture.

Recover and continue cooking for about 1 hour longer, or until the cheeses are melted and the onions are very tender and getting brown around the edges. Spoon any liquid in the bottom of the cooker over the onions.

Garnish each onion with a sprig of fresh mint and serve either hot or at room temperature.

SUGGESTED BEVERAGE: Okay, I can't resist. I'd like to suggest a well-chilled glass of retsina with this dish. Even the cheap, generic stuff would do, and probably bring back fond memories of the Greek islands. But several of Greece's new generation of winemakers have experimented with making artisanal retsina, and I'd like to suggest that if you can find one, you buy it and drink it. Gaia Estates' Thalassitis is one I can happily recommend.

4 Vidalia or yellow onions, peeled

1 cup water

1/2 cup chèvre

1/2 cup feta cheese

2 tablespoons olive oil

2 tablespoons currants

1 tablespoon chopped fresh mint leaves

2 tablespoons pine nuts

Freshly ground black pepper to taste

Several sprigs fresh mint, for garnish

GREEK LEMON, ARTICHOKE, AND EGG SOUP

∼ Serves 4 to 6 ∼

This classic Greek soup is one of my favorites when I want to "lighten up" from a gustatory standpoint. It makes the perfect chicken soup substitute when you are just not feeling up to snuff, or a good light dinner when you've had enough of the restaurant-and-fine-dining circuit. It is traditionally made with chicken broth and small bits of chicken, but I think the meatless version yields even truer, clearer flavors. A touch of ground cumin adds yet another dimension to the flavor.

Rinse the rice thoroughly and place it, along with the water, in the slow cooker insert.

In a sauté pan, heat the oil and sauté the onion, celery, and artichokes over medium-high heat until just beginning to brown, about 7 minutes.

Add the vegetables to the water and rice, cover, and cook on low for 4 to 5 hours, or until the rice is tender. Add the cumin and ¼ cup of the parsley to the soup.

In a medium bowl and using a whisk or a handheld immersion blender, beat the eggs and lemon juice together until frothy. Slowly add 2 ladles of broth, 1 ladle at a time, stirring constantly, to the lemon and egg mixture.

Add the lemon and broth mixture back into the soup, stirring constantly, and continue cooking for about 10 minutes more, or until heated through and beginning to thicken. (If you allow the soup to boil, the eggs will curdle.)

Add salt and pepper to taste, ladle into bowls, garnish with the remaining ¼ cup parsley, and serve immediately.

SUGGESTED BEVERAGE: A nice Sauvignon Blanc or an artisanal Greek retsina, if you can find one, would pair well with this soup.

½ cup basmati or long-grain rice

6 cups water

¼ cup olive oil

¼ cup finely chopped onion

½ cup diced celery (leaves and stalks)

1 (12-ounce) package frozen artichokes, thawed, or 1 (14-ounce) can artichoke hearts

Pinch of ground cumin

½ cup chopped fresh parsley

2 large eggs

½ cup fresh lemon juice

Salt and freshly ground black pepper to taste

POTATO, ARTICHOKE, AND MUSHROOM STEW WITH KALAMATA OLIVES

~ Serves 4 to 6 ~

The ingredients in this simple vegetable stew are made to order for the long, slow heat of the communal oven or the slow cooker. Flavors meld, juices blend together, and the whole thing is a fragrant, pleasurable afternoon's work.

Rinse the dried mushrooms, then soak them in a small bowl in about 1 cup of water for 30 minutes. Lift out the softened mushrooms, leaving any grit behind, and squeeze the excess liquid out of them.

Wash the potatoes thoroughly. If they are large, halve or quarter them. Add the potatoes, mushrooms, artichoke hearts, garlic, wine, and tomato sauce to the slow cooker insert.

Cover and cook on low for 6 to 8 hours, or until the potatoes are tender and the flavors are blended. About 30 minutes before serving, add the olives, olive oil, and salt and pepper to taste.

Serve in a bowl garnished with the chopped rosemary.

SUGGESTED BEVERAGE: Try a glass of northern Greece's signature grape variety, Xinomavro, if you can find it, or Kir-Yianni's Akakies, a delicious Greek rosé.

1/2 ounce dried porcini mushrooms

3 pounds small red or white rose potatoes

1 (12-ounce) package frozen artichoke hearts or
1 (14-ounce) can artichoke hearts

2 cloves garlic, minced

1/2 cup dry white wine

2 cups Tomato-Mushroom Sauce (page 63)

1 cup Kalamata olives, pitted

1/4 cup olive oil

Salt and freshly ground black pepper to taste

1 teaspoon finely chopped fresh rosemary or basil

STUFFED PEPPERS FLORINA

~ Serves 4 to 6 ~

Florina peppers are named for a city in western Macedonia (Greece), a part of the Greek countryside in which peppers are an all-important agricultural crop. They have a thick, red, sweet, firm flesh and are perfect for stuffing. I was first served them at the table of Mrs. Fany Boutari, the gracious matriarch of Greece's premier winemaking family. While Florina peppers are not easily found in the United States, you can buy them roasted and bottled, or you may be lucky enough to find some red Anaheim chiles that will work. In a pinch, you can use good old green Anaheims or the bigger poblanos, as I do. They won't be quite as sweet, but they will be good.

To roast the chiles, place them on a baking sheet lined with aluminum foil about 8 inches from the broiler. Broil them until the skin blisters and turns black on both sides. (Do not burn the chiles themselves.) Remove the baking sheet from the oven and quickly cover the chiles with a clean dish towel. Let them sit, covered, until they are cool. Using a paring knife or your fingers, carefully peel off the skins, then slit one side and remove the seeds and veins.

In a bowl, combine the onion, rice, cinnamon, cumin, currants, dill, and parsley and mix thoroughly with a fork. Using a garlic press, press the garlic into the rice mixture. Add salt to taste and mix well.

Oil the slow cooker insert with the olive oil.

Fill each pepper with as much of the rice mixture as it will hold, then carefully put the chile back together and lay it in the bottom of the slow cooker insert.

When all the chiles are in the slow cooker, sprinkle them with the feta cheese, cover, and cook on low for about 2 hours, or until the chiles are tender and the stuffing is hot all the way through.

Tip: I often make a double batch of the stuffing and then freeze half of it in a plastic bag. That way, it is available for instant stuffed veggies (it works in eggplant, tomatoes, and zucchini). Use within a month or two.

SUGGESTED BEVERAGE: Three Rs: retsina, rosé, or red.

4 to 6 red or green fresh Anaheim or poblano chiles

1/4 onion, finely chopped

2 cups cooked rice

1/2 teaspoon ground cinnamon

1/2 teaspoon ground cumin

1/3 cup currants

2 tablespoons chopped fresh dill

1/4 cup chopped fresh parsley

2 cloves garlic

Salt to taste

3 tablespoons olive oil

1/4 cup crumbled feta cheese (optional)

Moussaka with Artichokes, Tomatoes, and Potatoes

~ Serves 4 to 6 ~

Moussaka is a quintessential Greek dish, and one that every American knows. Usually a delicious dish of layered eggplant, ground beef or lamb, tomatoes, onions, and, best of all, a thick custard topping, moussaka is one of my personal favorites. This version calls for only vegetables, a not-uncommon variation found in rural Greece. It does well in the slow cooker, but may be just a bit juicier than if baked in an open casserole dish in the oven.

Layer the potatoes in the bottom of the slow cooker insert. Then layer all the eggplant slices on top.

Grind the cinnamon, cloves, peppercorns, and allspice to a powder in an electric coffee mill or a mortar and pestle.

In a large sauté pan, heat the oil and cook the onion until it begins to brown, about 7 minutes. Add the garlic, spices, wine, tomatoes, and artichokes and continue to simmer until the pan is nearly dry. Add salt to taste.

Pour the tomato-artichoke sauce carefully over the eggplant and potatoes. (The dish can be assembled to this point a day ahead of time and stored in the refrigerator overnight.)

Cover and cook on low for about 4 hours, or until a skewer inserted into the stew easily penetrates all the layers.

While the vegetables are cooking, make the custard topping. Combine the milk and flour in a blender and blend until smooth. Pour the mixture into a saucepan and cook over medium-high heat, stirring constantly, until the sauce thickens enough to thickly coat the back of a spoon. Gradually stir in the cheese, then turn off the heat and rapidly whisk in the egg yolks one at a time. Stir in a dash of nutmeg.

1 russet potato, peeled and sliced

1 eggplant, peeled and cut into $^1/_4$-inch-thick crosswise slices

1 cinnamon stick

5 whole cloves

6 black peppercorns

2 allspice berries

$^1/_4$ cup olive oil

1 large yellow onion, chopped

4 large cloves garlic, minced

$^1/_4$ cup dry red wine

3 large tomatoes, coarsely chopped

1 (14-ounce) can artichoke hearts, well drained and halved

Salt to taste

Carefully pour the custard over the vegetables, trying not to dislodge them. Cover and continue cooking for about 1 hour longer, or until the custard is set.

Turn off the slow cooker and let the moussaka sit for 15 to 20 minutes, then carefully spoon up individual portions into a pasta bowl.

Tip: I find that it helps to slice the dish into 4 to 6 portions right in the slow cooker insert with a sharp knife before removing the portions with a spoon. That way, each portion is a little tidier.

SUGGESTED BEVERAGE: I would love a good Greek wine. I would enjoy Kir-Yianni's Xinomavro. And if you can't find any, opt for a full-bodied red or any good dry rosé.

Custard Topping

4 cups milk

1/4 cup all-purpose flour

1 cup shredded Gruyère cheese

2 egg yolks

Freshly grated nutmeg

WILD MUSHROOM STEW ON NOODLES

❧ Serves 4 ❧

Wild mushrooms abound in the mountains of northern Greece, and like everywhere else in the world where wild mushrooms grow, they make their seasonal appearance in stewpots throughout the region. Much to the surprise of many nonresidents, pasta is very common in Greece, too.

Rinse the dried mushrooms, then soak them in a medium bowl in 2 to 3 cups of water for 30 minutes. Lift out the softened mushrooms, leaving any grit behind, and squeeze the excess liquid out of them.

In a large sauté pan, heat the olive oil and sauté the onions over medium-high heat until beginning to brown, 5 to 7 minutes. Add the wine and continue to cook for another 5 to 7 minutes, or until some of the wine evaporates.

Transfer the onions to the slow cooker insert. Add the mushrooms, cinnamon stick, crushed coriander seeds, and bay leaves, then sprinkle the flour over all and mix in. Add the water and stir to combine.

Cover and cook on low for about 8 hours, or until the sauce is thick and savory. Add plenty of salt to taste. Carefully stir in the yogurt just before serving.

Spoon over freshly cooked noodles, sprinkle with the chopped parsley, and serve.

SUGGESTED BEVERAGE: I'd probably choose either a Greek or a Côtes de Provence rosé, or a young, medium-bodied, fruity red wine with this one.

3 ounces dried wild mushrooms

1/4 cup olive oil

3 onions, cut in half and thinly sliced

2 cups dry red or white wine

1 cinnamon stick

1 teaspoon coriander seeds, crushed

2 bay leaves

2 tablespoons all-purpose flour

3 cups water

Salt to taste

1/2 cup Greek-style yogurt or sour cream

1 pound fettuccine or linguine noodles, cooked just before serving

1/4 cup chopped fresh parsley

YELLOW SPLIT PEA AND OREGANO PURÉE

∾ Serves 4 ∾

As I have mentioned, lentils and split peas are big in the rustic cuisines of so many countries. Greece is no exception. This very simple dish can either be served on a plate by itself as an appetizer for dipping warm pita or as a side with grilled vegetables and a salad.

Thoroughly rinse the split peas and place them, along with the water, in the slow cooker insert.

In a sauté pan, heat the oil, add about half the onion, and sauté until beginning to brown, 6 to 8 minutes.

Add the sautéed onion to the split peas, cover, and cook on low for 6 to 8 hours, or until the peas are soft and foamy.

Fluff the split peas with a fork or use a handheld immersion blender to thoroughly blend the split peas, then add the oregano, vinegar, and salt to taste.

Allow the split peas to cool, and then spoon onto appetizer plates or one large platter. Sprinkle with the parsley and the remaining onion.

SUGGESTED BEVERAGE: A dry rosé is perfect here.

1 cup dried yellow split peas

6 cups water

1/2 cup olive oil

1 onion, finely chopped

2 teaspoons chopped fresh oregano

2 tablespoons red or white wine vinegar

Salt to taste

1/4 cup chopped fresh parsley, for garnish

BABY LIMAS WITH SPINACH

⤜ Serves 6 to 8 ⤛

Here is another simple, delicious bean dish typical of what you might find in any Greek café. Be careful not to overcook the limas (unless you like them mushy), because they easily lose their shape with long cooking. The beauty of limas is that they have a very distinctive flavor and texture, both of which I adore. Serve the beans with a loaf of crusty country bread.

Rinse the beans thoroughly. Place the beans, water, onion, and garlic in the slow cooker insert. Cover and cook on low for 5 to 6 hours, or until the beans are tender but not falling apart.

When the beans are tender, stir in the spinach, olive oil, and lemon juice and add salt and pepper to taste.

Serve warm or cold.

SUGGESTED BEVERAGE: Again, if you can find it, why not try a Greek wine? Aghiorghitiko is a delicious red grape variety native to Nemea on the Greek mainland.

2 cups dried baby lima beans

6 cups water

1/2 onion, finely chopped

1 clove garlic, finely minced

1/2 pound fresh spinach leaves

1/4 cup olive oil

Juice of 1/2 lemon

Salt and freshly ground black
pepper to taste

The Middle East

Clearly, many Middle Eastern countries and cultures have a long tradition of soups and stews cooked for long periods in an oven or over an open fire, so there is no dearth of inspiration here for slow cooker adaptations.

The Lebanese Eggplant Stew is much like traditional Provençal ratatouille. Same vegetable repertoire, different seasonings. Harira is a Moroccan classic, usually made with lamb, and cooked for many hours during the Muslim month of fasting, Ramadan. For hundreds of years, its delicious smells must have filled homes with anticipation of that moment when the last rays of the sun disappear and devout Muslims can finally sit down at the table and dig in.

Although Armenia is not typically considered a Middle Eastern country, its heritage is much closer to that of ancient Persia than to most European countries, so I've chosen to include two rather unusual Armenian dishes in the collection. Khavits is close to American seven-grain breakfast cereals. So close, in fact, that you can use Cream of Wheat or a commercial seven-grain breakfast cereal for its base. The kicker is the topping of feta cheese, honey, and nuts. The Armenian Apricot Soup features one of our most popular stone fruits, which originated (like most of our stone fruits) in this region.

Hummus is a universal Mediterranean and Middle Eastern spread, and I have included a recipe for a sort of Egyptian "tostada," the Chickpea Fattet.

WINES WITH MIDDLE EASTERN FOOD

Pairing wines with the foods of the Middle East is an interesting proposition. On the one hand, you have a series of cultures and countries where grapes have been grown and wines made and consumed for several thousand years. On the other hand, you have the same cultures and countries from which the juice of fermented grapes has been all but banished since the time of the Prophet Muhammad in the seventh century.

Although the countries of the Middle Eastern region provided some of the first sites of serious wine production in the world (the pharaohs took wines with them to their tombs), wine culture today does not exist in most of them. This means that we are not likely to find traditional wine and food pairings in a Middle Eastern country. (The exception to the rule is Lebanon, a country with a significant Christian population, at one time referred to as the "Paris of the Middle East." Because of its pre–civil war affluence and its Christian population, Lebanon had a sophisticated level of wine appreciation and consumption. Today, fine wine production has met with a renaissance in this beautiful country.)

The good news is that the door is wide open, so to speak, and you have only your taste and your intuition to guide you in matters of food and wine pairing when exploring the foods of the Middle East. In the case of dishes that are strongly spiced, the rules for Indian cuisine might be useful: crisp, chilled whites, sparkling wines, cavas and champagne, rosés, and even younger, fruity reds. In the case of those dishes that are a bit more mild, such as the Chickpea Fattet made with hummus, I can easily envision enjoying a rosé, a red, or even a beer!

LEBANESE EGGPLANT STEW

~ Serves 4 to 6 ~

Many years ago as a student at the University of California, Berkeley, I was invited to a dinner given by professor Laura Nader, a Lebanese-American professor of Middle Eastern studies and sister of maverick politician Ralph Nader. Her dinner was simple and elegant, and the main course was a sort of Lebanese ratatouille. It was a delicious first for me, and contained many of the same elements as its French counterpart—eggplant, zucchini, tomatoes, and green pepper—but its seasonings, rather than being the basil and garlic of the French version, were more typical of the Middle East. You might serve the dish with rice and a simple salad of romaine lettuce, just as Professor Nader did so long ago. I would also offer some crusty bread on the side.

Combine the eggplant, zucchini, tomatoes, bell pepper, onion, and garlic in the slow cooker insert.

Using an electric coffee mill or a mortar and pestle, grind the peppercorns, allspice berries, cinnamon, and red pepper flakes to a powder.

Add the spices to the vegetables, cover, and cook on low for 3 to 4 hours, or until the vegetables are tender.

Stir in the olive oil and parsley, and add salt to taste just before serving.

SUGGESTED BEVERAGE: I think I'd choose a Merlot or Cabernet to accompany this dish.

1 eggplant, peeled and cut into 1-inch cubes

1 zucchini, cut into 1-inch pieces

3 tomatoes, cut into quarters

1 green bell pepper, stemmed, seeded, and cut into 1-inch pieces

1/2 onion, cut vertically into 8 pieces

3 cloves garlic, minced

1/2 teaspoon black peppercorns

1/2 teaspoon allspice berries

1-inch piece cinnamon

1/4 teaspoon red pepper flakes (optional)

1/4 cup olive oil

1/4 cup chopped fresh parsley

Salt to taste

Chickpea Fattet "Tostadas"

❧ Serves 4 ❧

Hummus is everywhere in Mediterranean cultures. In Greece, it is generally served as an appetizer, swimming in olive oil, accompanied by pita triangles, feta cheese, and olives. In the United States, it is also served as a dip for raw vegetables, and often has other ingredients, such as roasted red peppers or pine nuts, blended right in. The basic formula is pretty simple: chickpeas (garbanzo beans), tahini (sesame butter), lemon juice, salt, and olive oil. Proportions of the basic ingredients may be varied in accordance with your taste. Less garlic, more garlic, less tahini . . . whatever. Play around with it and see what you get. Fattet is a sort of Middle Eastern layered casserole or salad. Taking a left turn at traditional, it occurred to me that you could easily make a sort of Middle Eastern tostada using some of the common ingredients found in the dish.

To make the hummus, thoroughly rinse the chickpeas, then place them, along with the water, in the slow cooker insert.

Cover and cook on low for 6 to 8 hours, or until the chickpeas are tender. Drain the chickpeas, reserving $1/4$ cup of the cooking water. (You can reserve the rest of the cooking water for thickening soups or stews.) Measure out $1/2$ cup of the cooked chickpeas, coarsely chop them, and set them aside.

Place the whole chickpeas in the workbowl of a food processor. Press in the garlic, then add the lemon juice, tahini, olive oil, and 2 tablespoons of the cooking water and process until the mixture is smooth. Add the remaining 2 tablespoons cooking water only if needed to thin the consistency. Add salt to taste.

To make the fattet, in a toaster oven or under a broiler, toast the pita halves until lightly browned or crisp. Arrange the pita halves on individual plates, then spread each pita with about $1/3$ cup hummus. (Reserve the leftover hummus for another use). Sprinkle on 2 tablespoons of the

(continued)

Hummus

1 cup dried chickpeas

4 cups water

4 cloves garlic

$1/4$ cup fresh lemon juice

$1/4$ cup tahini

$1/4$ cup olive oil

Salt to taste

Fattet

2 whole pitas, split in half

$1^1/2$ cups Greek-style yogurt

1 teaspoon cumin seeds

1 cup chopped romaine lettuce

$1/4$ cup pine nuts, toasted

$1/4$ cup chopped fresh mint or cilantro leaves

chopped chickpeas, a generous dollop of yogurt, a pinch of cumin seed, $^1/_4$ cup lettuce, 1 tablespoon of toasted pine nuts, and 1 tablespoon of chopped mint.

Serve immediately.

Variations: Try adding artichoke hearts, kalamata olives, or roasted peppers when processing the hummus.

SUGGESTED BEVERAGE: If I were drinking wine with this, I would probably choose something light, aromatic, and white or something dry and rosy pink. That's *if* I were drinking wine with it. But "tostada" somehow makes me lust after a good beer.

HOT OR COLD LENTILS IN LEMON JUICE

⤳ Serves 4 ⤳

Here is another of those very simple, very refreshing, and delicious dishes using lentils. This is a Lebanese recipe, but it could just as easily come from Greece, Turkey, or anywhere in the Middle East. Serve warm or cold with pita, feta, and olives.

Rinse the lentils thoroughly, being sure to remove any small stones or dirt. Place the lentils in the slow cooker insert along with the water.

Cover and cook on low for about 2 hours, or until the lentils are tender but still hold their shape. (You want them slightly al dente.)

Drain the lentils and rinse them in cold water. Just before serving, add the garlic, olive oil, lemon juice, and salt to taste and mix thoroughly. Transfer to a serving bowl and garnish with the parsley.

Serve hot or cold.

SUGGESTED BEVERAGE: This is one of those dishes where I would enjoy a beer or even an icy-cold glass of Greek retsina.

1 cup dried lentils

4 cups water

4 cloves garlic, crushed

$^1/_3$ cup extra virgin olive oil

Juice of 2 lemons

Salt to taste

$^1/_2$ cup chopped fresh parsley, for garnish

ARMENIAN APRICOT SOUP

All right, Armenia can't really be considered "Middle East," but it is part of the botanically very important Trans-Causcasian region that begins in Iran. Botanically important because nearly all of our favorite stone fruits (cherries, peaches, apricots, etc.) had their beginnings in this region. This unusual soup combines the apricots of the region with lentils and vegetables. There are many variations and many ingredient possibilities, including bell peppers, tomatoes, mint, allspice, cinnamon, and paprika. In some versions, the lentils and vegetables are left whole; in others, they are puréed. Vary the soup to suit your taste.

Wash the lentils thoroughly, being sure to remove any small stones or dirt, and place them, along with the water, in the slow cooker insert. Add the onion, carrots, cumin, and apricots.

Cover and cook on low for 3 to 4 hours, or until the vegetables are tender. Add salt and pepper to taste.

If you wish, you can purée some or all of the soup, or leave it just as it is. In any case, garnish it with a dollop of the yogurt and a sprinkling of the mint.

SUGGESTED BEVERAGE: I think I would prefer a spicy, aromatic white wine, such as Gewürztraminer, well chilled, with this dish.

1 cup dried lentils

6 cups water

1 onion, chopped

2 carrots, diced

1 teaspoon ground cumin

1 cup dried apricots

Salt and freshly ground black pepper to taste

1/2 cup Greek-style yogurt or sour cream, for garnish

1 tablespoon chopped fresh mint, for garnish

Armenian Khavits

⌁ Serves 3 to 4 ⌁

Although there appear to be many recipes for the Armenian dish called khavits, *most of which entail frying semolina or cracked wheat in butter before boiling it, the toppings are what hooked me when I had it for breakfast at an Armenian café in my town. You can crack your own wheat in a blender (see page 59), or use semolina, store-bought seven-grain cereal, or even Cream of Wheat. For added fiber, I usually include a couple of tablespoons of ground flaxseed in each serving.*

Place the cracked wheat, water, and salt in the slow cooker insert. (If you are using something other than wheat you have cracked yourself, use the liquid instructions on the package as your guide.)

Cover and cook on low overnight, about 8 hours.

In the morning, stir the cinnamon into the wheat, then spoon the cereal into individual bowls and top each portion with 1 tablespoon of honey, 1 tablespoon of feta cheese, 1 tablespoon of pistachios, and 1 or 2 teaspoons of flaxseed.

Pour half-and-half over the top and enjoy!

SUGGESTED BEVERAGE: I would opt for a cup of freshly brewed black tea, especially one that has fragrant hints of smoke, such as Scottish breakfast tea.

1 cup cracked wheat berries
or seven-grain cereal

4 cups water (or according to
package instructions)

$^1/_2$ teaspoon salt

1 teaspoon ground cinnamon

$^1/_4$ cup honey

$^1/_4$ cup feta cheese

$^1/_4$ cup crushed pistachios
or walnuts or a mixture
of the two

4 to 8 teaspoons ground flaxseed
(optional)

$^1/_2$ cup half-and-half, low-fat milk,
or soymilk

CHICKPEA HARIRA

⤞ Serves 6 to 8 ⤝

During the monthlong observance of Ramadan, devout Muslims are asked to go without eating anything substantial from sunup to sundown. Harira is a soup that is traditionally served to break the fast after sundown in Morocco. Although harira is most often prepared with lamb or chicken, a mighty savory version can also be prepared without meat.

Throughly rinse the chickpeas and place them in the slow cooker insert along with the water, tomatoes, celery leaves, and onion. Cover and cook on low for 6 to 8 hours, or until the chickpeas are tender.

In an electric coffee mill or a mortar and pestle, grind the cloves, cinnamon, peppercorns, cumin, saffron, and red pepper flakes to a powder. Add the ground turmeric.

Add the spices to the soup 1 to 2 hours before serving. (If you plan to be gone all day, you can add all the ingredients at the start. However, the spices will be just a bit more pungent if you hold off adding them until the chickpeas have cooked for a while.)

Just before serving, stir in the olive oil, parsley, cilantro, and lemon juice. Add salt to taste and serve, topping each serving with a dollop of yogurt.

SUGGESTED BEVERAGE: Consumption of alcohol is generally not encouraged by Muslim religious practices, so it's probably best to leave this one to your imagination or taste.

1 cup dried chickpeas

8 cups water

3 tomatoes, diced

$1/4$ cup chopped celery leaves

1 onion, finely diced

6 whole cloves

1-inch piece cinnamon stick

$1/4$ teaspoon black peppercorns

1 teaspoon cumin seeds

$1/2$ teaspoon saffron threads

$1/4$ teaspoon red pepper flakes

$1/2$ teaspoon ground turmeric

$1/4$ cup extra virgin olive oil

$1/4$ cup chopped fresh
    parsley leaves

$1/4$ cup chopped fresh
    cilantro leaves

2 tablespoons fresh lemon juice

Salt to taste

$1/2$ cup Greek-style yogurt

Index